PENGUIN BOOKS

LIFE IS IN THE TRA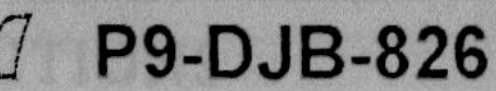

JONICA MOORE

BRUCE FEILER is the author of seven *New York Times* bestsellers, including *The Secrets of Happy Families*, *The Council of Dads*, and *Walking the Bible*. He's the writer/presenter of two primetime series on PBS, and his two TED Talks have been viewed more than two million times. A native of Savannah, Georgia, Bruce lives in Brooklyn with his wife, Linda Rottenberg, and their twin daughters.

Praise for *Life Is in the Transitions*

"This is a remarkably poignant read about the pivotal moments in our lives. Bruce Feiler gets to the heart of how turning points shape us—and how we can shape them. The wisdom and stories in this book will change the way you tell your own story."

—Adam Grant, bestselling author of *Originals* and *Give and Take*

"Crammed with cutting-edge research and compelling real-world examples, *Life Is in the Transitions* provides a framework of striking originality that explodes with thought-provoking insights. It has profound implications for how we view and handle the transitions—voluntary and involuntary—that increasingly disrupt our lives. And it's one of the rare books that is a pleasure to read in the moment and impossible to forget once you've finished the last page."

—Gretchen Rubin, bestselling author of *The Happiness Project* and *The Four Tendencies*

"As with any important book, it's a Rorschach test. Each reader will take away a different big lesson from it, and that lesson may be different if they reread it at a different stage of their lives. . . . Whatever life is going to look like in the coming years, we know it's going to be different. We know we're going to be different. So let's use this time."

—Arianna Huffington, *Thrive Global*

"I don't know what's more astonishing: the range of stories Bruce Feiler has found in asking people about their lives or the wisdom he extracts from them. There is no more powerful reminder that the stories we inherit define success—and that definition constantly needs updating. This beautiful book is an indispensable guide to accepting change—as it really is, rather than what it's supposed to be—and to becoming who we really are."

—Charles Duhigg, author of bestsellers *The Power of Habit* and *Smarter Faster Better*

"*Life Is in the Transitions* is essential reading for anyone in the act of becoming—which is to say, all of us. Timely, wise, and ultimately uplifting, the fifteenth book from Savannah native and self-described 'lifestorian' Bruce Feiler (*The Council of Dads*) offers an insightful, pragmatic tool kit for navigating the unexpected, uncertain, and often upending disruptions of our lives, and for rewriting the next chapters in our ever-changing stories." —*The Post and Courier* (Charleston)

"[Feiler] offers in this insightful work timely suggestions for anyone adapting to significant life changes. . . . He also presents evidence discrediting the notion of the midlife crisis and demonstrates that everyone's life contains multiple significant 'upheavals and uncertainties,' which should thus be accepted as normal, contrary to conventional wisdom. The findings buttress practical suggestions for responding to major change, including identifying emotions, giving up old mind-sets, testing alternatives, and seeking help from others. This logical, persuasive resource will resonate with any self-help reader." —*Publishers Weekly*

"This highly recommended title couldn't be more timely. . . . Feiler details a model for life transitions based on thousands of interviews with people from all walks of life and tells readers how to memorialize changes and give up old mind-sets. A helpful bonus is the complete outline for writing one's own story or that of others."

—*Library Journal*

"An engaging consideration of how people navigate the highs and lows in their lives . . . [Feiler's] relaxed, informal style is reassuring, and the numerous anecdotes gleaned from his wide variety of interview subjects keep the narrative fresh. His encouraging counsel will appeal to many." —*Booklist*

"In *Life Is in the Transitions*, Bruce Feiler listens to, synthesizes, and helps make meaning of the American story at this complicated moment. With a big, open heart, he helps us all better understand our own stories, what it means to be human, and how to navigate challenges and change. Along the way, he powerfully reminds us of the singular importance of honoring one another's stories and lives through listening." —Dave Isay, founder, *StoryCorps*

"Bruce Feiler has a real knack for helping us see what is not obvious but is right in front of our eyes. In this clear, terrifically compelling book full of instructive examples, he names and describes the 'lifequake' personal transitions that affect so many of us today and offers genuine wisdom, valuable counsel, and moving inspiration that make the journey easier. Read this book to open your eyes and lighten your heart!"

—William Ury, coauthor of *Getting to Yes*
and author of *Getting to Yes with Yourself*

Look for the Penguin Readers Guide in the back of this book.

To access Penguin Readers Guides online, visit

penguinrandomhouse.com

LIFE IS IN THE TRANSITIONS

Mastering Change at Any Age

BRUCE FEILER

PENGUIN BOOKS

PENGUIN BOOKS

An imprint of Penguin Random House LLC
penguinrandomhouse.com

First published in the United States of America by Penguin Press,
an imprint of Penguin Random House LLC, 2020
Published in Penguin Books 2021

Art credits: p. 28, detail from the tomb treasure of King Tutankhamun, 18th dynasty, held by the Egyptian Museum, Cairo, by Djehouty via Wikimedia; p. 32, James Catnach, "The Stages of Life," broadside circa 1830, via Wikimedia; p. 33 (top), James Baillie, "The Life and Age of Man: Stages of Man's Life from the Cradle to the Grave," print circa 1848, via Library of Congress Prints and Photographs Division; p. 33 (bottom), James Baillie, "The Life and Age of Woman: Stages of Woman's Life from the Cradle to the Grave," print circa 1848, via Library of Congress Prints and Photographs Division; p. 44, cover art from the book *Passages* by Gail Sheehy, originally published by Ballantine Books, an imprint of Random House, a division of Penguin Random House LLC, New York, in 1974.

ISBN 9781594206825 (hardcover)
ISBN 9781101980514 (paperback)
ISBN 9780698409965 (ebook)

Printed in the United States of America
2nd Printing

Book design by Daniel Lagin

For the next generation:

Max, Hallie, Tybee, Eden, Nate, Maya, Judah, and Isaac

Tell the stories

Life is in the transitions as much as in the terms connected.

WILLIAM JAMES

CONTENTS

LIFE IS IN THE TRANSITIONS

INTRODUCTION

The Life Story Project

What Happens When Our Fairy Tales Go Awry

I used to believe that phone calls don't change your life, until one day I got a phone call that did. It was from my mother. "Your father is trying to kill himself."

"He's what?"

Suddenly she was talking and I wasn't really following. Something about a bathroom, a razor, a desperate lunge for relief.

"Good God."

"And that wasn't the last time. Later he tried to climb out of a window while I was scrambling eggs."

As a writer, I'm often asked whether I learned to write from my dad. The answer is no. My father was uncommonly friendly, even twinkling—we called him a professional Savannahian, for the seaside city in Georgia where he'd lived for eighty years—but he was more of a listener and a doer than a teller and a scribbler. A navy veteran, civic leader, Southern Democrat, he was never depressed a minute in his life.

Until he got Parkinson's, a disease that affects your mobility—and your mood. My dad's father, who also got the disease late in life, shot himself in the head a month before I graduated from high school. My father had promised for years he wouldn't do the same. "I know the pain—and shame—it causes."

Then he changed his mind—or at least that part of his mind he could still control. "I've lived a full life," he said. "I don't want to be mourned; I want to be celebrated."

Six times in the next twelve weeks my father attempted to end his life. We tried every remedy imaginable, from counseling to electroconvulsive therapy. Yet we couldn't surmount his core challenge: He had lost a reason to live.

My family, always a bit hyperfunctional, dove in. My older brother took over the family real estate business; my younger sister helped research medical treatments.

But I'm the narrative guy. For three decades, I had devoted my life to exploring the stories that give our lives meaning—from the tribal gatherings of the ancient world to the chaotic family dinners of today. I have long been consumed by how stories connect and divide us on a societal level, how they define and deflate us on a personal level.

Given this interest, I began to wonder: If my dad was facing a narrative problem, at least in part, maybe it demanded a narrative solution. Maybe what my father needed was a spark to restart his life story.

One Monday morning I sat down and did the simplest, most restorative thing I could imagine.

I sent my dad a question.

What were your favorite toys as a child?

What happened next changed not only him, but everyone around him, and ultimately led me to reevaluate how we all achieve meaning, balance, and joy in our lives.

This is the story of what happened next, and what we all can learn from it.

This is the story of the Life Story Project.

The Story of Your Life

Stop for a second and listen to the story going on in your head. It's there, somewhere, in the background. It's the story you tell others when you first meet them; it's the story you tell yourself when you visit a meaningful place, when you flip through old photographs, when you celebrate an achievement, when you rush to the hospital.

It's the story of who you are, where you came from, where you dream of going in the future.

It's the high point of your life, the low point, the turning point.

It's what you believe in, what you fight for, what matters most to you.

It's the story of your life.

And that story isn't just part of you. It *is* you in a fundamental way.

Life is the story you tell yourself.

But how you tell that story—are you a hero, victim, lover, warrior, caretaker, believer—matters a great deal. How you adapt that story—how you revise, rethink, and rewrite your personal narrative as things change, lurch, or go wrong in your life—matters even more.

Recently, something happened to me that made me focus on these issues: I lost control of that story bouncing around in my head. For a while, I didn't know who I was; I didn't know where I was going.

I was lost.

That's when I began to realize: While storytelling has drawn significant academic and popular interest in recent years, there's an aspect of personal storytelling that hasn't gotten enough attention. What happens when we misplace the plot of our lives? When we get sidetracked by one of the mishaps, foul-ups, or reversals of fortune that appear with uncomfortable frequency these days?

What happens when our fairy tales go awry?

That's what happened to my dad that fall, to me around that time, to all of us at one time or another.

We get stuck in the woods and can't get out.

This time, though, I decided to do something about it. I set out to learn how to get unstuck.

How I Became a Lifestorian

What I did next—traveling around the country, gathering hundreds of life stories of everyday people, and then scouring those stories for themes and takeaways that could help all of us navigate the swerves in our lives—has a bit of a backstory.

I was born in Savannah, Georgia, to five generations of Southern Jews. That's two storytelling traditions of outsiders that collided in me. I left the South and moved north for college, then left college and moved to Japan. There, in a town fifty miles and fifty years from Tokyo, I began writing letters home on crinkly airmail paper. *You're not going to believe what happened to me today.* When I got back home, everywhere I went, people said, "I loved your letters!"

"That's great," I said. "Have we met?"

Turns out my grandmother had xeroxed my letters and passed them around. They went viral the old-fashioned way. *If so many people find these interesting, I should write a book,* I thought. With some luck, I landed a book contract. More important, I'd found a calling. Stories were how I'd always found myself. How I put my unease and outsiderness into coherent form.

Over the next two decades, I wrote stories—books, articles, television—from six continents and seventy-five countries. I spent a year as a circus clown and another traveling with Garth Brooks. I retraced the greatest stories ever told, from Noah's ark to the Exodus. I also got married and became the father to identical twin girls. Life was ascending.

Until I had a back-to-back-to-back set of experiences that shattered that linearity—and with it any illusion that I could control the narrative of my life.

First, I was diagnosed with a rare, aggressive bone cancer in my left leg. My disease was so nonlinear it was an adult-onset pediatric cancer. Frightened and face-to-face with death, I spent a brutal year enduring more than sixteen rounds of chemo and a seventeen-hour surgery to remove my femur, replace it with titanium, and relocate my fibula from my calf to my thigh. For two years I was on crutches; for a year after that I used a cane. Every step, every bite, every hug I've taken since has been haunted by the long tail of fear and fragility.

Then I nearly went bankrupt. The modest real estate business my father had built was gutted by the Great Recession. Three generations of dreams were dampened. I emptied my savings. At the same time, the internet decimated the world of print I had worked in for two decades. Friend after friend was out on the street. I woke up three nights a week in a pale sweat, staring at the ceiling, wondering.

Then came my father's suicide spree. The conversations that fall were almost unhaveable, the language inadequate for the choices we faced. For me, though, there was something achingly familiar about this period. It drew me back to what had always been my default reaction to a crisis: When in turmoil, turn to narrative. The proper response to a setback is a story.

That notion had been gaining currency. A year earlier, while researching a book on high-functioning families, I had gone to the home of Marshall Duke, a psychologist at Emory University. Marshall and his colleague Robyn Fivush had been studying a phenomenon first noticed by Marshall's wife, Sara. A teacher of students with special needs, Sara had observed that the children she worked with seemed better able to navigate their lives the more they knew about their family's history. Marshall and Robyn devised a set of questions to test this thesis: Do you know where your grandparents met? Do you know an illness or injury your parents experienced when they were younger? Do you know what went on when you were being born? Children who scored highest on this test had a greater belief that they could control the world around them. It was the number one predictor of a child's emotional well-being.

Why would knowing your family's story help you navigate your own? "All family narratives take one of three shapes," Marshall explained. First is the ascending family narrative: *We came from nothing, we worked hard, we made it big.* Next, the descending narrative: *We used to have it all. Then we lost everything.*

"The most healthful narrative," he continued, "is the third one." It's called the oscillating family narrative. *We've had ups and downs in our family. Your grandfather was vice president of the bank, but his house burned down. Your aunt was the first girl to go to college, but she got breast cancer.* Children who know that lives take all different shapes are much better equipped to face life's inevitable disruptions.

I was electrified by this research, and when I wrote about it in the *New York Times*, readers were, too. The article, "The Stories That Bind Us," went viral in the modern sense of the word. I heard from parents, scholars, and leaders around the world. All attested to the same thing: Stories stitch us to one another, knit generation to generation, embolden us to take risks to improve our lives when things seem most unhopeful.

Facing one of those unhopeful moments myself that fall, this idea gave me hope. *What if I ask my dad to tell his story?* Not too long, I thought; just a page or two. The first question I sent—about his childhood toys—worked, so I followed with another. *Are you still friends with any of your friends from high school?* Then: *What was your house like as a child?* As he gained confidence, I started emailing him questions every Monday morning. *How'd you become an Eagle Scout? How'd you join the navy? How'd you meet Mom?*

My father couldn't move his fingers at this point, so he couldn't type. He would think about the question all week, dictate his story to Siri, then print out a draft and edit it. A lifelong collector, he began adding photographs, newspaper clippings, love letters to my mom. As his writing grew bolder, I made the questions more probing. *What's your biggest regret?*

How'd you survive your first downturn? The process continued for the next four years, until my father, a man who had never written anything longer than a memo, backed into writing an autobiography. It was the most remarkable transformation any of us in the family had ever seen.

But what exactly explained this transformation? To learn more, I plunged into the neuroscience and biochemistry of storytelling; I interviewed experts on the psychological and emotional benefits of life reminiscence; I tracked down pioneers in the nascent disciplines of narrative gerontology, narrative adolescence, and narrative medicine. What I found was a young-but-growing field built around the idea that reimagining and reconstructing our personal stories is vital to living a fulfilling life.

But I also found something lacking. There was an aspect of what my dad was going through, what I was going through, what nearly everyone I knew was going through that seemed left out of the conversation. That missing ingredient touched on what Marshall had identified as the key element of family stories: their shape.

Our personal narratives, I began to think, have shapes as much as our family ones do. Each of us carries around an unspoken set of assumptions that dictate how we expect our lives will unfold. These expectations come from all corners and influence us more than we admit. We've been led to believe that our lives will always ascend, for example, and are shocked to discover they oscillate instead. Our society tells us we should be basking in progress, but our experience tells us we are beset by slip-ups. Might this gap help explain the anxiety so many of us feel?

All these issues came to a head for me one unlikely day. The occasion was my thirtieth college reunion. I had thrown out my back, and my classmate David offered to drive us from Brooklyn, where we both live. *We'll have a chance to catch up*, I thought. But David turned out to be closing a multimillion-dollar real estate deal and spent the entire car ride toggling between phone calls with ebullient lawyers on the one hand and distraught colleagues on the other. The day before, the nine-month-old baby of one of

David's business partners had gone down for a nap and never woke up. David was both on top of the world and completely flattened.

I was moderating a panel of prominent classmates that afternoon. In preparation I had assembled their résumés, all neatly typed and impressive. But I was so shaken by the story David had shared that by the time I took the stage, I looked out at the auditorium full of people, took the résumés, and ripped them in half. "I don't care about your successes," I said. "Tell them to your mother. I want to hear about your struggles, your challenges, what keeps you awake at night."

That evening, the class of '87 gathered under a massive tent. There was a bar on one end and a barbecue on the other. It took me two hours to walk from one end to the other as classmate after classmate came up and poured out their own heartbreaking stories.

My wife went into the hospital with a routine headache and died the next morning.

My thirteen-year-old slashed her wrists.

My mother's an alcoholic.

My boss is a crook.

I'm being sued for malpractice.

I'm being treated for depression.

I'm afraid.

What everybody said, in one way or the other, was the same thing: My life has been disrupted, my dreams shattered, my confidence punctured. There's a gap between the upward, dependable, "every problem can be cured with a pill, an app, or five minutes of meditation" life I was sold, and the unstable, unpredictable, utterly fluid life I'm forced to contend with.

The life I'm living is not the life I expected.

I'm living life out of order.

That night I called my wife. "Something's going on. No one knows how to tell their story anymore. I've got to figure out how to help."

"Tell Me the Story of Your Life"

What I did was create the Life Story Project. I crisscrossed the country, finding people with interesting life stories to tell; interviewed those people for hours about the transitions, disruptions, and reinventions of their lives; and then mined those stories for patterns and clues. I started organically, with people I knew, then gradually became more rigorous, seeking out people of all demographics. I did the oldest thing imaginable—go talk to people—and I did it in the most contemporary way: I conducted life stories in living rooms, bedrooms, hospital rooms, boats, bars, Airstreams, Native American reservations, Broadway theaters, and Franciscan nunneries; I did them in person, on cell phones, on landlines, and via Zoom, FaceTime, and Skype.

Two hundred years ago, the legendary loner and Danish philosopher Søren Kierkegaard used to interrupt his solitude by going on what he called *people baths*, plunging into the streets of Copenhagen, buttonholing acquaintances and engaging strangers in robust, afternoon-long conversations. That's what I felt like: I went on a three-year-long people bath.

And here's where I ended up: I gathered 225 life stories—all ages, backgrounds, and walks of life. All fifty states. The stories included a mind-boggling array of life experiences: lost limbs, lost jobs, lost homes; changed religions, changed careers, changed genders; those who got sober, got divorced, got out of cults; as well as scores who went through everyday transitions of hope, revival, and renewal. A small sample includes:

- a Wall Street bond trader turned romance novelist,
- a truck driver who became a nurse,
- the Army Ranger who discovered Saddam Hussein,
- a two-time cancer survivor who climbed Mount Everest,
- a CIA analyst who quit to train rescue dogs,

- a magazine writer turned mortician,
- a theoretical physicist who stepped down from a tenured professorship to devote himself to his YouTube band called Ninja Sex Party,
- a country music songwriter who became a Lutheran pastor,
- the most decorated Paralympian in American history,
- a pharmaceutical CEO who quit to raise his three sons after his wife killed herself,
- a United States senator,
- a Grammy winner,
- a former white supremacist,
- a reformed alcoholic who went door-to-door apologizing to two dozen people whose homes she robbed while drunk,
- three people who went to prison,
- four people who died and came back to life,
- five people who survived suicide attempts,
- six people who transitioned genders,
- and, at the very end, the partner of my friend David, whose baby went down for a nap and never woke up.

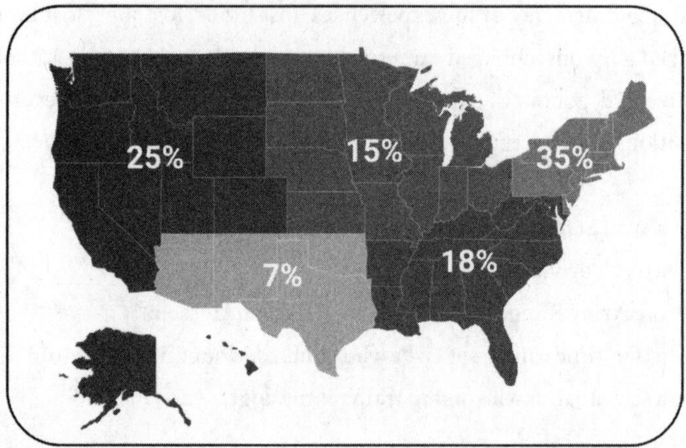

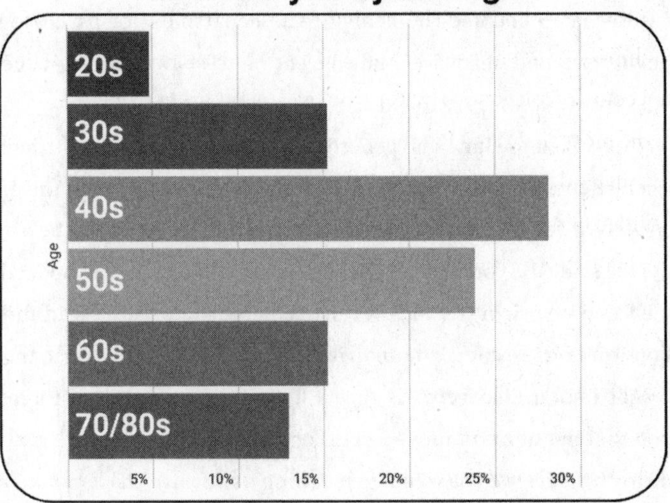

Life Story Project: Occupation

What I did with these people is what I called the Life Story Interview. More than thirty years ago, a little-known Harvard PhD named Dan McAdams designed a process of interviewing people about their lives as a way to understand how they developed and refined their sense of self. Dan went on to become the chair of the department of psychology at Northwestern, and narrative studies went on to spawn cutting-edge discoveries from adolescence to old age.

I reached out to Dan, who generously offered to guide me through my project. He encouraged me to take the template he designed in the 1980s but modify it for the issues I was interested in. "Don't try to be an academic," he said. "Be yourself." As he predicted, what quickly happened was that new and surprising themes began to emerge that I hadn't read about in the literature on life course, human development, and personal change.

What I soon discovered is that a host of unprecedented forces are reshaping contemporary life—technological, political, spiritual, sexual—yet the techniques we use to make meaning of our lives have not kept up. We're going through transitions more frequently, but our tool kit for handling them has not changed to keep pace.

The interviews I conducted were designed to understand and address this phenomenon. My first question was open-ended: "Please tell me the story of your life in fifteen minutes." Most people took more than an hour. Next I asked about major life moments: high point, low point, turning point; a meaningful experience; a major transition they handled well, another they handled poorly.

Since navigating such transitions quickly became an overriding theme, I spent a lot of time digging into this underdiscussed phenomenon. I asked subjects whether their biggest life transition was voluntary or involuntary, whether they used rituals to get through this time, what the biggest emotion was that they struggled with, how they structured their time, what old habits they shed, what new ones they created, how long this transition took.

In the final section, I asked about the prominent story lines that shaped their lives, and ended with my two favorite questions, the ones that produced the most enlightening insights:

Looking back over your entire life story with all its chapters, scenes, and challenges, do you discern a central theme?

Looking back over your life story in a slightly different way, what shape embodies your life?

The sheer breadth of raw material I ended up with was both deeply moving and nearly overwhelming. When I finished I had more than a thousand hours of interviews. All were on the record, all recorded. When I had them transcribed, the total reached six thousand pages. Stacked together, they reached the shoulders of my adolescent daughters. Reading them from beginning to end took me two months.

The next step was mining them. Modeled on a process used by my friend Jim Collins, the management guru, as well as Dan McAdams, I assembled a team to help analyze the stories. We spent a year building a massive database, coding each story for fifty-seven different variables. The variables ranged from which phase of transitions people found most difficult to which types of advice they found most helpful, from when their defining life events took place to what their dreams were for the future. And we haggled over our findings in daylong *murder boards* in which no idea went unchallenged and everyone was sent back to the transcripts and existing research to double- and triple-check our findings. I can say with confidence that 90 percent of the patterns we uncovered have never been written about before. And we have the data to back them up.

Transitions Are Coming

Before digging into that data—and the stories behind them—I'd like to begin with an overall observation. If I could put what I learned into a simple formula, it would be this:

THE LINEAR LIFE IS DEAD

↓

THE NONLINEAR LIFE INVOLVES MORE LIFE TRANSITIONS

↓

LIFE TRANSITIONS ARE A SKILL WE CAN, AND MUST, MASTER

I realize these statements risk sounding a little obvious, and a little opaque. *What do you mean by "linear life"? How can you be sure that life transitions are more plentiful? How am I supposed to master such things if I don't even know what they are?* Fair enough. But to me, the patterns are clear, the warning lights are blinking, and the urgency is upon each of us to update how we make sense—and meaning—of our lives.

With that caveat, I'd like to begin by suggesting what I think is causing much of the unease so many of us have been experiencing and by laying out what I hope to achieve with this project. Specifically, I have three goals, two warnings, one promise, and one final moon shot dream for this book. Let's start with the goals.

The first is to put a name to a little-understood phenomenon in contemporary life, one that appears to play an oversize influence in how we think about ourselves: Our lives no longer follow the traditional, linear path. At the start of my project, if you'd asked me to describe the shape of my life, I would have said it was a line. One that stretched backward through my family, then moved forward, up, and down across my life, based largely on my outward success. And I would have thought everyone would say something similar.

I would have been wrong—deeply, dangerously wrong. Worse, I would have missed something fundamental about how we live today.

The smartest minds today—including those studying computers, biology, math, physics—have come to understand that the world no longer adheres to predictable, linear mandates. Instead, life is filled with chaos and complexity, periods of order and disorder, linearity and nonlinearity. In place of steady lines, observers now see loops, spirals, wobbles, fractals, twists, tangles, and turnabouts.

Curious about how this applied to our day-to-day lives, I began asking everyone I met, "What shape is your life?" I was flabbergasted by the answers. People mentioned all manner of shapes—circles, hearts, butterflies, boomerangs, rivers, trees, mountains, spirals. When I asked them to explain, they unfurled a pent-up tangle of desires, defeats, and disappointments, all of which were reflected in the multidimensional shapes of their personal narratives.

The idea that life follows a series of carefully calibrated progressions—childhood to young adulthood to middle age to old age; dating to marriage to children to empty nest; low-level job to mid-level job to senior-level job to retirement—seems preposterously outdated. Instead of passing through a series of preordained life stages interrupted by periodic *crises* on birthdays that end in zero, we experience life as a complex swirl of celebrations, setbacks, triumphs, and rebirths across the full span of our years.

What's more, Gen Xers feel this way more than boomers, and millennials even more than Xers. The once routine expectation that people will have one job, one relationship, one faith, one home, one body, one sexuality, one identity from adolescence to assisted living is deader than it's ever been. This is what it means to live a nonlinear life, and it has profound consequences for decisions we all make every day.

The biggest of those consequences is that for all the benefits of living nonlinearly—personal freedom, self-expression, living your own life rather than the life others want you to live—it obliges us all to navigate an almost overwhelming array of life transitions. That leads to my second goal: understanding this proliferating breed of life event.

Conflict is the one precondition of a story. For there to be a narrative at all, something unforeseen must happen. The *plot twists* in Hollywood lingo; the *peripeteia* in Aristotle's naming. "Everybody agrees that a story begins with some breach in the expected state of things," writes Jerome Bruner, the pioneer of narrative psychology. "Something goes awry, otherwise there's nothing to tell about." The story is the tool to resolve this breach.

A central finding of my conversations—and for me an unnerving one—is that the frequency with which these disturbances are popping up these days is rapidly increasing. We are facing an epidemic of breaches—*disruptors*, as I call them. Many reasons explain this (see chapter 2), but for now let me simply say that we tallied up every single variation of unsettling life event I heard. The total came to fifty-two types. That's fifty-two different sources of conflict, upheaval, or stress a person can face. These range from the voluntary (losing weight, starting a company) to the involuntary (being fired, discovering your child has special needs); from the personal (getting sober, losing a loved one) to the collective (joining a social movement, being hit by a natural disaster). The number of disruptors a person can expect to experience in an adult life is around three dozen. That's an average of one every twelve to eighteen months.

We manage to get through many of these disruptors with only minor upset to our lives. We adjust, draw on our loved ones, recalibrate our life stories. But every now and then, one—or more commonly a pileup of two, three, or four—of these disruptors rises to the level of truly disorienting and destabilizing us. I call these events *lifequakes*, because the damage they cause can be devastating, they're higher on the Richter scale of consequence, and their aftershocks can last for years. The average person goes through three to five of these massive reorientations in their adult lives; their average duration, my data show, is five years. When you do the math, that means nearly half our lives are spent responding to one of these episodes.

You or someone you love is almost surely going through one now.

Few anticipate this volume of life-altering events, which leads to my third goal: Since we face more of these experiences than we expect—and that number is only likely to increase in the coming years, as I'll explain—mastering the skills necessary to pass through them becomes all the more acute. Lifequakes may be voluntary or involuntary, but navigating the transitions that flow from them can *only* be voluntary. We must choose to deploy the skills.

So what exactly are those skills? I believe the most exciting thing I uncovered is a clear, detailed tool kit for navigating these transitions. Many people perform a number of these steps instinctually, but knowing (or doing) the entire list is quite rare—not least because many of these ideas contradict a century of thinking about how we navigate personal change.

Assembling this tool kit also represents the biggest single change I went through while working on this project. At the outset, I expected that how people handled crises in their personal lives or work lives or spiritual lives would be quite different from one another. Each transition must have its own playbook. I was mistaken. What I found was far more similarities—and a far more unified tool kit—than I ever would have imagined. The second half of the book (beginning in chapter 7) lays out that tool kit in explicit detail.

This leads to my twin warnings:

TRANSITIONS ARE COMING. BE PREPARED.

And to my promise: I think we can help. The *we* in this case is not just me, or even the team who helped me quantify these findings. It's the hundreds of people I explored these issues with, who were brave and forthcoming in their honesty, and who shared with me the daring and inventive ways they navigated their personal triumphs and trials. The ideas in the book are mine; if they are misguided or misdirected, I am responsible. But I did not impose them on the people I met; I discovered them. They are not top down; they are bottom up. They reflect, I believe, the truth about how people are actually responding to this period of unprecedented change.

Which brings me to my moon shot dream, the ultimate cultural windmill I'd like to tilt against. I'd like to redefine what life transitions mean. As long as we all have to go through these tumultuous periods, and not just once or twice, but three, four, five, or even more times in our lives; as long as we have to experience all this stress and distress, heartrending and heartmending; as long as we have to readjust our personal narratives, realign our priorities, and rebalance the shapes that bring meaning to our lives; why do we insist on talking about these periods as something dire and defeating, as miserable slogs we have to grit, grind, or grovel our way through?

As long as life is going to be full of plot twists, why not spend more time learning to master them?

William James, the father of modern psychology, said it best nearly a century and a half ago, and his wisdom has been sadly forgotten. *Life is in the transitions.* His point is even more true today: We can't ignore these central times of life; we can't wish or will them away. We have to accept them, name them, mark them, share them, and eventually convert them into a new and vital fuel for remaking our life stories.

The Wolf in the Fairy Tale

The Italians have a wonderful expression for how our lives get upended when we least expect it: *lupus in fabula. Fabula* means "fairy tale." The *fabula* is the fantasy of our lives, the ideal version, our lives when everything is going right. *Lupus* means "wolf." The *lupus* is the trouble, the conflict, the big, scary thing that threatens to destroy everything around it.

Our actual lives, in other words.

Lupus in fabula means "the wolf in the fairy tale." Italians use it as the equivalent of *speak of the devil.* Just when life is going swimmingly, along comes a demon, an ogre, a dragon, a diagnosis, a downsizing, a death.

Just when our fairy tale seems poised to come true, a wolf appears.

That's what happened to me all those years ago, to my dad in his moment of hopelessness, to everyone I know at one time or another.

We get stuck in the woods and can't see a way out.

We lose sight of happily ever after.

I don't feel that way now. This project was a giant wolf killer for me. It gave me more tools to fight problems, more compassion to help others, more capacity to expand and rewrite my life story than I ever thought possible. Along the way, it helped me make peace with my illness, with my career insecurity, with my own misjudgments and screwups. Listening to these stories every day filled me with awe for the breadth of human experience and with appreciation for the range of abject human miseries I've been lucky enough to avoid—at least for now.

And it taught me this: We all ache. We all hurt, suffer, and yearn. We all wallow in our bad decisions, mourn our losses, obsess over our flawed body parts, our poor choices, and our missed opportunities. We know we would be happier, richer in satisfaction, maybe even literally richer if we didn't do these things. And yet we can't help ourselves. We have what appears to be a genetic imperative to retell our story over and over again, sometimes tarrying a little too long on our poorest performances or weakest moments.

We can't get past the wolves.

And that's okay. Because if you banish the wolf, you banish the hero. And if there's one thing I learned: We all need to be the hero of our own story. That's why we need fairy tales. They teach us how to allay our fears, and help us sleep at night. Which is why we keep telling them year after year, bedtime after bedtime.

They turn our nightmares into dreams.

I

THE SHAPE OF YOUR LIFE

CHAPTER 1

Farewell to the Linear Life

The End of Predictability

Christy Moore always hated school. "I hated it from the very first day," she said. "I would pretend to vomit at the bus stop. My mom got to the point where she'd make me show her where I'd gotten sick in order for me to stay home." If she couldn't show her, Christy had to get on the bus. "But then I'd just make myself sick at school so she'd have to come and get me."

A tomboy, Christy had no interest in girly things, from dresses to babies. "I took apart my sister's Barbie doll house on Christmas morning." By high school she was a rebel. "I had no idea what I wanted to do in life. I just knew I didn't enjoy learning." She started dating a football player; she became a cheerleader, because that's what sixteen-year-olds did in South Georgia; she played hooky and hung out at the beach.

And then, the summer after her junior year, she became pregnant.

"I told Roy upfront, 'I'm having the baby,'" she said of her boyfriend. "'If you're gonna be in our lives, I'll keep it. If not, I'll put it up for adoption." Roy was offended; of course he would stick around, he said. She went to tell her mother.

"At the time I didn't know Mom was an alcoholic," Christy said. "She was literally a closet drunk; she went into her closet every night and drank, then passed out. We always thought she went to bed early." Christy sat next to her on the couch and said they needed to talk. "You and Roy are getting close," her mother said preemptively. "Maybe you need birth control." *Hmmm. A little late for that,* Christy thought.

Christy's mom proposed they buy some maternity clothes, then pick up a book on grandparenting to give to her dad, who worked late. They left the book on his pillow. "I woke up at midnight to my dad screaming at my sister, because she was the 'bad one.' 'It's your other daughter,' my sister said, and that's how he found out.'"

Six weeks later, Christy and Roy were married. He dropped out of college and got a job at Kentucky Fried Chicken. Christy dropped out of high school. They lived in a duplex.

"I thought this not only ruins our lives, this completely changes the trajectory of our lives," she said. "I really had no desire to have kids, I was gonna be a really good aunt. But I instantly went from *I'm never gonna be a mom* to *I'm going to be the best stay-at-home mom ever and raise good citizens.*"

In the next eight years, Christy and Roy had three children. He worked multiple jobs in fast food, rising from assistant manager to manager; she took a paper route from three to six in the morning. They had to switch from the Methodist church to the Baptist church because her old community shunned her. They eventually scraped up enough credit to get a loan and buy a small Japanese restaurant in a strip mall on Wilmington Island, Georgia. But Roy suffered repeated bouts of ulcerative colitis, had two major surgeries, and was out of work for months, tumbling them into medical debt. "We were that typical family with 2.5 kids and one paycheck away from being homeless, and we didn't want that. We needed security."

Then something unthinkable happened.

Christy used to take her daughter to the public library for toddler time. One day the kids went off to do arts and crafts, and Christy, pregnant with her second child and bone tired, plopped down in the nearest comfy chair. Unable to move, she stretched out her arm and grabbed the only book she could reach. It was *Wuthering Heights.* "I didn't understand half of what I read, so I had to read it twice." When she finished, she went on to the next book. It was *To Kill a Mockingbird.* "That book changed my life," she said. "To this day, I read it every year. I start on Thanksgiving night and read it slowly through Christmas Eve. My kids laugh at me. *Mom, it's not going to change.* But every time you read it, you get something else out of it."

Every Tuesday and Thursday, Christy would go to the library, sit down, and reach for a book. She slowly made her way through the entire shelf of classics—*Pride and Prejudice, The Great Gatsby, Moby-Dick.* And it was there, in that chair, on that shelf, that she found the answer she and Roy had been looking for. She would go back to school. She would turn to the one thing she always hated as a child, education.

On the day she dropped her third child at preschool, Christy drove straight to Armstrong Atlantic State University. "I cried the entire way. *What have I done? I'm a stay-at-home mom.* I sat through my first class, in psychology, and thought, *I have no idea what this man is talking about.* All the eighteen-year-olds sitting around me obviously knew because they were shaking their heads and taking notes. I went back to my car and started crying. *You're out of your mind. You're a high school dropout. You're not smart enough.*"

But she got right out of the car and went to her second class, then to her third. Every day she would drop her youngest off, then drive to school. "I would pray to God: 'I don't know if I can do this, just put the information in my head.'" She survived the first semester, then signed up for another. Her grades improved. With a full load, three children, a sick husband, ballet rehearsals, and baseball games, her life was orchestrated to the second. She entered everything onto a paper calendar in different colors of ink and crammed her life into a blue L.L.Bean book bag. And she made mountains of flashcards.

"My kids just learned: At the red light, the cards would come out; when the light turned green they'd say, '*Mo-ommm*,' and I'd put them down and drive to the next place. I even studied at Disney World."

In four years she earned a bachelor's degree in respiratory therapy. The girl who didn't like babies until she had babies of her own became an expert in keeping premature babies alive. Then she went on to get a master's degree, which took three more years. Finally, after a bout of thyroid cancer, she took the biggest leap of all. She enrolled in a doctorate program in adult education.

Six years later, a full sixteen years after picking up *Wuthering Heights*, twenty-four years after dropping out of high school, and thirty-eight years after purposefully throwing up on the first day of kindergarten, Christy donned a tank top and shorts on a 102-degree day in August, pulled on her royal-blue cap and gown, and marched down the aisle. She had pulled off the unimaginable: She had gone from GED to PhD. She called it the happiest day of her life.

"Although my life is completely out of order," she said, "if I had done it in the expected order, I wouldn't have the husband I have, the children I have, or the life that I have, which I adore. I would have been on the corner doing drugs or toothless flipping burgers somewhere."

Instead, today she has a job counseling nontraditional students—precisely those who don't love school—on the virtues of bucking the traditional path and continuing their education. And she considers the upside-down way she lived her life to be the greatest testament she can make to the value of finding your own life course.

The Circle of Life

In her book *A Short History of Myth*, Karen Armstrong makes the point that every time humans take a step forward, they revise and update their understanding of the world. This revision usually involves a host of issues, from religious beliefs to sexual taboos. Few would disagree we're in such a moment of transformation today. In what seems like overnight, we've seen whiplashing breakthroughs in technology, a weakening of religious institutions, a realignment of gender roles. Yet few people seem to acknowledge—or even understand—that we're in a similar readjustment in our expectations for what shape our lives should take.

I realize the word *shape* might seem out of context in a discussion of human life. *Wait, are you saying my life is a circle, a triangle, or a line?* In a way, yes, because that's what society tells us. I'm using the word—and the idea underneath it—the way it's been used for centuries to refer to the deep-seated assumptions and unspoken paradigms that define our view of the ideal human life. Specifically, whether our lives are expected to follow a path that's circular, ascending, descending, oscillating, or something else entirely. While these distinctions may sound abstract, they have thousands of real-world implications, governing everything from when we should get married to when we should work, from when we should get sick to when we should take risks.

In short, who should control the *should*s of our lives?

The easiest way to understand this change is to first look back at prior cultures and how they understood these shapes and *should*s. Broadly speaking, there have been three significant evolutions in our understanding of life shape, which relate directly to our conception of time. We've shifted from a concept based on natural time (seasonal, cyclical) to one modeled on mechanical time (regular, syncopated, linear) to one characterized by the more variable understanding of time as dynamic, unpredictable, nonlinear. Let's start at the beginning.

The earliest ways of thinking about time reflected humans' observations of the world around them. With no timepieces, early civilizations from Babylon to Egypt likened time to nature—the seasons, the weather, the reassuring cycle of regularity. There was virtually no sense of chronology in the ancient world, of history, of one life event influencing the next. Instead, most cultures believed that humans followed a preexisting *circle of life*. (The

Egyptian ouroboros, in which a serpent devours its own tail, is one early representation.) In this cyclical worldview, the highest form of living was not to forge your own path—to be the hero of your own story—but to reexperience what already happened—to replicate the universal story.

All this began to change in late antiquity with the arrival of linear time. The Bible played a big role in this, as it introduced the idea that time followed a historical progression from Adam and Eve through the patriarchs, kings, prophets, and so on. With Christians, this advancement reached its ultimate peak with Jesus. Gradually life changed from being a *circle* to something more linear and capable of progress. Now each of us could follow a path that elevated our condition; now each of us could aspire to a life of personal fulfillment. That led to a new consensus shape in the West: life as a series of *stages*.

"Shit Was About to Get Real, Quick"

Davon Goodwin's life was not cyclical at all. He went through so many unpredictable pivots that he considered his life to be a pentagon.

Davon was raised by a single mom in the projects of Pittsburgh. His father was imprisoned on drug charges. "My brother was always angry," he said. "But I was like, *Yeah, everybody has their dad to go play with. Cool, I have a mom!* Davon visited his grandma one summer in North Carolina and started digging in her backyard. "The dirt changed my whole life," he said. "I wanted to be a botanist. I wanted to be playing with flowers. Most people in my world said, 'You're gay; you gotta be gay.' But I just loved plants."

Back in Pittsburgh, the head of Davon's school invited him to take over an abandoned greenhouse, so he spent half of every day building a tropical forest, the rest going to wrestling practice. "I started looking for a college that had wrestling and botany," he said. "That's not a lot of places!" He accepted a scholarship to the University of North Carolina at Pembroke.

Halfway through freshman year, he quit the wrestling team. "I told the coach, 'Thank you, but I want to party, I want to eat more than one meal a day, I want to experience college.'" Soon his grades dropped, he lost his scholarship, he had no way to pay his bills. An army recruiter offered him $60,000 to cover his tuition, so Davon enlisted. His mother was horrified. "Why the hell did you do that?" But he was driving trucks in a nondeployable unit, he assured her, and he could stay in school while he served.

Then he got deployed. At first it was just Kuwait, which was relatively safe, but then his sergeant came in and announced, "We just got called to Afghanistan. Pack your stuff. We're leaving in an hour." *Shit was about to get real, quick*, Davon thought. "I knew it was going to be bad when as soon as the plane landed on the tarmac, they opened the back door and said, '*Jump!*'"

For a while, things were stable; Davon even went home on leave. Two weeks after he returned, he was assigned to drive an Oshkosh M1070 Heavy Equipment Transporter, the largest vehicle in the army, on a mission in Helmand Province, west of Kandahar. "The Taliban were everywhere," he said. The night before, Davon had a bad feeling and couldn't sleep. He told his commanding officer, "I don't know what it is, but something tells me not to drive." The officer responded, "Then at least get your ass in the passenger seat."

Fifteen minutes later the truck drove over a five-hundred-pound IED—an improvised explosive device—directly under his feet. The vehicle was shredded. "The only thing I remember asking was, 'God, get me out of this truck.'"

Davon broke his L1 and L2 vertebrae that morning and suffered what he calls "a hell of a lot of traumatic brain injury." He was flown to Germany, then to Fort Bragg in North Carolina. He suffered from acute back pain, depression, and severe narcolepsy. "I started drinking heavily. I had suicidal ideations. One night I went into the bathroom and stared in my medicine cabinet. I said to myself, *If I take all these pills, what do I have to lose?* Right then the phone rings. *Don't answer it*, I thought. But I looked over and saw it was my mom. She told me she was quitting her job in Pittsburgh and moving to North Carolina. 'I'll be right there if you need my help.'"

The week she arrived, she made Davon go to church. Halfway through the service, the preacher asked new visitors to share their stories. Davon demurred, but his mother insisted. "You've got to tell your story, because your story matters." So he told it. "I was crying and crying, and she was like, 'See, it's out now. You don't have to feel ashamed.' That was the day I started living again."

Davon's rehab officer insisted he could never read again, but Davon didn't believe him, so he checked out of his program and reenrolled in college. He started with one class, then added more. He got married and had a son. "That gave me even further reason to live," he said. He graduated but struggled to find work. No one wanted to employ a narcoleptic. "People would say, 'You're great, but we can't let you do anything.'"

He was down to his last month's rent when he met a local doctor who ran a five-hundred-acre farm on the side. They were looking for a manager.

He went for the interview, stuck his hands in the soil, and immediately remembered his childhood love of gardening.

"It's hard to explain," he said, "but it felt like there was healing in that soil. I had forgotten my earlier dream—to be a botanist, to cure cancer, to travel the world. The day I got blown up in Afghanistan—that ended my first life's mission. But now I have a new mission: to help communities of color have access to fresh produce. All I can say is, that bomb was not a bomb; that bomb was a blessing. It forced me to come up with a new dream."

The Stages of Life

A few steps from the Thames, in the Blackfriars neighborhood of London, is a brutalist concrete office building occupied by BT. Tom Cruise broke his ankle here while performing a stunt for the sixth *Mission: Impossible*. In the courtyard is an aluminum sculpture in the shape of a totem pole consisting of seven faces. The sculpture pays homage to the most famous speech in Shakespeare's *As You Like It*, one that perfectly captures the next biggest turn in how people viewed the shape of their lives.

All the world's a stage,
and all the men and women merely players;
They have their exits and their entrances,
And one man in his time plays many parts,
His acts being seven ages.

By the early modern era, the idea of life following a circle finally died away, replaced by the idea of life proceeding through a series of *ages*, *phases*, or *stages*. Few people knew, or cared, about their exact chronological age; instead people viewed their lives as consisting of periods—youth, apprenticeship, marriage, parenthood, sickness, death, and so on. A series of expressions arose that captured this progression. Everyone now followed a *life course*, a *life span*, or a *life cycle*. The word *career*, from the Latin for "wheeled vehicle," was invented at this time to capture what it felt like to navigate this course.

The primary visual metaphor for this way of living was a rising and falling *staircase*. Individuals were expected to climb through their early lives, peak in middle age, and then slowly decline. Men and women had their own staircases, but the general shape was the same: Children play, those in their prime work, the old hobble. What's striking is that unlike more recent paradigms, here middle age is the pinnacle.

As life became more urban during these years, city pleasures rose. First among these: theater. Since plays are performed on stages, the *stage* quickly became the chief way of talking about life. Each step on the staircase was a *stage* in which you were an *actor* performing in the great *drama*

of life. Shakespeare's seven stages included the infant, the schoolboy, the lover, the soldier, the shrunken, and the second child, "sans teeth, sans eyes, sans taste, sans everything."

It's hard to overemphasize how influential these constructs were. They normalized the notion that life was universal, rigid, unforgiving. Life went up, then it went down. There were no exceptions, no second chances, no *getting clean at forty* or *finding new love at sixty*. You have only one shot, and it's downhill from there. To reinforce that message, hourglasses were common in these staircases. Everyone was *running out of time* before Father Time himself appeared to inform you your "time was up."

You might think we would have ditched this doom and gloom in the modern world. We would have done everything in our power to free ourselves from this rigid up-and-down shape. Instead, we made it worse.

"He Said to Me, 'I Expect Great Things From You'"

David Parsons is proof that strict up-and-down models don't work.

David was born into American automobile royalty in Detroit, at a time, 1952, when American automobiles were the envy of the world. His family had eight cars, "one for each member." Three of David's grandparents immigrated through Ellis Island. One was a potato farmer from Sweden who moved to Michigan and invented the concealed door hinge, which made him prosperous, connected, and Republican. His son, David's father, followed the same path. He was in the first class of recipients to be awarded the National Medal of Technology, along with Steve Jobs and Stephen Wozniak.

"In high school I was expected to be an athlete," David said. "I was on my way to Dartmouth, probably to play football and study pre-law, when I got the part of Curly in *Oklahoma!* my senior year." There's a moment in the show when Curly kisses Laurey, then turns to the audience and declares his love. "I was absolutely sucked in," he said.

David told his parents he wanted to ditch the Ivy League for music school. His father took him to dinner with the governor of Michigan, the state's senior United States senator, and a former All-American quarterback—all of whom were lawyers, all of whom attempted to change his mind. All of them failed.

David enrolled in music school at the University of Michigan and went on to get undergraduate and master's degrees in performance. Unlike his peers, he also got work—at the Santa Fe Opera, the Houston Grand Opera, and when he moved to New York, the first five operas he auditioned for. "A good average is if you get one in ten auditions," he said. "Then you're making a living. I was making a career." He was raved about in the *New York Times*, featured on *CBS News Sunday Morning*, invited to Edinburgh by Alistair Cooke.

And on top of it all, he married Miss America. They met while he was again playing Curly, at Cincinnati Opera, and she was playing Laurey. She broke a date with baseball icon Johnny Bench to go out with David. "We just fell in love," he said. They quickly began a glamorous life of travel, music, artistic residences in Europe. Their home was in New York but their heart was in the stage lights. And all this time he kept a dark, hidden secret.

David was a stone-cold drunk.

"I started drinking when I was eleven," he said. "Significantly. Seriously. I grew up in a world where people would give you ashtrays for Christmas. My parents had a liquor cabinet stocked with every kind of liquor you could want, with extra cases in the basement. It was easy to take things."

After his wedding, David began to lose control. He had a botched surgery on his vocal cords that ended his opera career. He began teaching. He joined the church choir. He took a job at a sporting goods store selling ski equipment. "I just said my life is over. The only thing I've ever done is be a singer. I felt, well, for some people things just don't work out."

And then, things got worse. David's oldest brother, Carl, became gravely ill with AIDS. Carl had lived in Los Angeles since the late sixties, where he was Zsa Zsa Gabor's secretary and designed homes for stars. He and David had remained close. Carl was the one who had flown in for every one of David's openings. Now Carl had to fly home and move in with his parents. "They had no idea he was gay," David said. "Denial is a powerful tool."

On David's last visit with Carl, he was surrounded with purple flowers. "He had this kind of corona around him of purple," David said. "And he said to me: 'I expect great things from you.'"

Carl died in the third week of December. Four days later, David was in western Oklahoma, where his father-in-law was a conservative pastor. David asked if he could sing in the Christmas service. "It was better than I'd ever sung," he said. "I went home and went through a bottle of scotch with such ferocity and anger. And the next morning, I woke up, got down on my knees, and said, 'I can't do this another day.'" David didn't know anything about recovery, he said. He had never been to an AA meeting. "I just said, 'God, please help me not drink today. If I make it, I'll thank you tonight, and I'll ask you again tomorrow morning.'" He paused. "I haven't had a drink since that day."

Soon after, David told his wife that he was called to join the Lutheran ministry. He had been spending more time in church, he said. He saw the resistance to gays and lesbians like his brother and wanted to expand the mission of the church. "I'll pay for you to go to law school," she said, "but I won't be a preacher's wife." David couldn't resist. He enrolled in Union Theological Seminary in New York, and at the end of the first year she called to say she wasn't coming home. "I kept saying this was going to be great, and she kept saying it wasn't."

David started work at St. John-St. Matthew-Emanuel Lutheran Church in Brooklyn two days before 9/11. When I met him, he was living in the parish house, along with his second wife and their eleven-year-old daughter. He had become a leading voice in the Lutheran Church for LGBT inclusion. He sang in the choir but dreamed of returning to the stage one day. When I asked the shape of his life, he said, "The cross."

"Every pastor is a theologian of the cross," he said. "But in my case, I believe in the Jesus story. I know that freaks people out, especially in New York. But I lived a very dissipated life, and now I live a life of service. There was a very specific point in time when God came down and touched my life. That's the crossroads that led me where I am today."

The Linear Life

The fascination with time that began in the early modern era became all-consuming by the industrial age. Humans in the nineteenth century became time-obsessed. They started eating when the clock told them, working when the clock told them, sleeping when the clock told them. A large reason for this preoccupation was that timepieces were suddenly ubiquitous. Pocket watches became widespread in the 1800s, followed by wristwatches and grandfather clocks. A song from 1876 told how Grandfather adored his beloved clock, bought on the day he was born. It followed him through the stages of life, until it "stopp'd short, never to go again, when the old man died." The sheet music sold a million copies.

It was inevitable that as humans started tracking their day by the clock, they began tracking their lives by the clock as well. The dominant shapes of life in the twentieth century were all mechanical, industrial, sequential. The *arrow of progress*, the *conveyor belt of life. Up by your bootstraps, rags to riches*, "Forward, forward let us range," in Tennyson's phrase.

In this climate, it was no surprise that the new field of human psychology adopted similar language. The regimentation of the human day led to the regimentation of the human life. Beginning around 1900 a plethora of new time periods became popular: *adolescence, midlife, retirement, geriatrics*. Each new *time of life* came with its own barrage of studies, conditions, and self-improvement products.

Sigmund Freud, for instance, said all humans were permanently shaped by a series of psychosexual stages they were expected to pass through between zero and twelve—oral, anal, genital, etc. Jean Piaget identified a different series of development stages and a different calendar—sensorimotor (birth to twenty-four months), preoperational (two to seven), and so on. These ideas revolutionized our understanding of children. They represent milestones in thought.

But they also had lasting consequences that are not always understood, and not always positive. Namely, they acculturated all of us to the idea that life proceeds for children *and* adults through a series of set, well-established metamorphoses that unfold on a uniform timetable. Even the term *human development* likens people to cars or washing machines. In the beginning we are *not yet done*, then we become *ready for use*, and somewhere down the line we become *obsolete*.

Sure enough, in the wake of these ideas about childhood, a flood of prominent theories about adult development appeared. Suddenly there were six stages of moral maturation and five of self-actualization. John Bowlby, the British psychologist who explained how children *attach* to loved ones in stages, extrapolated that we *unattach* in a reverse process. Elisabeth Kübler-Ross introduced the widely popular idea that both when we are dying and when we grieve, we pass through five successive stages: denial, anger, bargaining, depression, and acceptance. Joseph Campbell's iconic hero's journey is a staged model of spiritual growth.

By far the most influential of these linear models is Erik Erickson's eight stages of development. Born in Germany to a Danish father and Jewish mother who quickly divorced, Erickson was mocked as a Jew in school and as a goy in synagogue. He fled the Nazis, ended up in America, and turned his extraordinary life into grist for a series of crises everyone had to master—trust versus mistrust in infancy, intimacy versus isolation in early adulthood, integrity versus despair in old age. Failure to pass through any stage in the "predetermined order" prevents one from having a healthful life.

Erickson openly acknowledged the influence of industrial metaphors on his thinking. "As our world-image is a one-way street to never ending progress," he wrote, "our lives are to be one-way streets to success."

Erickson's contribution is that he extended Piaget's stage model past childhood all the way to old age. But his disservice is equally profound. He validated the rather flimsy idea that adulthood passes in three carefully delineated time periods. To read him today is to be stunned by the bias: progress marches on whether you're on schedule or not.

And yet: What happens if you get pregnant at the wrong time (as Christy Moore did), get a life-threatening injury at the start of your adult life (as Davon Goodwin did), or find that you succumb to addiction, lose your livelihood, lose your brother, and have your marriage end (as David Parsons did) on a calendar that's not "predetermined"?

Today, each of these staged constructs has been diluted, debunked, or discredited in some way. They're too pat, too narrow, too grand, too male. As Columbia University's George Bonanno, a leading grief researcher, wrote, the stage models are simply too tidy, they're based more on wishful thinking than empirical data, and they put too much pressure on people to meet someone else's expectations. Bonanno goes so far as to call them "dangerous," doing "more harm than good."

It's the *should* problem all over again. You *should* be feeling this at this specific time in your life; if you don't, there's something wrong with you.

Yet as harmful as these ideas were, they were trumped by the impact of the mesmerizing but ultimately misleading idea put forward by the greatest of all popularizers of the linear life. Her name is Gail Sheehy and her idea: Life is a series of *passages*.

"It's Raining Cancer in My Life"

Ann Ramer's life has followed no linear trajectory. It was more like a comfy pair of slippers, she said. Until, one day, the comfort melted away.

Unlike Christy Moore, Ann wanted only to be a mom. "I was a stay-at-home mom, and I was enjoying that very much," she said of her life in Cleveland, Ohio. "I wasn't ambitious. I felt like, *I don't have to do anything big or grand in the world. I need to raise good human beings.*" And her plan was working. Ann and her husband, Dan, an architect, had a son, Alex; then a second son, Brent; then a daughter, Lauren. "I was very content," Ann said.

At seventeen months, though, Lauren began growing pubic hair. "My pediatrician told me it's because I started taking birth control pills while I was breastfeeding." Ann was skeptical, so she called her OB. "No, this is not from that. You bring her to see me today."

Lauren was diagnosed with adrenal cancer. "It's hideously rare," Ann said. Lauren had an operation to remove the tumor, went through chemotherapy, and was declared cancer-free. "Pretend this never happened," doctors said. Ann wanted another child, but her husband balked. "What if that child gets cancer, too?" he asked. Ann prevailed, and Olivia was born three years later. Three years after that, cancer did return. Only this time it wasn't Olivia, or even Lauren. It was eleven-year-old Brent.

Brent came home from school one day and announced that his soccer coach had held him out of practice because of his leg. "Do you have pain?" Ann asked. "No, I have a limp." The next day Brent couldn't run across the field. "I looked in the back of his pelvic bone and there was no muscle there," Ann said. "That wasn't right. He was a huge athlete."

Brent was diagnosed with an osteogenic sarcoma, another extremely rare cancer.

"I had an ugly feeling right away," Ann said. "'I need to see a geneticist immediately,' I said, 'even before seeing an oncologist.'" The geneticist confirmed her worst instincts. Brent had Li-Fraumeni syndrome, a hyper-rare hereditary disorder that results from a mutation of the p53 gene that predisposes carriers to get multiple cancers. Brent wasn't the only child to have the mutation; Lauren did, too. Her two other children did not.

"We also tested me and Dan," Ann said, "and this part is fantastic. The geneticist came in and gave us the good news. 'So, neither you nor your husband has this mutation.' Then she said, 'I have to ask you, are we sure about the paternity of these children?'"

"Really?" I said.

"Oh, it was an awesome day," Ann said. "I told her, 'Well, it's not like I've been cruising the cancer ward to step out on my husband.'"

Every doctor the family consulted said that Brent needed to have his leg amputated, except one, John Healey, an orthopedist at Memorial Sloan Kettering, in New York City, the same surgeon, as it happens, who saved my leg. Brent began chemotherapy; his surgery was scheduled for early January. The family decided to celebrate Christmas early, on December 23. "That morning, the telephone rang," Ann said. "It was Lauren's doctor, saying they'd found a golf-ball-sized tumor in her brain."

Nine-year-old Lauren had brain surgery on December 28. While she was still in the hospital recovering in Ohio, eleven-year-old Brent had surgery in New York.

"I mean, this is not how this is supposed to go."

"*This* being life?"

"Just think: It's raining cancer in my life. Nobody expects that."

That rain soon became a full-blown storm. Brent had three follow-up surgeries in the coming months, then three more procedures the summer after that. "He was able to walk, went back to school, was doing great," Ann said. "Then I got a phone call that he had metastatic melanoma and had to do a year of interferon. There were a good three hours when we were in the clear." The treatment did not work. Brent soon came down with acute myeloid leukemia. The only option was a bone marrow transplant.

While all this was going on, Lauren's brain tumor came back. "So we're doing kids with cancer for the second time," Ann said. Lauren's surgery was scheduled for the same time as Brent's transplant. Alex, their older brother, agreed to be Brent's donor. "So I had three kids on the oncology floor in the same month."

Lauren's surgery was successful. Brent, too, did well for a while and was able to resume school, but the following year he developed necrotizing fasciitis, a flesh-eating bacterium. He was a good candidate for a drug trial but was ineligible because he was a minor. A skin graft from his brother helped for a time, but his body was weakening. Lauren, meanwhile, got an osteosarcoma herself. Once again, Lauren and Brent were in the same treatment center in Houston, on the ninth and seventh floors.

This time, though, the situation did not last. Brent Ramer died on December 30, two months after his eighteenth birthday, which would have made him eligible for the trial.

"Our whole family was there," Ann said. "I grabbed Lauren off her floor so we could all be together."

Ann, the mild-mannered, stay-at-home mom with no aspirations for herself, was transformed into an activist. She lobbied elected officials in Washington to change eligibility requirements for drug trials; she hunted down medical researchers and beseeched them to reconsider their restrictions for minors; she started a Li-Fraumeni support group online. "I developed great friendships with the ladies in the group, but in the end I had to step away because my story was starting to frighten the newbies."

That story, though, was a source of strength for Ann. I was struck that in our conversation, Ann barely mentioned her childhood, her early career as a schoolteacher, her love of gardening and cooking. "Because none of what happened before this whole situation matters," she said. "Before my daughter had cancer five times, before my son had a horrific six-and-a-half-year battle with cancer, before this entire period that I call *cancering*."

Perhaps most challenging: The woman who wanted only to be a mom couldn't always be the mom she wanted to be. "For a long time, I didn't even feed my own family. People would bring meals in. As you might imagine, I'm in New York for two months, Alex needed to get to practice, Olivia needed to get to preschool. And people stepped in. As a stay-at-home mom and a person whose identity was taking care of my family, that was a huge change for me. To give up that control. To accept that charity."

But she did accept it and came to embrace this new narrative of herself.

"I learned things about life I didn't think I could understand," Ann said. "I challenged myself in ways I didn't think possible. I learned to seek out answers, to speak up, to do things I wasn't comfortable doing. This wasn't the life I expected, but it was the life I got. My work used to be my children; now my work is cancer and my children. And I'm still content with that."

Gail Sheehy and the Delusion of Predictability

The man who invented the midlife crisis had a midlife crisis of his own: His idea bombed. In 1957, a Canadian psychoanalyst named Elliott Jaques gave a speech before a distinguished audience in London in which he claimed people in their midthirties went through a depressive period. Reactions to this time of life included concern over health, compulsive vanity, promiscuity, and religious awakening. The audience hated the idea, so he dropped it.

Nearly a decade later, he revisited it, this time in a paper called "Death and the Mid-life Crisis." Jaques was inspired, he said, by the oversimplification of how we talked about life shape. "Up till now, life has seemed an endless upward slope, with nothing but the distant horizon in view." Now, he went on, he'd reached the crest of the hill, "and there stretching ahead is the downward slope." It ends, inevitably, in death. The most common age for this crisis: thirty-seven.

Jaques's idea, while tantalizing, was not grounded in research. It was based on his reading of biographies of 310 famous men, from Michelangelo to Bach. He didn't include women in his study, he said, because menopause "obscured" their midlife transition. No wonder the London audience scoffed at his theory!

But others ran with it. In the early seventies, Roger Gould, of UCLA, sent questionnaires on midlife to several hundred subjects. Daniel Levinson, of Yale, interviewed forty people (also all male) and identified what he called *four seasons of a man's life.* "There is a single, most frequent age at which each period begins," he went on: seventeen, forty, sixty, and eighty. Everyone lives through the same developmental periods at the same time. Again, the rigidity is stunning. Levinson was so precise—and doctrinaire—that he insisted the midlife crisis *must* start in the fortieth year and *will* end at forty-five and a half. Eighty percent of men go through one of these crises, he said.

Rather than question this idea, Americans embraced it, largely because of the brilliance of one woman. Gail Sheehy was a former home ec major turned freelance journalist, and a divorced single mom, when, in 1972, while in Northern Ireland, a young boy she was interviewing was shot in the face. The shock produced an existential crisis about how she felt on reaching her midthirties. Sheehy picked up on the research of Gould and Levinson and used them for the basis of an article in *New York* magazine.

Gould, who went uncredited in the story, sued her for plagiarism and won, securing $10,000 and 10 percent of the royalties of *Passages*, the book that grew out of the article. Published in 1976, *Passages* tapped into a moment of deep change in America, with the sexual revolution, surging divorce rates, and economic anxiety all converging. The book went on to sell five million copies in twenty-eight languages. It spent three years on the bestseller list. The Library of Congress named it one of the most influential books of the century.

Subtitled *Predictable Crises of Adult*

Life, *Passages* is the bible of the linear life. Using her unmatched talent in naming, Sheehy said all adults go through the same four stages: the Trying Twenties; the Catch-30 around your thirtieth birthday; the Deadline Decade of your thirties; and the Age 40 Crucible. (She mentioned no passage after age forty, which she admitted later was an embarrassment.)

After Sheehy, the midlife crisis was no longer a theory; it was simply a fact of life. Even in my interviews, forty years later, people used expressions like *my first midlife crisis, I had my midlife crisis at twenty or thirty-two or fifty-four, my midlife crisis happened after I retired*. The slipperiness of the term hints at a larger truth.

Sheehy's idea is deeply flawed. Clearly she mined a rich vein in the culture; she took a century of thinking about fixed, linear development and burst it from the ivory tower onto every kitchen table. But as countless studies have since shown, she almost single-handedly created a set of expectations that often differed from reality. She said not only *might* we all go through these changes, we *would* and *should*.

Half a lifetime later, I believe that this expectation that life will proceed in an orderly, predictable manner is a significant source of the dissatisfaction I experienced in my own life, and that I encountered in my hundreds of interviews. Christy Moore had the big pivots in her life at sixteen and thirty; Davon Goodwin at seven, seventeen, and twenty-three; David Parsons at eleven, sixteen, thirty-eight, and forty-three; and Ann Ramer at twenty-eight, thirty-four, and forty-eight. And they're not alone. Most lives simply do not follow the tidy templates of linearity. They follow a different shape entirely.

CHAPTER 2

Embracing the Nonlinear Life

What It Means to Live Life Out of Order

A hallmark of our time is that life is not predictable. It does not unfold in passages, stages, phases, or cycles. It is nonlinear—and getting more so every day. It's also more manageable, more forgiving of missteps, and more open to personalization, if you know how to navigate the new outbreak of twists and turns.

"I Feel Like the Theme of My Life Has Been Change"

Take J. R. McLain.

J. R. was born in a small hospital in West Point, Mississippi. His parents moved a lot, first to Alabama and then Louisiana, so he went to nine different schools in his first twelve years. "My mom said I had a new friend every time before the truck was unpacked." When J. R. was in junior high, the family lived in a nice house with a pool. "Then my father got this wild hair and decided to become a Baptist minister, which meant he got this tiny church in a rural community making $12,000 a year."

One day J. R. was playing football out front with seven black friends.

"Suddenly a pickup truck came screaming into the churchyard. One of the deacons jumps out and starts yelling, 'You niggers get out of this churchyard right now!' My dad came running out with his fists clenched. 'As long as I'm here, these kids are all right playing in the churchyard.' The deacon left in a huff, and a few short weeks later we were asked to move along."

J. R. battled ADHD and left high school without a diploma. He drifted into a series of minor jobs before joining the navy as an aviation machinist. After serving stints in Florida, Europe, and Asia, he got married and was spooked enough about the challenges of military marriages that he left the service and moved with his wife and two daughters back to Alabama, where he began driving 18-wheelers.

"To make a living, you had to spend a lot of time on the road," he said, which put stress on his family. One day he took a load to Georgia. "I had already told the company, 'I need to be home for my daughter's birthday this weekend.'" When they detoured him to Chicago, he turned the rig toward home. "The dispatcher screamed, 'If you don't turn that truck around, I'm gonna tell the police you're stealing our truck.' 'Fine, I'll park it by the interstate and hitch a ride home.'" The boss called. "Don't ditch the truck. We'll talk on Monday." By then J. R. had decided to quit driving and enroll in nursing school.

"I'd always envisioned myself as an EMT," he said. "When I was a kid, my favorite class was health, and I loved the show *Emergency!*" Though he got detoured several times, including taking a year off to care for his wife, who became ill while pregnant with their third child, he eventually graduated at the top of his class. "I thought that was pretty good for a guy who never did well in school." When a hospital in Oregon offered him three times what he was making in Alabama, he leapt at the opportunity.

"Honestly, it didn't have anything to do with any midlife crisis," he said. "I was just trying to make a better life for my family." Also, his mother had become intrusive, he and his wife were going through a rough patch in their marriage, and their elder daughter was having social issues. "We were all ready for a change."

In the next five years, J. R. went through a tsunami of change. Having already changed professions and regions, next he changed religious affiliations—from Baptist to nondenominational Christian. He changed political orientations. He enrolled in the nurses' union and helped lead the Oregon campaign for single-payer health care. But the hardest change of all was switching parenting styles, he said. "Before, I was a Mom-and-Dad-are-the-boss-and-you-do-everything-we-say-or-we-spank-you type of parent. But we wanted a more collaborative relationship with our kids."

That came in handy when their fifteen-year-old daughter, Zoe, became pregnant. "I was originally taken aback," he said. "If that had been me, my father would have used corporal punishment. But she was my oldest baby. I kept thinking back to when she was a girl in my lap. I thought, *I love her. We're going to figure out what to do from here.*"

Zoe elected to keep the baby, started dating a woman, and eventually moved back in with her parents. In their forties, J. R. and his wife became primary caretakers for their grandchild.

The effect of all this upheaval was at first physical. "There was a weightlessness I felt. My wife felt free to be out of the South; my daughter could love who she wanted; I could stop trying to please other people." And that affected how he viewed life itself. "I imagine it's a common experience," he said, "but I feel like the theme of my life has been change. That goes back to the nine different schools, to the navy, to moving my family across the country. And now I realize: Change is life. It's what keeps life interesting."

The Butterfly Effect

The moment that's considered the origin of modern science—the big bang of the linear life, if you will—came in 1583 when a young student named

Galileo at the University of Pisa used his pulse to time the pendulum swings of a hanging lamp in the cathedral. The moment that's considered the origin of postmodern science—the big bang of the nonlinear life—came in 1961 when a middle-aged meteorologist named Edward Lorenz at MIT observed the irregular pattern of clouds outside his office.

Lorenz attempted to quantify the variable phenomenon using the vacuum tubes of his computer. He couldn't, which led him instead to the more shocking discovery that he later called *the butterfly effect*. The idea is that weather is not regular and periodic; it's irregular and nonperiodic. Tiny influences in one part of the system can transform the outcome in other parts. As Lorenz memorably asked in the title of a 1972 paper: "Does the Flap of a Butterfly's Wings in Brazil Set Off a Tornado in Texas?"

Lorenz wasn't the first to see such irregularities; Da Vinci talked about the mystery of flowing water centuries earlier. But Lorenz's discovery set off a new race to explore previously ignored complexities across science—from the path of lightning to the swirl of cream in a cup of coffee to the conduct of neurons in the brain. Each of these phenomena is what mathematicians call a *nonlinear system*.

Linear thinking, writes physicist F. David Peat, views the world in terms of quantification, symmetry, mechanism; nonlinear thinking frees us from those confines. "We begin to envision the world as a flux of patterns enlivened with sudden turns, strange mirrors, subtle and surprising relationships." As James Gleick, an early chronicler of this new science of chaos, wrote: "Nonlinearity means that the act of playing the game has a way of changing the rules." It's like walking through a maze whose walls rearrange themselves with each step you take.

In previous breakthroughs in science, once observers had identified a phenomenon like nonlinearity in the world, the rest of us would begin to recognize it in our own lives. Some of that has happened. Person after person in my conversations described their lives as *fluid*, *fickle*, *changeable*, *adaptable*. But for whatever reason, no unifying expression has emerged to capture this variability.

The time has come to fix that. Since our world is nonlinear, we should acknowledge that our lives are nonlinear, too. Just as the *cyclical life* was replaced by the *linear life*, the *linear life* is being replaced by the *nonlinear life*.

Once you appreciate that life is nonlinear, you see the examples everywhere: Lin-Manuel Miranda picking up a random biography of a forgotten Founding Father at a bookstore in Manhattan. Lana Turner being discovered at a diner on Sunset Boulevard. Waylon Jennings giving up his seat on Buddy Holly's chartered plane at the last minute. J. R. McLain changing jobs, homes, churches, ideologies, and parenting styles—all in a three-year span.

Nonlinearity suggests that instead of resisting upheavals and uncertainties like these, we should accept them. Yours is not the only life that seems to be following its own inscrutable path. Everyone else's is, too.

More to the point, nonlinearity helps explain why we all feel so overwhelmed all the time. Trained to expect that our lives will unfold in a predictable series of stately life chapters, we're confused when those chapters come faster and faster, frequently out of order, often one on top of the other. But the reality is: We're all the clouds floating over the horizon, the swirl of cream in the coffee, the jagged dash of lightning. And we're not aberrations because of this; we're just like everything else.

Acknowledging this reality is both a rebuke to centuries of conventional thinking that imposed order on our life stories where there was none, and an invitation to see in the seeming randomness of our everyday lives patterns that are far more thrilling than we could ever imagine. The fundamental ingredient of those patterns—the base unit of the nonlinear life—is the everyday events that reshape our lives. I call these events *disruptors*. The most startling revelation: They're far more prevalent than anyone expects.

The Deck of Disruptors

Let's start with a definition. A disruptor is an event or experience that interrupts the everyday flow of one's life. I chose *disruptors* as opposed to *stressors*, *crises*, *problems*, or any other label they've been given over the years because the term is more value neutral. Many disruptors, like adopting a child, say, or starting a new job, would not traditionally be defined as negative, yet they're still disruptive. Even the most customarily negative life events, like losing a spouse or being fired, sometimes become catalysts for reinvention. Disruptors are simply deviations from daily life.

I combed all 225 life stories to generate a master list of the events that meaningfully redirected people's lives. These events ranged from getting married to caring for an aging parent, from being fired to being sexually harassed, from overnight fame to public humiliation. The total number of disruptors was fifty-two. The parallel to a deck of cards is irresistible, so I named the list life's *deck of disruptors*.

I further divided the list into the five story lines that emerged in my conversations as the shared fabric of personal identity. In order of number of disruptors, the story lines are *love*, *identity*, *beliefs*, *work*, and *body*. At 35 percent, love, defined as the larger realm of family and relationships, has the clear plurality of disruptions. All the others are bunched in the teens.

The closest analogy to this list is the Holmes-Rahe life stress inventory, created in 1967 by psychiatrists Thomas Holmes and Richard Rahe. They identified forty-three *life change units* and weighted each one for the stress it caused. The highest were death of a spouse (100) and divorce (73); the lowest were major holidays (12) and minor violations of the law (11).

The differences between their list and mine, made fifty years apart, are fascinating. Most items are similar, but they have some everyday annoyances—major holidays, family get-togethers—that rarely came up in my conversations. They have only one category relating to religion (change in church activity) while I have three (change in religious observance, change in religious affiliation, personal calling), which I suspect reflects the fluidity of spiritual identity today.

In a measure of the rise of entrepreneurship, Holmes and Rahe have eight categories about work, all of which I cover, but none about starting your own business or nonprofit. They have divorce, but no custody battles, which of course have become more common. And most striking, none of

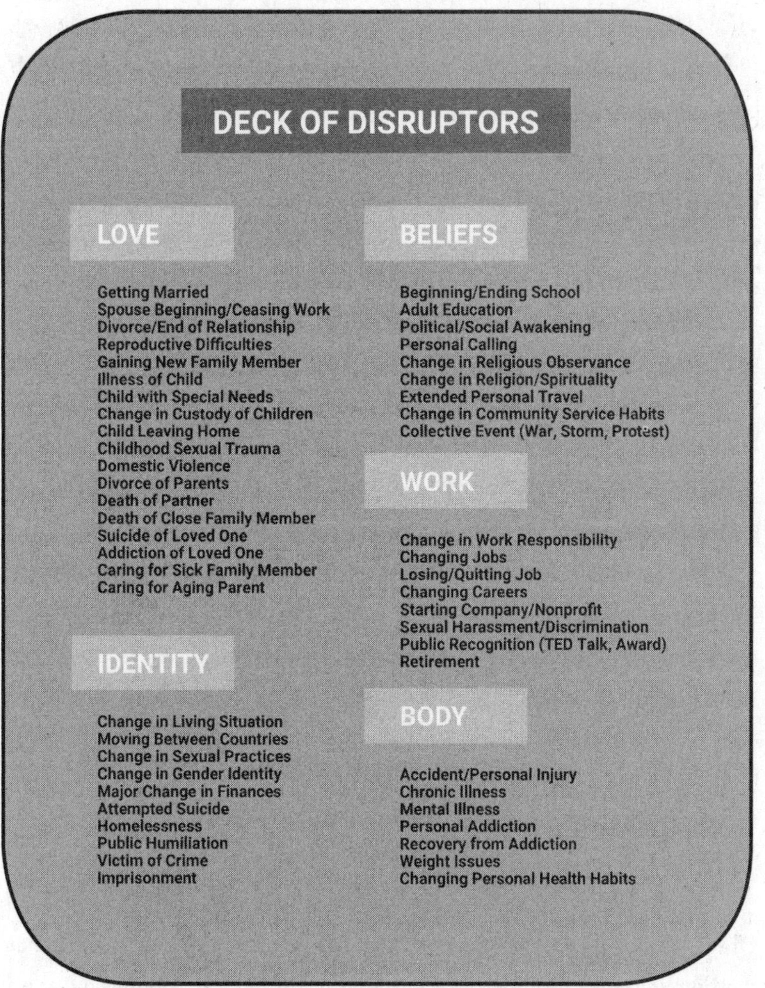

the more contentious social flash points of our time appear on their list. They have no sexual harassment or domestic violence; no mental illness, suicide, or addiction; no public humiliation, which has become more prevalent because of the internet. All of those were dominant, poignant themes of the Life Story Project.

Since these disruptors are the foundation for everything that follows, I'd like to go into some detail on the census of life changes people face today. It is my conclusion that the variety of these disruptors is increasing, the span of life in which they occur is increasing, and the raw number is increasing. Let's start with the variety.

Love

The range of ways our interpersonal relationships are disrupted is vast.

Tiffany Grimes was born into a deeply religious family in an old gold rush town in the foothills of California. Both her parents had seven brothers and sisters. "I have thirty-six immediate first cousins, so Christmases, holidays, and birthdays were all just big," she said. Tiffany enrolled in Southern Oregon State College. "In my first month I met a guy and fell deeply in love."

After graduating, Tiffany and her boyfriend, Eric, backpacked through South America, then returned to Oregon, got married, and started building an eco-friendly home with straw-bale insulation.

Tiffany never moved into the house. "During the construction, I realized I was feeling attraction to women. I had grown up in a Christian household, so I didn't know a single gay person. We thought about staying together and never having sex again, because we loved each other, but in the end, Eric moved into the new house, and I stayed in our old house."

Tiffany embraced her new status. "I dated all five lesbians in southern Oregon," she said. One day she went to an event called Les Get Together at the bowling alley and met an electrician. "She was very butch dyke, no fingernail polish, but very feminine, too." She also had a deeply religious family and was fresh out of a divorce. They even shared a name: Tiffany.

"We had a good laugh about that."

Two years later the two Tiffanys were married in Thailand. Tiffany2 changed her name to Dade to reduce the confusion. Tiffany1 started trying to get pregnant. "We were in love. We wanted to pop out kids."

A few weeks after the honeymoon, the couple was watching a documentary that contained a transgender character. "That's interesting," Dade said. Neither mentioned the topic again. Six months later, Dade picked Tiffany up from work, took her to a diner, and announced that she was a man.

"I was so pissed off," Tiffany said. "I felt tricked. And I screamed, 'I CAN'T BE WITH A MAN. I JUST LEFT A MAN TO BE WITH A WOMAN, AND NOW THE WOMAN I'M WITH WANTS TO BE A MAN.'" Tiffany made her own announcement. "Either you stay female bodied and we stay married, or you're male bodied and we're separating."

For the next eight months, neither of them spoke about it. "I was all caught up in my own phobias," Tiffany said. Finally, they found a therapist, who said, "Tiffany, you have to shut up long enough to listen. Dade, you have to speak up long enough to be heard."

"And that's when I had the epiphany," Tiffany said. "My wife is essentially dead, and there is this new person in front of me trying to be themselves."

The next weekend they went to Lake Tahoe. The first morning, Dade took a cup of coffee to the balcony and skimmed a stone across the water. "It was such a visual moment," Tiffany said. "And I just remember feeling, *I'm not done. I love him. I love everything about him.* So I told him, 'I'm not going anywhere.'"

The next week Dade began taking hormones. Tiffany and Dade had to get legally remarried after he officially became a man. They even started a YouTube channel to share their story. And soon, Tiffany became pregnant.

"Everything felt so fast and big," Tiffany said. "Until one day, my body had done this complete transformation into motherhood, and his body had done this complete transformation into manhood, and we said, 'Now we have to go on another journey to figure out how to love each other as we are.'"

I asked Tiffany how she defines herself today—gay, straight, or something else. "I'm forty-three, happily married, and a mother of two," she said. "Beyond that, who cares?"

What's remarkable about Tiffany's story is how unremarkable it is in many ways. The world of family and relationships is in a period of profound volatility. Just a few statistics make the point. Marriage is less consequential today than at any time in the last five hundred years. Since 1950, the marriage rate has fallen by two-thirds, replaced by domestic partnerships, open relationships, polyamory, and more. Fewer than half of American households are headed by married couples.

All this volatility has upended the traditional family. A quarter of children are raised by single parents—triple the number since 1960. Half of children will see their parents divorced; half of those will live through a second. Adoption has soared, as have gay families and three-parent families. Also, a growing number of adult children move back home. For the first time ever, more adults between eighteen and thirty-four live with their parents than with romantic partners.

Some examples of the love disruptors I heard:

- Allen Peake, a rising conservative lawmaker in Georgia, conducted a longtime consensual extramarital affair with a woman he met on the website Ashley Madison; the episode later ruined his career when a list of the website's users was leaked.
- Rosemary Daniell, a poet and novelist, got married at sixteen to a man who was abusive and tried to drown her on their honeymoon; her

second husband confessed to a dark family secret on their honeymoon; her third husband asked for an open relationship; her fourth marriage has lasted thirty years.

- Kacie Case, a ninth-generation Mexican Texan schoolteacher, learned that her oldest child had a blood disorder that would make school difficult, so she and her husband sold their house, moved into an Airstream, and homeschooled their children on the road.

Identity

The stories of identity disruption are equally diverse—and multiplying.

Lev Sviridov was born in the Soviet Union in the height of the Cold War to a blacklisted journalist and single mom who had grown up under Joseph Stalin. "My mother doesn't like it when I say it, but I was very much a bastard." When Lev was five, the food system collapsed; when he was ten, the country collapsed. When he was eleven, he and his mother came to New York with two suitcases and a toy for a six-month fellowship. On the day they were scheduled to return to Moscow, a coup broke out. En route to the airport, Lev begged his mother to stay.

"She agreed, but that meant we became undocumented," he said, "which also meant we became homeless."

For the next year and a half, Lev and his mother lived on the streets of Manhattan. "She would say, 'We're tourists! We're seeing the city at the night!'" In the morning, they would go to a library or a bus station to wash up, try to take a nap, and find a quiet corner, or a couch. "I had pneumonia, so we walked to Cornell hospital because we were too afraid to call for an ambulance. I had a total of seven different pneumonias."

Eventually his mother found a human rights organization that helped her get a grant as a journalist. They moved into an apartment in the Bronx and he enrolled in public school. At first Lev didn't fit into his new life at all. "I had absolutely no foundational relationships with any of my peers," he said. "I was raised on two things: *The Simpsons* and *The Price Is Right*."

Yet he also developed a deep love for America.

"My entire concept of life is that this country is a huge privilege. We were completely destitute, yet we got access to health care, to a great education. You just begin to understand how incredible the whole idea of America is."

Lev has devoted his life to repaying that debt. He turned down the Ivy League to enroll at the City College of New York, where he was elected student body president. He won a Rhodes Scholarship, earned a PhD in chemistry, and returned to his alma mater to run a program that helps first-generation students get a foothold in the American dream. The highlight of his life: buying his mother her first apartment near Yankee Stadium.

Until relatively recently, most people accepted the identities they were born with—their community, religion, sexuality, gender, and class were largely fixed. Today all of those are up for grabs. Most people change at least one; many change more than one. (I count four of these under identity; religion falls under beliefs.)

On community: The average person moves 11.7 times in their lives; two-thirds of us live in a community other than where we were born. On sexuality: An entire new alphabet has arisen. In addition to L (lesbian), G (gay), B (bi), we now have T (transgender); A (asexual or ace); Q (questioning or queer); P (pansexual); and K (kink). On gender: Facebook has seventy-one different gender options, including androgyne (a person identifying as neither man nor woman), genderqueer (a person whose gender is beyond the binary), and two-spirit (a Native American who has attributes of both men and women). On class: 36 percent of Americans move up the socioeconomic ladder in their lives; 41 percent move down.

Some of the identity disruptors I heard:

- Linh Nguyen was on the penultimate helicopter out of Saigon in 1975. His family was sponsored by the Episcopal Church and relocated to South Carolina, where he found himself as a refugee teenager who couldn't speak English. Five years later he was admitted to Yale.
- Chavie Weisberger was raised in an ultra-Orthodox family in New York, had an arranged marriage at eighteen, and quickly had two children. But she also felt drawn to women and later came out, rejected Judaism, and won a landmark case to share custody of her children.
- Sal Giambanco signed a vow of poverty to become a Jesuit at age twenty-three but left a decade later, made millions in Silicon Valley, and has since had three marriages to men.

Beliefs

Our belief systems may be even more fluid than our identities.

Brittany Wilund was born in 1994 in West Columbia, South Carolina, to parents who had started a church together in college and homeschooled their three children. Brittany was raised with a "very, very conservative Christian narrative," she said. She was a perfectionist and liked to follow the rules, which helped in this environment; she was also a rebel and gender-nonconforming, which didn't. "I got kicked out of the girls' bathroom by accident when I was eight because my hair was cut short. I only wore my brother's clothes. I screamed every time I had to put on an Easter dress."

Brittany enrolled in public high school and began questioning her beliefs. "I had to sort out whether I was Christian or not," she said. She was particularly challenged by the concept of hell—"Those flames and fire seemed to have nothing to do with how good you were"—and the idea that her friends who didn't believe in Jesus were damned. "It didn't make sense and didn't seem fair. There were so many other points of view, I wanted to hear them," she said.

She also felt attracted to women. "When I was younger, I was homophobic, because everybody I knew was. But I was kind of a little bit gay, too, and that was confusing."

Brittany gradually drifted from her family as she enrolled in college, took up art, and began channeling her emotions into daring performance pieces like building a metal cage inside of which she played a recording of all the demeaning things she'd heard and thought about herself.

"My parents are wonderful, and I didn't want to cause them any pain," she said. "But I finally had to sit them down and say, 'I'm sorry, I'm not a Christian anymore. This is not what I believe.' I asked them to accept my decision, and they said that they'd keep praying that I found the truth."

After graduation, Brittany moved to Hawaii to start a new life. She decorated windows for Anthropologie, started dating a (male) surfer, and the two of them experimented with the off-grid #vanlife, eventually moving into a run-down school bus that she turned into a ceramics studio. With some friends, Brittany approached the owners of an abandoned sugar mill about converting it into an artists' co-op. The connection to her parents' starting a church was not lost on her, and their standoff started to thaw. When I asked her dream for the future, she said, "Reconnecting with my family through art."

We are in a period of unprecedented churn in American beliefs. Part of this is faith. Half of Americans will change religions in the course of their lives; four in ten of us are in an interfaith marriage. A quarter of Americans now say they have no religious affiliation. Political beliefs are also surprisingly malleable. Four in ten Americans identify as independents today, up from three in ten two decades ago. Half of millennials have switched party affiliations. Travel contributes to this openness. One in four Americans travels outside of the country every year, a number that's quadrupled in the last twenty years.

Some of the contemporary belief disruptors I heard:

- John Mury was born to an American military dad and a Korean mom who divorced when he was nine, leaving him angry, bitter, and divided between two worlds, until he was walking across a snowy bridge at nineteen and felt called by God to become a youth preacher.
- Jocelyn Wurzburg was a sheltered Jewish housewife in Memphis who was stirred by the assassination of Martin Luther King Jr., and built a network of all-women black-and-white luncheons.
- Mark Lakeman quit his architecture firm in Portland after uncovering unethical practices, spent a year traveling to indigenous communities around the world, and then returned home to set up a renegade nonprofit to build outdoor tea shops in busy urban intersections.

Work

No area of life is more fraught with surprising change than work.

Brian Wecht was born in New Jersey to an interfaith couple. His father ran an army-navy store and enjoyed going to Vegas to see Elvis and Sinatra. Brian loved school, especially math and science, but also loved jazz saxophone and piano. "A large part of my identity came from being a fat kid who was bullied through most of my childhood," he said. "I remember just not having many friends."

Brian double majored in math and music and chose graduate school in jazz composition. But when his girlfriend moved to San Diego, he quit and enrolled in a theoretical physics program at UC San Diego. Six months later the relationship failed; six years later he earned a PhD. When he solved a longstanding open problem in string theory ("the exact superconformal *R*-symmetry of any 4d SCFT"), Brian became an international star and earned fellowships at MIT, Harvard, and the Institute for Advanced Study in Princeton, New Jersey. He secured an unimaginable job: a lifetime professorship in particle physics in London. He was set.

Except.

Brian never lost his interest in music. He met his wife while playing for an improv troupe. He started a comedic band with his friend Dan called Ninja Sex Party. "I was always afraid it was going to bite me in the ass during faculty interviews because I dressed up like a ninja and sang about dicks and boning."

By the time Brian got to London, the band's videos were viral sensations. He cried on the phone with Dan: Should they try to turn their side gig into a living? Brian and his wife had a daughter by this point. The choice seemed absurd. "You can't quit," his physics adviser said. "You're the only one of my students who got a job."

His wife was supportive but said she couldn't decide for him. *If I take the leap and it fails*, he thought, *I may be fucking up my entire future for this weird YouTube career.* He also thought, *If I don't jump, I'll look back when I'm seventy and say, "Fuck, I should have tried."*

Finally, he decided: "I'd rather live with fear and failure than safety and regret."

Brian and his family moved to Los Angeles. When the band's next album was released, Ninja Sex Party was featured on *Conan*, profiled in the *Washington Post*, and reached the top twenty-five on the *Billboard* charts. They went on a sold-out tour across the country, including the Brooklyn Bowl in Las Vegas.

The world of work is in a sustained period of upheaval. The average worker today holds twelve different jobs before the age of fifty. Those with higher education can expect to change jobs fifteen times and alter their skill set three. The typical job now lasts four years; among those under thirty-five, it drops to three. Half of American workers are said to be at risk of losing their jobs to automation. It's no wonder that 90 percent of workers are disengaged from their jobs and six in ten would choose a different career. Or that four in ten have a *side hustle*. The bottom line: Americans view their careers less as a *path* these days and more as a *portfolio*.

Some of the work disruptors I heard:

- Amy Cunningham was a freelance women's magazine writer and the mom of teen boys in Brooklyn when her father's funeral in South Carolina so moved her that she enrolled in mortuary school and became an environmentally friendly funeral director.
- Gena Zak, a Coast Guard veteran and onetime saleswoman for 1-800-Flowers, quit her safe job at Verizon in her fifties to open a lifestyle business in Maine caring for second homes.
- Michael Mitchell had such difficulty adjusting to retirement after stepping down from a distinguished career in pediatric urology that he took up teaching, mentored young doctors, and asked his wife to give him long to-do lists to make up for his absence when their children were young.

Body

The last category of disruptors—the human body—shows equal flux.

Randy Riley was born on Friday the thirteenth, "which somewhat shapes my life," she said. "I grew up blue collar. I was a smart kid. I made my way through school—no health problems, nothing." She played for the Indiana state-champion softball team and was homecoming queen. "I was very happy."

After her freshman year at Purdue, she started gaining weight. "I thought it was just the freshman fifteen, but I was running a lot of 5Ks that summer, bruising really easy, with a lot of stomach pain." One weekend she threw up blood. A friend said, "Do you have liver problems? Your eyes are really yellow."

Her boyfriend drove her to the hospital. Tests showed an uncommonly high liver enzyme, but the local doctors didn't know why. When her body started crashing, they airlifted her to the University of Chicago, where she was diagnosed with Wilson's disease, a rare autoimmune blood disorder that causes copper to accumulate in the body. Her liver was destroyed; her lungs filled with fluid; she was hours from death.

"I felt like my heart was drowning."

Randy had her first liver transplant three months later. She returned to school, graduated with a degree in nursing, and got married. She also had eight pancreatic stents over the next two years. "They prescribed enough painkillers to kill a donkey," she said.

On the surface, Randy was completely normal. She worked in a blood lab, was happily married, raised her young daughter and son. "I was totally functioning," she said. "It was almost creepy. Because along with all that chronic pain came a dependency on pain medicine. I was completely addicted to opioids."

Randy struggled to reduce her dependency, but when she needed a second liver transplant—then a third—she got hooked again. It ultimately took her three years, and a maintenance drug, to get clean. "Look, if you didn't know me, you would never think I was an addict," she said. "I'm very well spoken. I've got two little kids. I go to church on Sunday. I'm a typical midwesterner." She's also not a thug, she added. "People don't understand that doctors sometimes overprescribe, and it's very easy to get hooked. It hits you or someone you know and then it gets real, very real, very quick."

You might think that modern medicine would make the body less ripe for disruption, yet every advance seems to be met with a host of new worries. Americans today experience puberty earlier, menopause later, and a more drawn-out end of life. We are also facing an unprecedented epidemic of depression, anxiety, and suicide. For the first time since World War I, American longevity began a prolonged dip in the late 2010s. Six in ten Americans suffer from at least one chronic condition like heart disease, high cholesterol, arthritis, or diabetes; four in ten have more than one. A third of us will get cancer, a quarter of us an anxiety disorder, a fifth of us chronic pain. All of these problems worsen with age, and more of us are old. The percentage of those over sixty-five went from 5 percent in 1920 to 16 percent today. The number of older people is expected to balloon by as much as 75 percent by 2050.

Some of the body disruptors I heard:

- Jeffrey Sparr was a freshman tennis player at Ohio State when he got a case of jock itch he couldn't ignore, checking himself dozens of times a day, the first sign of the obsessive-compulsive disorder he now fights with medication and art therapy.
- Leigh Wintz already suffered from sleep apnea and diabetes from traveling one hundred thousand miles a year leading an international nonprofit when she discovered her own ovarian tumor, prompting her to get a divorce, hire a trainer, and lose sixty pounds.
- Carolyn Graham, a survivor of sexual abuse from a female scout leader, was so debilitated by Lyme disease she mixed a lethal dosage of an antidepressant into a McDonald's shake and walked into the Atlantic Ocean off Cape Canaveral, the first of two suicide attempts she survived before turning to alternative therapies that cured her.

The collective toll of all these ways our lives are being upended constitutes the first rule of disruptors: They're becoming more prevalent. The second rule is that they occur over a wider span of time.

The Whenever Life Shake-Up

From the start, the midlife crisis was a dodgy concept. The idea that every person in the culture would go through the exact same crisis starting at the exact time (between forty and forty and a half!) should have seemed, on the surface, absurd. As it happened, it took scholars no more than a few years to debunk the idea. And to be clear, what they found—and certainly what

I found in the Life Story Project—is not that some people don't experience transitions during this window. It's that this window is just one of dozens in which these kinds of transitions occur.

There are three core flaws with the idea of the midlife crisis. First, empirical data finds no evidence for it. *Passages* set off a wave of studies. The biggest, called "Midlife in the United States," was conducted in 1995 and involved thirteen scholars and seven thousand subjects, aged twenty-five to seventy-four. It concluded: "There is relatively little evidence to support the idea that most Americans experience a midlife crisis or, more generally, a universal course of life with expectable periods of crisis and stability." Only a quarter of participants reported experiencing challenges during this period, and those were attributed to events, not despair over mortality. By contrast, people were shown to grow happier as they move through middle age and into old age. The *New York Times* put it this way: "New Study Finds Middle Age Is Prime of Life."

Second, the term *midlife* itself has become so elastic it's virtually meaningless. As adolescence has moved earlier and old age later, the period of midlife has grown longer. Studies show that young people view middle age as occurring between thirty and fifty-five, while older people view it as between forty and seventy. Like being middle class, everyone is middle aged these days!

Third, life events that were formerly experienced by broad segments of the population at a similar time—like getting married, buying a home, or having children—are now spread out over decades. Many still have children in their early twenties, for example, while others wait until their early forties, and some have a second set of offspring even later. Meanwhile, events that used to be associated exclusively with midlife—like switching jobs or swapping mates—now happen across adulthood.

This final point is worth dwelling on, as it's the essence of the nonlinear life. We're all undergoing change all the time. What's more, we're wired to do so. The first generations of psychologists stressed that we all finish developing by age twenty-one. That notion is now dead. A wave of recent brain research has shown that we're capable of change at any age. As one neuroscientist put it, "The brain remodels itself throughout life."

The upshot of all this is that we should finally bury the idea of the midlife crisis and replace it with an idea much closer to reality: the *whenever life crisis*, or, to be more neutral, the *whenever life shake-up*. I asked everyone I interviewed for a high point, a low point, and a turning point. I graphed each answer, and what I found was overwhelming: Significant life events are equally distributed across our lives.

Consider the low point, the closest analogy to the alleged "midlife crisis." Those in their thirties said their low points were fairly evenly divided among every half decade of their adult lives; those in their forties show a similar diversity. Those in their fifties show low points gaining ground through their thirties and forties, but remaining high in their fifties, while those in their sixties show the widest distribution. Turning points are even more dispersed.

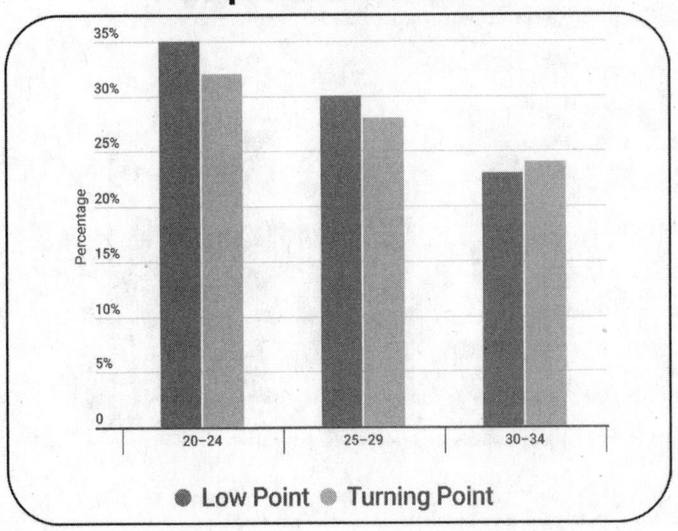

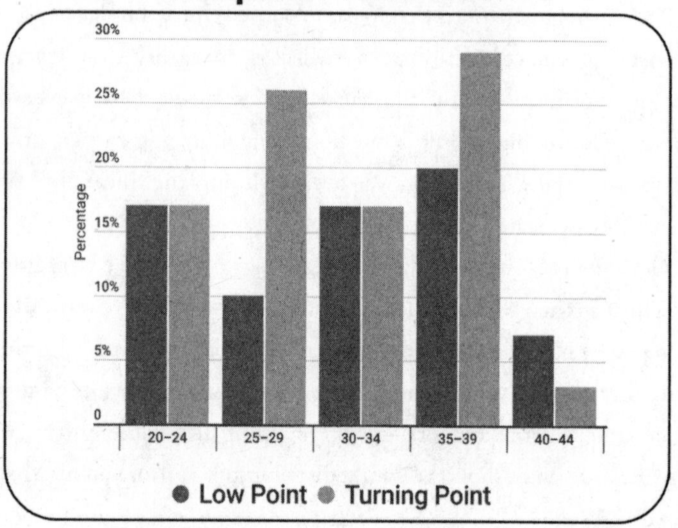
Low Point & Turning Point:
People in Their 40s
30%
25%
20%
15%
10%
5%
0
Percentage
20–24
25–29
30–34
35–39
40–44
Low Point
Turning Point

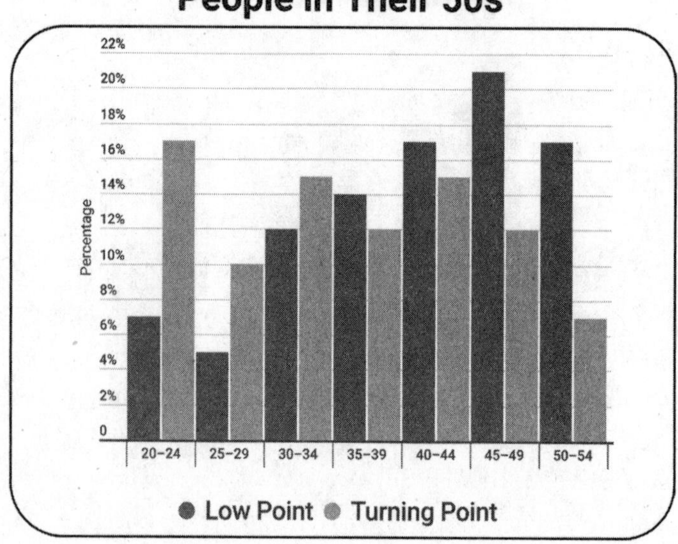
Low Point & Turning Point:
People in Their 50s
22%
20%
18%
16%
14%
12%
10%
8%
6%
4%
2%
0
Percentage
20–24
25–29
30–34
35–39
40–44
45–49
50–54
Low Point
Turning Point

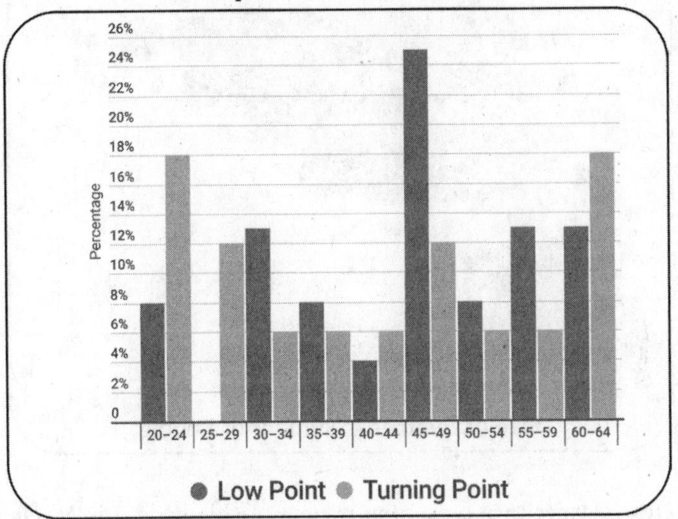

I then took this analysis one level deeper. To remove age from the equation, I took how old each person was at the time of their major turning point, then divided that number by how old the person was at the time of our interview. The resulting figure represents where the turning point fell in the person's life, regardless of age. I found that these low points were remarkably evenly distributed across the life span.

In sum: I found absolutely no evidence of any bump in major life disruption between thirty-five and forty-five. Instead, these disruptions happen *whenever.*

Here's how the whenever life shake-up plays out in real life:

Some people are conceived in turmoil. Amy Cunningham was "born into a grieving womb." Her older brother died at thirteen months, and her mother announced she wanted another baby immediately. Will Dana was the fourth of four children born to an already feuding couple who soon divorced. "I was born in the midst of this turmoil that I had no awareness of."

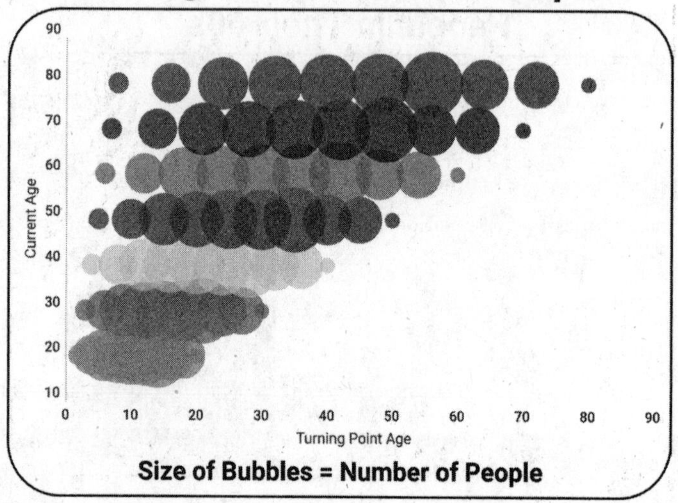

Others experience a defining trauma in childhood. Liz McGuire's mother became seriously ill when Liz was an adolescent, forcing Liz into a spiral of loneliness as she had to mother her wheelchair-bound mom. Buddy Casey grew up at the end of a dirt road in North Carolina in a house that had no running water and with parents who had no education; he was raped by another boy when he was six.

Lots of people have ordeals in their twenties. Seth Mnookin started using drugs in high school, graduated from Harvard, but cratered so far into heroin use in his twenties that he was estranged from his family and living in his car. The defining moment in his life was getting clean on his twenty-sixth birthday. Jill Cameron Michel was called to ministry as a teenager, pastored a church in Missouri while in college, and got married at twenty-four. Two weeks later her husband informed her that he was gay.

Others undergo massive shifts later in life. Shirley Eggermont was a mother of seven in Minnesota who docilely worked alongside her husband of forty-one years in the pinball business until she learned he had been having an affair for ten years, forcing her out of her shell. For nearly fifty years,

John Smitha held the shame of killing forty people in Libya as part of a US military operation until he found God and peace helping disabled vets.

Sexual awakenings are a perfect example of how the whenever life shake-up works. Adam Foss became a sex addict at fourteen. Xanet Pailet felt so disconnected from her body following the death of her father and mental breakdown of her mother when Xanet was age three that she didn't have a meaningful sexual relationship (including with her husband) until her fifties; now she's a tantric sex coach. Sean Collins was aware of being gay at age five but joined a Benedictine monastery at eighteen to mask his sexuality; five years later he left after realizing "celibacy was not the answer."

Disruptors are a fact of life—and a fact of all decades of life. They adhere to no biological clock, no social clock, and no artificial clock. They toll on their own schedule.

How Many Disruptors Will I Face?

So how many will each of us face? The answer is the final rule of disruptors: more than you think.

I took two approaches to calculating this number. First, I tallied up all the publicly available data. For example, we know the number of jobs the average person has (13), the number of moves (11.7), the number of accidents (3). We also know the ratio of people who get married (7 in 10), cheat (1 in 5), get divorced (1 in 5). Half of us will have heart attacks, a quarter of us will become addicts, a third of women will be sexually assaulted, as will a sixth of men. I didn't even consider the number of diets (55) or financial struggles (1 in 3) because it's too hard to quantify when these are truly disruptive.

All in, I concluded that the total number of disruptors the average adult faces is between thirty and forty.

Next I looked at my interviews and counted the frequency with which subjects described disruptive events. Obviously I didn't hear about every move, breakup, or job change. Still, the patterns were clear. People experience an average of three dozen disruptors in their adult lives.

When I layered in these two numbers, a bright, blinking rule of thumb appears:

THE AVERAGE PERSON GOES THROUGH ONE DISRUPTOR EVERY 12–18 MONTHS

When I shared this finding with others, they reacted with a mix of shock and resignation. *Wow*, followed by *yeah*. And remember, these are the run-of-the-mill disruptors, not the ones that truly destabilize us. (We'll get to those in chapter 3.) More significant is that when you begin to accept that we're all being battered by the crosswinds of contemporary life (*Wait! I'm not done dealing with this crappy situation and now I've got a new one*), it's only logical that some of these disruptors show up at inconvenient times. How we feel when that happens is a key part of modern malaise. We're upset, we're confused, we're exhausted.

What we really are, I believe, is haunted by the ghost of linearity.

Primed to expect that our lives will follow a predictable path, we're thrown when they don't. We have linear expectations but nonlinear realities. Even people who are linear in one area (a stable career, say, or long-running marriage) are nonlinear in others (recurrent health problems or frequent changes in their religious identity). Nearly everyone I spoke to said that at least one aspect of their lives was *off schedule, off course, out of sync, out of order.*

We're all comparing ourselves to an ideal that no longer exists and beating ourselves up for not achieving it.

Living life out of order means different things to different people. It's sixty-three-year-old Loretta Parham forced to raise two granddaughters after Loretta's daughter was killed in a car accident. It's twenty-nine-year-old Sarah Cooper forced to move back in with her parents after her first marriage lasted merely three months. It's Fred Schloemer coming out as gay in his fifties, and Wendi Aarons unable to socialize in her twenties because she was the only one of her friends who was married. It's Sarah Holbrooke thrust into the dating pool with a newborn after learning her husband had been having an affair while she was pregnant, and Katrina Alcorn buying a home with a second husband while still married to the first.

It's me getting a pediatric cancer as a forty-three-year-old new dad.

The good news of living life out of order—of surviving the fifty-two-card-pickup craziness of the deck of disruptors—is that we're freed from the shackles of expectations, whether they come from our parents, our neighbors, or ourselves. The *should* train has slowed. Each of us can make our choices and decide what brings us peace.

The bad news is that it can be more difficult. Faced with limitless choice, we choose none. We get writer's block trying to write our own story. The difference between success and failure—between a life of fulfillment and a life of frustration—is how well you manage the challenge of making meaning in your life. Fortunately, there's a growing body of know-how to make that process easier.

CHAPTER 3

Lifequakes

What Happens When the Big One Hits

The idea that dozens of disruptors are lurking around every corner of our existence is an unnerving enough feature of the nonlinear life. But there's another feature that's even more unsettling. Every now and then—and for many of us more frequently than that—we get hit by a blunter, more explosive force of change. These are the signature events that shape or, more accurately, reshape our lives, often in ways we can't imagine and with an intensity we can't control.

These are the wolves that upend our fairy tales.

On the surface, these events often seem sui generis—the one-hundred-year flood, the rare disease, the fluke confluence of two otherwise unrelated events. But look at enough of these episodes and certain patterns appear. What are those patterns, and what can they teach us about how to navigate these times? These were consuming questions of the Life Story Project.

"The Fear of Staying Was Greater Than the Fear of Leaving"

Consider Lisa Ludovici.

Lisa was the youngest of three children born in Pittsburgh to two alcoholics who divorced when she was three. "I feel like I raised myself," she said. "My dad didn't pay any child support. My mother knocked down my door when I was twelve and said, 'Get a job!' I said, 'I'm twelve. What can I do?' She said, 'Go be a mommy's helper.'" On top of that, Lisa had seventeen migraines a month for years.

"I would be up all night, screaming, projectile vomiting, head in the toilet, clawing at my eyes trying to rip them out," she said. "I missed tests, trick-or-treating, all kinds of holidays. That was my childhood. By the time I got to Penn State, I could control the nausea, but I still felt pain. I'd read a paragraph, then get a migraine and have to stop."

She graduated with a C average; no one in her family bothered to show up for the ceremony. She worked as a film casting assistant in Pittsburgh and, drowning in student and medical debt, lived in her Mazda Protegé. She eventually landed a job in radio advertising, which led to an interview at a little-known startup called America Online. Eleven reorgs, nine bosses, three moves, one failed marriage, and seventeen years later, Lisa was a powerhouse internet ad executive in Manhattan. She was earning good commissions and had prestige clients—Pfizer, Kimberly-Clark, Walmart—but was working fourteen hours a day and still wilting under the migraines. Also, she hated her boss, who belittled his employees. She cried every night at her desk.

One day, a colleague shared that her coworkers were intimidated by her work ethic and customer service. Lisa thought to herself, *If today was the last day of my life, would I want to spend it with these people?* She walked home to her one-bedroom apartment and combed through her Amex bills, wondering how she could cut costs. She tallied what she had in stocks and savings and figured if she could eliminate her cable, stop eating out, and buy no more clothes, she could hold on for five years. She walked into her boss's office the next day and quit.

"I did something I'd read about for decades and I always thought was a great concept: *Jump and the net will appear.*" Where did she get the courage?

I asked. Her answer was nearly identical to Brian Wecht's explanation of how he quit physics to join Ninja Sex Party: "The fear of staying was greater than the fear of leaving."

Two weeks later Lisa was sitting on her couch, watching public-access television (she'd cut the cable), when a woman came on and spoke about the power of the subconscious. She, too, had left the corporate world and now helped people discover their inner selves. Lisa tracked down the woman, who agreed to a call. "By the time I hung up the phone, I said, *This is what I'm going to do with my life. I'm going to help people live better.*"

Within weeks she was enrolled in hypnotherapy school in Santa Fe. "On my tenth day in class, on the tenth of February 2010, at ten thirty in the morning, I was sitting at my desk with my head in my hands, when the director came up to me and said, 'What's going on?'" Lisa explained she was having a migraine, it was no big deal, she'd had one every few days for forty-one years. The director asked her to come into her office and sit in a large easy chair. She then proceeded to hypnotize Lisa and walk her through a guided exercise using metaphors to begin rediscovering the unsick, unpained self she hadn't known since she was three.

"That was the very last day I ever had a migraine," Lisa said. "And when we got to week seven in the course and started learning about how in utero we absorb our mothers' thoughts and emotions, how I had been carrying the stress and anxiety of my parents' problems since before I was even born, I knew this was the beginning of my life of people-healing."

Lisa got her degree in hypnotherapy. A decade later she was the leading certified medical hypnotist in New York City, having worked with patients facing Parkinson's, cancer, traumatic brain injury, curled toes, "and some of the most incredible things I've ever heard." She lectures medical professionals around the world. She was hired by the VA to treat Vietnam vets still suffering from gunshot wounds fifty years after the war. "I'm the first hypnotist to be hired by the United States government to work in the world's largest healthcare system, and we published work showing a

50 percent success rate eradicating chronic pain when no one else is showing even 30 percent success."

She had transitioned from corporate ad executive to hypnotist. She switched her primary story line from work to body. And she changed her life from one absorbed in pain and fear to one illuminated with forgiveness and healing. "That's the definition of our soul," she said. "And my life is to make sure all of us tap into that as much as possible."

"Monster Curveballs"

Tumultuous episodes of the kind we're talking about are hardly new. Beethoven was thirty-one and already the virtuoso composer of his first symphony when he learned he was going deaf. F. Scott Fitzgerald, already the bestselling author of *The Great Gatsby*, was thirty-eight and suffering from marriage woes, financial worries, drinking problems, and tuberculosis when he fled to the mountains of North Carolina and had what he described as a "crack-up." Mark Felt was fifty-nine when he was passed over to become head of the FBI by Richard Nixon, prompting him to flip and help bring down Nixon as the anonymous mole Deep Throat.

These moments go by many names. Max Weber coined the term *metanoia* to capture a massive change in a person's outlook. William James deemed them *mental rearrangements*. Hollywood likes *turning points*. Entrepreneurs, like my wife, use *inflection points*. Others have tried *pivots*, *U-turns*, *crossroads*, *crises*. Each of these terms has virtues and weaknesses.

Some of my subjects devised their own shorthands. The comic book artist Bob Hall, who cocreated *The West Coast Avengers* and drew *Spider-Man* for a while, likened them to the *boom!* in a comic strip: "It's a change from one action to another. Not in a gradual sense, but in the sense of *poof*." Kate Milliken, who grew up in a prominent family of Connecticut WASPs and has had three such experiences—her failure to get into Dartmouth, the breakup of her engagement, and her diagnosis at thirty-four with multiple sclerosis—called them *monster curveballs*. Lev Sviridov called them *ampersands*. "You enter in one place, go through an elaborate squiggle, then come out in another."

I call them *lifequakes*, because the magnitude with which they upend our lives is exponentially worse than everyday disruptors. Lifequakes involve a fundamental shift in the meaning, purpose, or direction of a person's life. I think of them as BCE/CE moments (or BC/AD in the old vernacular), in which a person's life story gets divided into a before and an after. A full decade following my cancer diagnosis, I still use the experience to demarcate time: *I haven't been to that restaurant since I got sick.* My wife does the same with the birth of our daughters, my brother with the Great Recession.

Yet just going through such an experience is not enough to make it a lifequake. You must assign it meaning it might not otherwise have; you must be aware that a change is happening and accept that it will lead to some kind of transition. I interviewed countless people who underwent what others might consider a cataclysm—a divorce, a job loss, the death of a loved one—and were not thunderstruck. My mother had breast cancer, twice, but unlike those who don pink ribbons, march, and lobby, she went through treatment, returned to her routine, and made it clear to everyone she'd be happy never to talk about it again.

My definition: A lifequake is a forceful burst of change in one's life that leads to a period of upheaval, transition, and renewal.

How many will you face? Everyone I spoke with, even those in their twenties, had been through one or two; no one over forty had been through fewer than three; some people had been through six or seven. We calculated the average to be between three and five in a lifetime. That sets up an interesting formula: One out of every ten disruptors becomes a lifequake.

What do these events have in common? I identified two essential variables: personal versus collective and voluntary versus involuntary.

Personal means something that happens to you individually (a career change, a health crisis, losing your home), while *collective* is an event that happens to you along with many others; it could be your neighborhood, your community, your country, or larger (a recession, a war, a natural disaster). We found that 87 percent of lifequakes were personal, 13 percent collective. What's notable about this finding is how people are less and less shaped by shared, communal events. Had I done these interviews in the twentieth century, with its back-to-back wallops of two world wars, the Great Depression, civil rights, and women's rights, surely the number of collective events would have been higher.

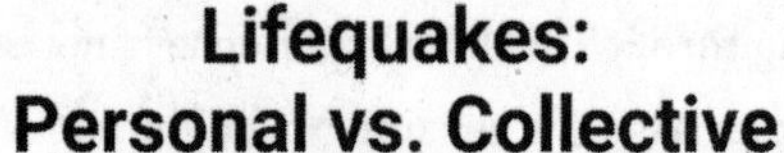

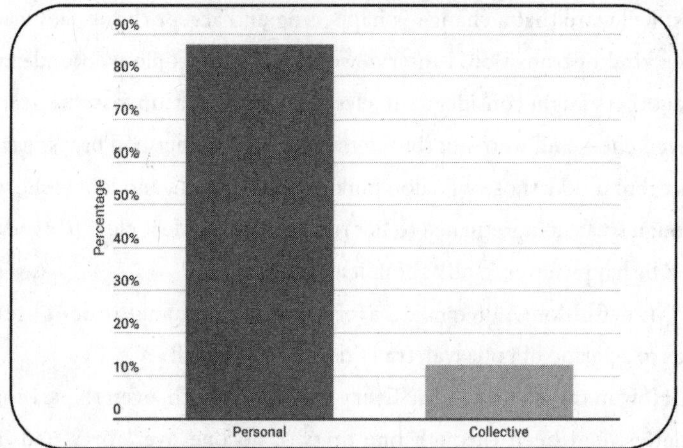

Voluntary means that the person initiated the change (having an affair, switching jobs, changing religions), while *involuntary* means it happened to you (your spouse has an affair, your house burns down, you're fired). Forty-three percent of our lifequakes were voluntary, 57 percent involuntary.

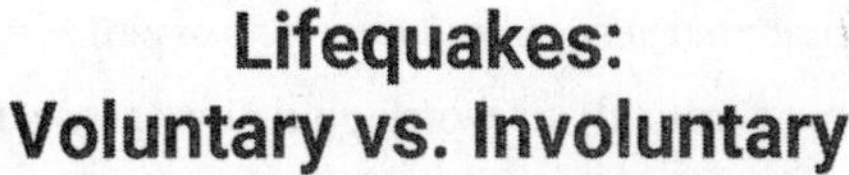

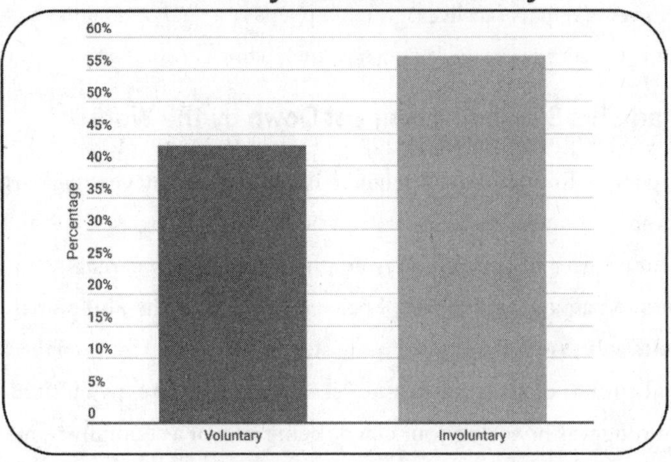

Layering these two variables on top of each other, I created the *lifequake matrix*:

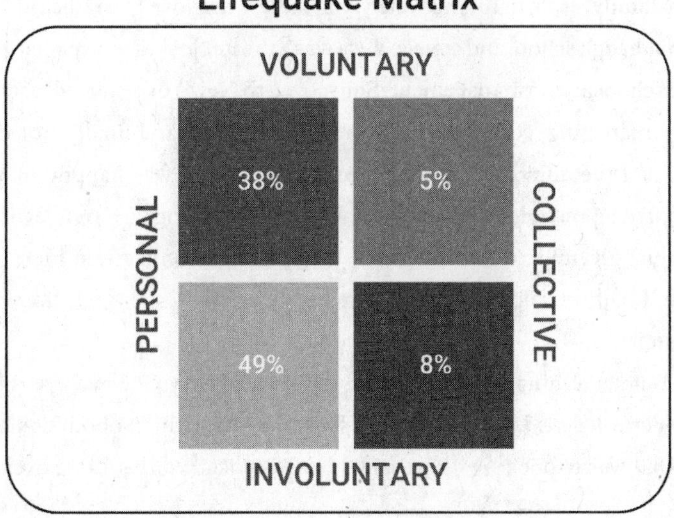

Since the breadth of these experiences is so expansive, and the distinctions among them so critical, it's worth going into some depth about how these events impact our lives.

"I Had This Sense of Being Let Down by the World"

The personal-involuntary lifequake is the largest category—nearly 50 percent.

Lisa Porter was born in Vermont to Peace Corps parents who soon moved to Saipan, a small island between Japan and the Philippines. Her parents split, and Lisa and her mom stayed. "I grew up in the tight, communal culture of an Asian island," she said. "I feel like my cultural programming was honoring your elders, being part of a community, making yourself appear less rather than more. So when we moved to Cambridge, Massachusetts, when I was a teenager, I was miserable and wanted to return."

At fifteen, Lisa walked into a theater class one day and suddenly discovered the community she'd been longing for. "I had found my family. My own family was small and lonely, but here I felt loved, and heard." All through high school and college, Lisa was a theater jock; she attended graduate school in arts management. She moved to New York, started teaching stage-managing, got married, divorced, remarried, and finally, at thirty-five, had the adult family she'd been seeking. She was happily in love, accepted a prestigious job at the University of California San Diego, and had just given birth to a daughter, Daisy. "I had connection, I had purpose, I had worked myself out of a lot of dark boxes and felt life was a constellation."

But something was never quite right with Daisy. She had eye issues, never crawled, and didn't walk until she was nearly two. "Nobody could tell us what was happening," Lisa said. Finally a social worker came over and gingerly suggested there was a nearby preschool for children with special needs; perhaps they should take Daisy for a visit.

"I was like, '*What?*'" Lisa said. "It's that moment when people are trying to tell you something they don't want to tell you."

Daisy turned out to have a neurological disorder on the autism spectrum. The shock was intense. "I felt one more time I was back in that dark box," she said. "I had this sense of being let down by the world. I had overcome the universe, this strange upbringing, parents who weren't ready to be parents. And now it was happening all over again."

But she and her husband, Anders, quickly decided not to have a "pity party." Anders agreed to flip the script and become the primary caretaker. Lisa plunged into the science of neuro-atypical children. "I got my first big book on the brain. Suddenly I had to learn about the nervous system, the sensory network, plasticity. Though I love teaching more than anything, I had to become the student. Daisy became the teacher in a class with no syllabus."

The fact that personal, involuntary lifequakes are by far the most common is a reminder that the nonlinear life is, at its core, not something most people seek out. We prefer to think we control the trajectory of our lives; the reality, unfortunately, is far more tenuous.

As I dug into the variety of these experiences, the reasons became clearer. The biggest category clustered around the body story line. A third of personal-involuntary lifequakes involved illness, injury, or some other medical event. For all our illusions of progress, we still have limited control over our health. The other subcategories involve death of a loved one, end of a relationship, or financial setbacks. My own experience confirms these patterns: Two of my involuntary lifequakes involved health (my cancer and my dad's medical crisis); two were financial (the Great Recession and uncovering theft by a trusted employee).

Other personal-involuntary examples I heard:

- Eric Westover was a six-foot-four former high school wrestler and Costco forklift driver who spent weekends riding his motorcycle in the sand dunes near Lake Michigan, when he drove headfirst into a Jeep and lost his right leg above the knee and his left one below it.
- Nisha Zenoff was home by herself in Northern California on a Saturday night when the doorbell kept ringing and ringing, revealing two policemen who informed her that her teenage son Victor had fallen off a mountaintop in Yosemite that afternoon and died.
- Gina Bianchini, a California native with two Stanford degrees and stints in Congress and at Goldman Sachs, was the rare female CEO of a tech startup in the all-male bastion of Silicon Valley, when her cofounder, the iconic Marc Andreessen, fired her, making her an "unperson" in her own community.

"Bob Dylan Wrote a Bunch of Great Songs That Only Had Three Chords"

The second biggest category was personal and voluntary. Nearly four in ten fit this description.

Elisa Korentayer was born on Long Island to Israeli American parents who moved around a lot. She attended six elementary schools, from Pennsylvania to New Zealand. "That kind of shaped the rest of my life," she said, "in terms of my love for cultural overlap, my strong feelings about building empathy, my desire to respect differences."

Elisa repeated her mix-and-match lifestyle in college, where she tried multiple majors, and in her twenties, during which she moved to Israel to promote coexistence with the Palestinians, to London to work at a hedge fund, and then to Massachusetts to start Geekcorps, "Peace Corps for geeks." By twenty-five, she was burned out and feuding with her cofounders, when a friend from high school gave her a copy of Julia Cameron's *The Artist's Way*, a step-by-step guide to discovering your inner creativity.

"There's an exercise where you have to say, *If you could be anything right now, what would you be?* And the two things that came up for me were singer-songwriter and theater director. I taped my answers on the wall and said, 'Well, I've never written my own songs. I only know how to play a few chords on the guitar, but, hey, Bob Dylan wrote a bunch of great songs that only had three chords. At least I know three.'"

Elisa wrote a song and a few weeks later performed it at an open mic in New York City. The crowd loved it. "I thought, *This is incredible! I'm going to leave my job and pursue being a singer-songwriter.*" She applied to nineteen artist-in-residence programs; all rejected her. Her twentieth application was to the New York Mills Regional Cultural Center in Otter Tail County, Minnesota. "I'm, like, opening the atlas trying to find this place in the middle of nowhere." She was accepted. After learning that the best thing to do in northeast Minnesota was go canoe camping in the Boundary Waters, she reached out to the center for a guide recommendation. When she arrived, however, the guide, Christopher, informed her that the other participants had dropped out. "Are you sure you want to go?"

"I did this mental calculus in my head," Elisa said. "Was he an ax murderer?"

A year later they were married. She packed up all her belongings and cat, drove across the country, and set out to become a midwesterner. "I assumed I would have absolutely no difficulty," she said. "I had studied in London, lived in Tel Aviv, worked in Ghana. I mean, no problem, right? But it became very clear to me right away that the most boring place I had ever been was rural Minnesota. I would have to make all the most difficult transitions—changing jobs, losing friends, starting a relationship—all at the same time."

The fact that four in ten people say they initiated their own lifequakes shows how intimate and urgent the nonlinear life has become. The majority of life changes may happen to us, but we still like to upend the status quo ourselves. A plurality of personal-voluntary lifequakes (37 percent) involve work—switching careers, quitting a job, or retiring; 16 percent involve leaving a marriage; the rest of this category are divided among changing religions or political parties, moving, recovering from addiction, and transitioning genders.

A whopping 87 percent of these lifequakes involve leaving or rejecting a stable condition, whether a career, family, worldview, or home. This strongly suggests that the larger atmosphere of nonlinearity has given people greater permission to turn their backs on something safe in the service of striving for greater personal fulfillment.

Other personal-voluntary examples I heard:

- Eric Haney came from a long line of Appalachian hillbillies mixed with Cherokee fighters, was a member of the first-ever class of Delta Force (he participated in the aborted Iranian hostage rescue mission and the invasions of Grenada and Panama), and then left to start a paramilitary security company (clients included Saudi princes, the Haitian president, and oil executives held hostage in Latin America). But in his forties Eric switched from being a "man of action" to a "man of letters" and wrote a memoir, *Inside Delta Force*, that sold a million copies, followed by a string of spy novels.
- Coco Papy couldn't wait to escape her oppressive childhood in Savannah, which didn't take well to her cursing, body art, and liberalism. She fled to art school in Atlanta and later Manhattan, then starving-artisthood in Brooklyn, until her boyfriend's mother trashed the South one night and she realized she missed the place, prompting her to move back home.
- Lester Johnson was born into a family of middle-class African American Catholics in the civil-rights-era South, became enamored of the Nation of Islam in high school, rejected that, but in college became a devout Sunni Muslim, grew a beard, changed his diet, and became a lawyer who worked for social justice.

"Um, There Goes the House"

The collective-involuntary lifequake is the next biggest category, though it affected fewer than 10 percent of participants.

Kate Hogue considered her life linear and straightforward. Her parents were high school sweethearts in Joplin, Missouri. Kate was a tomboyish soccer player at eight who went on to participate in beauty pageants at ten. At thirteen, she felt called to the pastorate. "I was a cradle Presbyterian, and we had a youth pastor who encouraged us to listen to God." She delivered her first sermon, on love, while still in middle school.

Kate enrolled in Missouri State, where she worked in campus ministry and met her future husband in her first week. They planned to get married over Christmas her senior year. That summer she lived at home, planned her wedding, and volunteered at the church. On the morning of Sunday, May 22, she preached on being open to change.

That afternoon Kate was watching a *Harry Potter* marathon with her parents when a tornado siren went off. "The theme has always been that my dad monitors the weather outside while my mom and I go to the basement crawl space, which is maybe three feet high, lined with gravel, where we have a cot and a flashlight. It also doubled as my father's wine cellar, because he's a vintner."

This time, though, her dad joined them within minutes. "This was the first time in my twenty-one years that he has ever come into the basement," she said. "He brings two wine buckets, and my mom says, 'What are these for?' He says, 'Put them on your head.'"

Kate gulped, but did what he asked.

"Three minutes later, the lights start blinking and you can hear a rushing sound like a freight train," she said. "It's the loudest thing you've ever heard. And then, shattering glass. My dad says, 'Um, there goes the house.' I'm sitting there not knowing what to do, so I keep saying the prayer 'God, be with us. Keep us safe.'"

By the time the noise stopped, the water heater had fallen, blocking their escape. Natural gas was pouring in; water was raining down. "I'm freaking out about the possibility of now being killed in this space that had recently given us safe haven," Kate said. "My dad says, 'We survived the tornado, we're not going to die this way.'"

Just then, neighbors appeared overhead. "They assumed everyone was dead, because the house was leveled," Kate said. "It was a pile of matchsticks." Kate's dad tied a jacket to a piece of PVC pipe and waved it like a flag. "It was my seventy-eight-year-old grandfather who spotted it. He had driven as close as he could get, which was a mile away, then run to where we were. My dad explained the situation to him and said, 'We have some tools in the garage.' My grandpa looks over and says, 'You don't have any tools.'"

A passerby did, though, and three hours later the family was freed. They had survived the deadliest tornado to hit the United States in seventy years and the seventh deadliest overall. One hundred fifty-eight people died; another 1,150 were injured. Damages reached $2.8 billion.

In the subsequent decade, Kate would become obsessed with weather, suffering recurring nightmares and PTSD. She used her platform as an ordained pastor to turn her experience into touching rituals to help others adapt to trauma. But on that Sunday afternoon, she had something else on her mind. After surveying the devastation, taking in their fractured life and discarded memories, Kate's eyes settled on a tree still standing in what used to be their front yard. In its limbs, "a miracle of miracles," was a hanger. On it was her wedding dress, waving in the breeze.

In a series of seminal books over the last forty years, the sociologist Glen Elder described the long-term impact of collective events like the Great Depression and the 1980s farm crisis. My data suggest these types of shared events may no longer hold similar sway over people's lives. It could be that there are fewer of these events, or that people prefer to see their lives as unique and not subject to the same influences as everyone else. By far the most common collective-involuntary event people mentioned was 9/11, which played a meaningful part in a large number of lifequakes, from changing careers to ending marriages. Others included the Great Recession, the civil rights movement, Vietnam, #MeToo, and, in the case of Allen Peake, the Republican state rep from Georgia, the release of the Ashley Madison list of adulterers.

Other collective-involuntary examples I heard:

- Doc Shannon was born in the same Alabama town as Gomer Pyle actor Jim Nabors and became an IRS officer until he was drafted and sent to Vietnam, where he watched two buddies die in a double killing over drugs; he was so traumatized he became an international narcotics agent and spent the rest of his life avenging their deaths.
- Gayla Paschall dropped out of college in San Antonio to care for her younger brother and started trading commodities, but when the stock market crashed in 1987, she watched grown men cry and fortunes evaporate and was so unsettled she quit to earn a PhD in clinical psychology.
- Naomi Clark was born male-bodied in Seattle, lived in Japan as a teenager, and began to have thoughts of being female. She repressed those feelings for years, until being blocks from ground zero on 9/11 brought her face-to-face with her mortality. *I have only one life*, she thought. *I would rather risk everything than die without being myself.* She began to transition soon after.

"I Was a Total Corporate Bitch"

The smallest category of lifequake is collective and voluntary—but they do exist.

Shannon Watts has had three distinct phases of her adult life. First was her commitment to self. Born in upstate New York to a mom who never went to college and a corporate dad, she was a difficult teen with an undiagnosed learning disorder. "I was ambitious and competitive despite struggling to get through school," she said. "And I was obsessed with Watergate, which made me want to be a journalist."

Shannon studied journalism at the University of Missouri, eloped at twenty-three, had three kids by thirty, and became a hard-driving corporate communications executive. "I'm a very type A person, and I was in crisis communication, which is not just nine-to-five, it's all-day, all-weekend," she said. "I was a total corporate bitch. I was very talented, and I did well financially, but it was just not fulfilling."

Neither was her marriage. And in a classic, voluntary-personal lifequake, in a two-year span in her midthirties she quit her job, left her marriage, and became a stay-at-home mom. She remarried a few years later and became a stepmom to two more daughters. Those were the years she focused on family, and it was a struggle. She was a doting, slightly frantic mother; a loving, mostly supportive wife; and an enthusiastic, mildly frustrated volunteer. "This was a complete role reversal," she said. "I had been the primary breadwinner. I tried to do all these things well, but there were a lot of tears. I wasn't really sure what to do with myself."

Then came the shooting at Sandy Hook Elementary School, in which twenty-eight people were killed and two injured. It was the deadliest elementary school shooting in US history.

"I remember being so upset and agitated by the news, but also just sad and devastated," Shannon said. "I had been at yoga teacher training class—I was really horrible at it—and I said to my husband and stepdaughter in the kitchen, 'I think I'll start a Facebook page.' He said, 'Are you sure?' I think he sensed what might happen."

He was right. "By the time I went to bed," she said, "I was getting threatening texts and calls from people who saw my information online. But I was also getting calls from women who were so outraged they said, 'You know, I'm gonna start a chapter of this.'"

She called the group Moms Demand Action for Gun Sense in America. Within a few years she had five million volunteers and three hundred fifty thousand donors. She had gone in less than a decade from career to family to starting a purpose-driven movement. She quickly became one of the country's most visible advocates for gun safety, which brought widespread acclaim and influence, but also acute vitriol and the pain of missing many family milestones. The *corporate bitch* had become a "more thoughtful, activist crusader and badass woman."

The fact that voluntary-collective lifequakes are such a small percentage (5 percent) is more evidence that people are more fixated on their own life stories these days than becoming a part of larger social narratives. People still engage with causes. Movements like Black Lives Matter, Lean In, interfaith relations, and the Tea Party did come up, but more as everyday disruptors than earth-shattering reorientations. For better or worse, we live in a time when most of our stories start with *I* not *we*.

Other voluntary-collective examples I heard:

- Ann Imig was a frustrated musical theater actress and stay-at-home mom in Madison, Wisconsin, when she became an early leader of the mommy blogger movement. Looking for a way to elevate women's voices, she started the viral phenomenon "Listen to Your Mother," a nationwide series of staged readings for mothers to share their real-life experiences.
- Dawan Williams grew up without a father on the streets of Philadelphia and was arrested for the first time at sixteen and imprisoned for armed robbery at twenty-two. The father of three, Dawan enrolled in a voluntary group therapy program for incarcerated dads called Fathers and Children Together. Dawan was so transformed by the experience that after completing his sentence he went to work for the organization that administers the program.

- Adam Foss, the child of a rape victim in Colombia who became a prosecutor in Massachusetts, was so alarmed by the way his office was treating young African American criminals that he quit to join the grassroots movement to reform the criminal justice system. Recruited by John Legend to join his Let's Free America campaign, Adam gave a TED Talk, got a book deal, and met four presidents.

How Disruptors Become Lifequakes

What these various life stories, whatever their classification, have in common is that they feature an event, episode, or moment that redirects an entire life. But considering we go through about three dozen disruptors in our lives but only three to five lifequakes, what makes an otherwise routine intrusion rise to the level of remaking our lives? I found three primary factors.

The first is timing. Sometimes a disruptor comes along at a moment of particular vulnerability, exhaustion, or frustration and provides just enough spark to ignite a major change. Dwayne Hanes was married to his high school sweetheart and working to rehabilitate sex offenders in Detroit, but when he got passed over for a promotion, he became so angry he cheated on his wife and sunk his marriage. Leigh Wintz had been yo-yo dieting for years to mask her unhappiness, but a health scare finally jolted her into action, prompting her to drop sixty pounds, which gave her the confidence to get divorced, change careers, and remarry. Kellee Milheim's first child brought little change; she adjusted and kept working as an intelligence analyst. But after three miscarriages while trying to have a second, she broke down in tears one morning in the CIA parking lot. "I remember thinking, *All right, God, I can't take it anymore. I put myself in your hands.*" She joined a Bible study group, got pregnant, and then quit to follow her passion, training rescue dogs.

The second factor is that the disruptor falls at the end of a long string of disruptors; it's the last straw. Deb Copaken had been sagging under family financial tensions and frustrating communication with her husband for some time until she had a piercing pain in her abdomen and needed an appendectomy. When a colleague she was speaking with on the phone asked who was taking her to the hospital, she said, "Nobody." "What about your husband?" "It never occurred to me to call him," she said. The next year they were divorced. Richard Sarvate suppressed his dream of being a stand-up comedian for years, working instead at a soul-draining voice mail company to please his strict Indian American father, until he got caught in a riptide in Puerto Rico and almost drowned. *I cannot die having not gone onstage,* he thought. The next week he performed at his first open mic (his opening joke: "Oh, can you guys imagine Gandhi as a boxing instructor?"); the next year he moved to Hollywood.

But the third factor in why some disruptors become lifequakes was not something I expected: Disruptors seem to clump together. There's a confluence of destabilizing events that collectively create even more instability. Just when you get fired, your mother-in-law gets cancer; no sooner do you question your faith than your car gets totaled and your daughter is found to be anorexic. I struggled over what to call this phenomenon, until one day I saw a clip of an old movie in which one wobbly Model T crashed into another, then another car careened into the wreckage, then another. *That's exactly what it feels like!* I thought.

It's a *pileup.*

As in the movies, there are two-car pileups: Amy Cunningham's grief over her father's death led her to quit journalism and become a mortician. Jan Boyer and his wife were fighting so much over how to treat their teen daughter's drug and alcohol addiction that it led to the end of their marriage. Henry Ferris had two two-car pileups in his life: In his twenties, he learned he needed a kidney transplant while his wife was pregnant with twins; in his fifties, he was fired from his job as a book editor just before his wife left him for another man.

There are three-car pileups: Amber Alexander lost her boyfriend in a car wreck, her grandfather to a stroke, and her aunt in an overdose, all within six months. Ivy Woolf Turk was tending to her father in the hospital after a massive heart attack and caring for her mother, who was emotionally walloped by the event, when she came home to find that her husband had emptied their home of all its belongings in a rampage. Bob Hall was in his late forties and drawing comic strips in New York when his marriage failed, he moved home to Nebraska, and he learned he was adopted.

There are even four-car pileups and more: Khaliqa Baqi, a hospice chaplain in Oregon, went through menopause, got divorced, returned to school, and started a new job—all within a few years. Erik Smith, a young minister in Virginia, preached his mother's funeral, his father's funeral, left the church to become a special-needs teacher, had suicidal thoughts, got addicted to painkillers, and lost sixty pounds—all within two years.

Some of these concurrences are accidental. The diagnosis, the death, the tornado just happened to occur at a moment of vulnerability. But more, I've come to believe, are connected. It's as if our immune system becomes compromised by one disruptor so that when another one, two, or three come along, our entire identity gets the flu.

Sometimes we even initiate the pileup ourselves. Will Dana was in a loveless, sexless marriage for a dozen years when he lost his job as the managing editor of *Rolling Stone* after an article the magazine published about a rape scandal at the University of Virginia proved inaccurate. A month later he met a woman at a conference and began what he described as a "mad affair." "I had this thought of *Why not blow it all up at once?*" His marriage finally ended and his teenage son blamed him, leading to a painful estrangement.

Lifequakes are massive, messy, and often miserable. They come at inconvenient times that usually make them more inconvenient. They aggregate. But they also do something else: They initiate a period of self-reflection and personal reevaluation. They set in motion a series of reverberations that lead us to revisit our very identity. They force us to ask what we don't ask often enough: *What is it that gives me meaning and how does that influence the story of my life?*

CHAPTER 4

The ABCs of Meaning

What Shape Is Your Life?

While the chief promise of the linear life was regularity, the chief upshot of the nonlinear life is irregularity. Instead of ticking off a predetermined series of life events, each of us is bombarded by our own idiosyncratic fingerprint of booms, busts, ampersands, exclamation points, monster curveballs, lucky breaks, and every other conceivable life detour and twist.

A primary side effect of all this volatility is unease, a low state of anticipation and dread, a lingering sense of anxiety over whether what's coming next will be good or bad. *How did I end up in this situation? Why am I feeling so unsettled? What do I do now?* It's as if all that turbulence breeds a kind of existential agitation.

We throw lots of solutions at this condition these days—work, liquor, porn, pot, prayer, meditation, food, exercise. Many of these succeed for a time; some of them succeed longer. But sooner or later, an existential crisis demands an existential solution. We are called upon to answer life's ultimate questions: *What kind of person do I want to be? What story do I want to tell? What gives me meaning?*

Fortunately, we have a growing body of knowledge to help answer these questions. A century after the search for meaning catapulted to the center of modern thought, we have increased clarity over what each of us can do to sharpen our definition of what matters most to us. A generation after the importance of narrative identity advanced to the heart of modern psychology, we have greater appreciation that each of us has a personal story—or, more accurately, a collection of personal stories—that we use to nurture our well-being.

But my conversations suggest there's a connection between these two strands of thought we may have overlooked. Our varied sources of meaning and our multiple personal stories are more aligned than many of us realize. What's more, those building blocks of meaning and those assorted story lines also connect to a notion that has permeated society for millennia: what shape best captures our lives. Understanding the connections among what gives us meaning, which personal stories we emphasize at any given time, and the visual representation of those pillars of identity was a challenging and ultimately thrilling part of the Life Story Project.

In this chapter, I'll unpack the results.

"That's What the Communists and Jews Want You to Do"

Let's start with someone who has a nontraditional life shape.

Christian Picciolini was born to Italian immigrants who moved to Chicago in the mid-1960s, opened a beauty shop, and struggled. "They were often the victims of prejudice," he said. Christian was sent to live with his grandparents in the suburbs, where he felt like an outsider. "I hung out in my grandparents' closet, watching other kids through the window riding their bikes and wishing I could join them. I was lonely for the first fourteen years of my life."

When he was fourteen, Christian was standing in an alley one day smoking a joint when a '68 Firebird came speeding by, kicking up gravel and dust. "The car screeched to a halt in front of me, and this guy gets out. He's got a shaved head, boots. He grabs the joint from my lips, smacks me in the head, and says, 'That's what the Communists and Jews want you to do.'

"I was just a kid," Christian continued. "I had no idea what the hell a Communist or a Jew was. But he said, 'You're Italian. Your ancestors were great warriors and thinkers and artists. It's something to be proud of.' Suddenly, I wanted to be just like him. He seemed to have the one thing I had been searching for my entire life: community."

That man was twenty-six-year-old Clark Martell, the founder of the Chicago Area Skinheads, one of the leading neo-Nazi groups in the United States. Overnight, Christian became a zealot. He tattooed his body from head to toe with swastikas and Nazi eagles; he participated in gang attacks on blacks and Jews; he formed a band and wrote hateful lyrics: "The Holocaust was a fucking lie because six million Jews could never die."

"For the first time in my life I had purpose," he said. "And that purpose was saving the world. I thought everybody who didn't think like me was a fool, and I was carrying their dead weight on my shoulders."

When Martell was sent to prison two years later, Christian became the leader of America's neo-Nazis. He opened new branches from Minneapolis to San Francisco. With his dashing good looks and flair for recruiting, he became the international face of the movement. He was on CNN at seventeen.

When he was nineteen, Christian performed in front of four thousand skinheads in Germany. Afterward, they rioted. "It was at that moment when I started to recognize the impact of my lyrics," he said. "It never really struck me how accountable I was for the ideas I put out in the world."

Back in Chicago, some black teenagers walked into the McDonald's Christian frequented. "I was belligerent and told them this was my effing McDonald's and they had no right to be there." Christian and his pals chased them outside. One of the teenagers pulled a gun and began firing, but the gun jammed. "I proceeded to beat him up," Christian said. "I was kicking him in the face; it was swollen and bloody. He opened one of his eyes, and I connected with it. And I thought: *This could have been my brother, my mother, my father.* It was my first moment of empathy."

Christian was running a record store that specialized in white power music, but also sold hip-hop and punk. "People started coming in who were African American, they were Jewish, they were gay. I didn't want them at first, but I was happy to take their money. But they kept coming back, and the conversation would grow, become personal."

Christian also fell in love. "My girlfriend hated the movement," he said. "I had to beg her to go on a date with me." They married and had a baby. "I was in the delivery room, holding my son for the first time, and he was so innocent. I realized he could be manipulated, and maybe I had been, too. Suddenly I began to have another identity, another community, another purpose."

He began to withdraw from the movement. He closed his record store. He had another son. His wife thought he was moving too slowly, so she left him, taking their boys with her. By the time he stepped away for good—seven years after he first entered—Christian had lost his livelihood, his family, his community. For the next five years he sank into depression, drank heavily, did cocaine. He rarely left the house except to see his children.

Finally, one of his friends pushed him to apply for a tech support job at IBM. This was before the internet, so his identity was easier to conceal. He got the job. His first assignment was to install computers at the high school he'd been kicked out of, twice. The last time he was there he was dragged out in handcuffs and given a restraining order for attacking the African American security guard. On his first day on the job, he recognized the guard, Mr. Holmes. Christian followed him to the parking lot and tapped him on the shoulder.

"He turned around, took a step back, and was horrified. All I could think to say at that moment was 'I'm sorry.' We talked. I found some more words eventually, explained to him what I'd been through in the last five years, and he embraced me. He told me he forgave me and asked me to forgive myself. And he encouraged me to tell my story."

Christian went on to generate a quarter of a billion dollars in sales revenue for IBM. He married his supervisor. He started giving speeches about his past. And eventually he helped found an organization called Life After Hate that helps former extremists, from white supremacists to Islamic fundamentalists, transition out of violence. "It starts with compassion," he said. "Everyone is looking for an identity community and they hit potholes somewhere along the road. Those potholes can be trauma, they can be abandonment, they can be witnessing your father commit suicide. The people have misery, but they don't have company. And sometimes they find acceptance in pretty negative places. My job is to fill potholes. My motto is: 'I treat the child not the monster.'"

After all these years, he was still that vulnerable boy staring out the window, hungering for love. And that yearning for connection is what defines who he is. When I asked him to pick a shape that represents his life, he chose a bowl.

"A bowl is a place for people to spill their guts into. It's a place to fill with your thoughts, your demons, your dreams. It's the place I was looking for as a boy, sitting in my grandparents' closet. And it's the place I help provide today, where you hold people in your hands and help them feel like they belong."

The Meaning Movement

The father of the modern meaning movement, Viktor Frankl, was four years old in 1909, living at number 6 Czernin Street, Vienna, a few blocks from where Johann Strauss composed "The Blue Danube." One night before sleep, he was startled by a piercing thought: *I, too, will have to die.*

"What troubled me then," he later wrote, "as it has done throughout my life, was not the fear of dying, but the question of whether the transitory nature of life might destroy its meaning."

His answer would guide his life and that of tens of millions of others in the coming century: "In some respects it is death itself that makes life meaningful."

Vienna was the hometown of meaning. Freud gave birth to psychotherapy there; Hitler moved there when he was a teenager; Frankl grew up there and went on to launch a revolution. At sixteen, Frankl gave his first lecture, "On the Meaning of Life." At twenty-eight he formed the "Third Viennese School of Psychotherapy." His core idea: We should not ask what the meaning of life is because it is we who are being asked. Each of us is responsible for finding our own reason to live.

In many ways Frankl was the latest iteration of the centuries-long conversation about what it means to live a fulfilling life. Aristotle described the tension between hedonism—the pursuit of happiness—and eudaemonia—the search for dignity, authenticity, and what came to be called meaning. Frankl became the preeminent modern champion of the idea that seeking meaning is the core motivation of humans and the key to our very survival.

In 1941, Frankl was just finishing a book on his ideas when the Nazis began systematically implementing the Final Solution. As a doctor, Frankl was able to secure entrée to the United States, but he anguished about leaving his parents. Returning from picking up his visa, Frankl covered the Jewish star on his coat and ducked into a cathedral, praying for a sign from God. When he got home, his father was in tears, staring at a piece of marble on the kitchen table.

"What's this?" Frankl asked.

"The Nazis burned our synagogue today," he said. The chunk of marble was the only remains from the Ten Commandments above the bimah.

"I can even tell you what commandment it's from," his father said. "Only one uses these letters."

"And what's that?" Frankl asked.

"Honor thy father and mother."

Frankl ripped up the visa on the spot. The following year, the entire family was sent to a concentration camp, where Frankl's father died in his arms. Two years later, Frankl, his wife, and his mother were sent to Auschwitz. His mother and wife were gassed. Frankl was forced into hard labor, slept ten to a bed, and ate only crumbs a day. One night he witnessed a man having a nightmare but resisted waking him. "No dream, no matter how bad, could be as horrible as the reality of the camp."

And yet, what allowed him to survive was his commitment to meaning, he said. Frankl had stitched the only copy of his book into his jacket, but it was confiscated and destroyed. At night he kept himself occupied by repeating passages to himself. When he was liberated in 1945, he sat down and wrote an account of his experience. It took him nine days. He wrote it anonymously at first, but friends urged him to attach his name.

The book was published in 1946 and instantly became a defining book of the century. *Man's Search for Meaning* has gone on to sell over twelve million copies. Frankl's message was that even in the face of unimaginable bleakness, humans can find hope. "You do not have to suffer to learn, but if you don't learn from suffering . . . then your life becomes truly meaningless." The key, he said, is to imagine a better time, to have a *reason* to live. He quotes Nietzsche: "He who has a why to live for can bear almost any how."

Frankl's book arrived amid the smoldering ruins of Hiroshima and the Holocaust, during what was widely considered an epidemic of meaninglessness. Frankl called it the "sickness of the century." Carl Jung called it an "illness." "Meaninglessness inhibits fullness of life," Jung wrote. "Meaning makes a great many things endurable—perhaps everything."

From this ground zero, a modern meaning movement began to rise, eventually growing to include philosophy, psychology, and neuroscience. If the symptoms of meaninglessness were alienation and emptiness, the balm was fulfillment and personal sense-making. The "central concept of human psychology is *meaning*," wrote Jerome Bruner. And the central task of every individual is to make your own meaning. There is no single formula.

But there is guidance. Seventy-five years of thought and research have produced a robust body of ideas about what it means to live a meaningful life. In our coding sessions, we cross-referenced these ideas with the words, phrases, and expressions people used most frequently in my conversations. We then compared these results with the themes people selected for their lives.

In the end, we identified three key ingredients of a well-balanced life. Let's call them the *ABCs of meaning*. The *A* is *agency*—autonomy, freedom, creativity, mastery; the belief that you can impact the world around you. The *B* is *belonging*—relationships, community, friends, family; the people that surround and nurture you. The *C* is *cause*—a calling, a mission, a direction, a purpose; a transcendent commitment beyond yourself that makes your life worthwhile.

These three essential ideas, as powerful as they are, aren't the only means we use to live with harmony, fulfillment, and joy. They correspond to another set of tools: the three strands of our narrative identity. The first is our *me story*—the one in which we're the hero, the doer, the creator; we exercise agency and, in return, feel fulfilled. The next is our *we story*—the one in which we're part of a community, a family, a team; we belong to a group and, in turn, feel needed. The third is our *thee story*—the one in which we're serving an ideal, a faith, a cause; we give of ourselves to others and, by extension, feel part of something larger.

It turns out that we all have all three of the ABCs of meaning within us—and all three of these personal stories. What's more, we are constantly weighting and reweighting these elements in response to life events. We're like Lady Justice in that way, with three scales instead of two. When our sources of meaning are in balance, our lives are in balance. When they're out of balance, our lives are out of balance.

I learned something else, too: We tend to prioritize one element over the others. We each have what we might consider a home base, a *core construct*, as psychologists might call it. We're agency-first people, belonging-first people, or cause-first people. We also have a secondary priority, and a third. (I would be an ABC in this model, my wife a CAB.)

There's one more way to understand and visualize these sources of meaning. That relates to the final question I asked in every interview.

The Shapes of Our Lives

One notable curiosity of the science of chaos is how researchers trying to capture how the world actually works kept circling back to shapes. In the midst of order, they found chaos, but then, in the midst of chaos, they found order. The turbulence in water generates complex dimples and swirls; clouds drift in and out of tufts and puffs; the perimeter of a country appears from above as the familiar outline you see on a map, but the closer you get, the more you see an endless variety of juts, bends, coves, and bays. Chaos created an entire new vocabulary of shapes to capture these phenomena: fractals, intermittencies, folded-towel diffeomorphisms, smooth noodle maps, strange attractors, bend curves, spiral vortices, metawobbles, the drunkard's walk.

It was this fascination with shapes in science that first inspired me to ask people what shape best captures their lives. The earliest responses threw me, because they seemed all over the place. They included a house, tree saw, spiral, heart, sunset, winding road, the Brooklyn Bridge, a circle, and, from Brian Wecht, a chaos researcher himself before he jumped to YouTube star, a Calabi-Yau manifold. This was beginning to seem like a party game with little point.

Still, I kept asking, in part because the answers were so vivid, but more because how people explained their answers was so revealing. It was obvious that people had fierce opinions and that their shapes represented something essential about how they viewed themselves. Saying your life is like a stock market chart versus a heart versus Jesus on the cross communicates something powerful about what matters most to you.

But what exactly does it communicate? The last thing I want to do is free people from the restrictive boxes of the past, only to cram them back into new boxes. But at a time when the predominant shapes of the past have become outmoded—the cycles, staircases, and arrows of progress that once reigned—exploring whether any rubrics might come to replace them seems worthwhile. These shapes are clues to the priorities people hold most dear.

At root, the shapes fall into three buckets. The first bucket includes shapes that reflect some sort of trajectory. This group characterized their lives as primarily moving through time, rising and falling, usually in response to their individual success or failure. I would have chosen this shape, and it was the most popular. Examples include a river, a winding road, a zigzag, a mountain range. Because of the linear nature of this category, I label this bucket *lines*.

As obvious as this shape seems (especially to those who chose it!), it was by no means the only category. The second bucket consists of shapes that are more spatial in nature. These shapes are enclosed; they have borders, outlines, walls, or other features that could contain things, usually loved ones. Two in five selected this category. Examples include a heart, a house, a basket, and, like Christian Picciolini, a bowl. Given the way these shapes suggest assembling people, I label this bucket *circles*.

The final bucket includes shapes that are some sort of object. People

Self-characterization

Agency

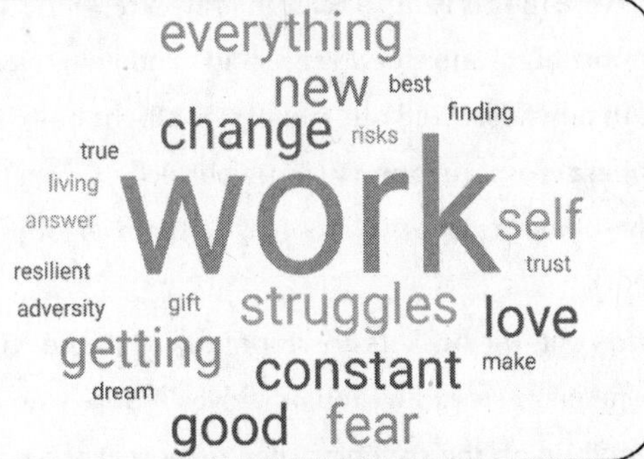

Belonging

Cause

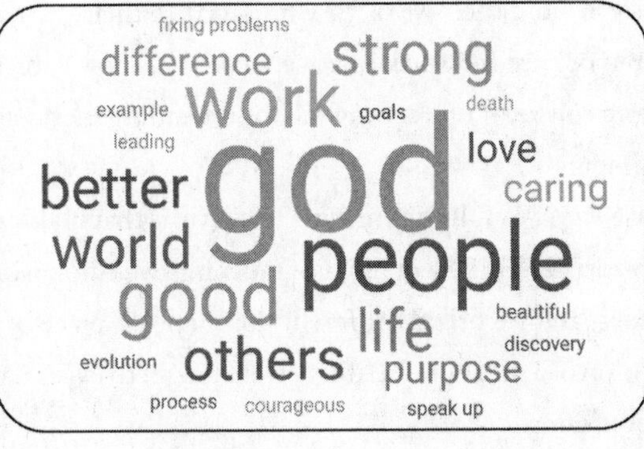

who chose this category took *shape* to mean a symbol, an icon, a logo, if you will, that represented a guiding principle or commitment in their lives. Three in ten were in this camp, including my wife, who runs a global nonprofit to support high-impact entrepreneurs and who selected, in a nod to her interest in new ideas and aha moments, a light bulb. Other examples include a globe, a cross, an infinity sign, a butterfly. Given the inspirational quality of these objects, the way people see them as lodestars, I label this bucket *stars*.

As it turns out, the buckets correspond well to the ABCs of meaning and to three primary stories we tell ourselves. Those who chose lines tend to be more focused on their agency; they're more work- and achievement-oriented. Their *me story* comes first. Those who chose circles tend to be more focused on belonging; they're more relationship-oriented. Their *we story* is primary. Those who chose stars tend to be more cause focused; they're more oriented toward their beliefs, saving the world, or serving others. Their *thee story* is paramount.

For a visual demonstration of the words people in each category use to describe their lives, please see the piece of art on the previous page.

Just because a person picks one shape doesn't mean they don't value the others. We all have multiple sources of identity. What it does suggest, I believe, is that we foreground one of these shapes during certain times of our lives. We're all familiar with this idea. We all know people who build their identity around their work, or who sacrifice their own ambitions to raise children or care for a sick relative, or who eschew careers with high financial return in favor of teaching school, spreading the gospel, or saving the environment.

What we've yet to fully appreciate, I believe, is that making this choice means we prioritize a different pillar of meaning, we emphasize a different personal story, and we prize a different life shape. In place of the one singular definition of a meaningful life we were taught to expect, we now have multiple definitions.

Let's take a closer look at these various strands of meaning and how people prioritize among them.

A Is for *Agency*

Deb Copaken grew up in a split-level *Brady Bunch* house in Potomac, Maryland, that was riddled with tension. "There were no sidewalks and there was no escape," she said. At fourteen she would drive her parents' car just to get away; at seventeen she fled to Japan, taught English, and sold her first piece of journalism to *Seventeen*. "I was like, *I can freakin' do this.* I can travel, I can sell articles, and I can get someone else to pay for it."

She returned home, had a fling with a cover boy from *Tiger Beat*, and enrolled at Harvard, where an experiment with LSD opened up new worlds. "I finally saw who I was," she said. "And I wanted to explore that person instead of the person others wanted me to be." She ditched her safe major for photography and channeled her rage from an attempted rape into bold, daring work in which she ventured into difficult neighborhoods and shot gritty portraits. "I felt like a prey," she said, "so I became the hunter."

And she got hooked. She moved to Paris and became a war photographer—Israel, Afghanistan, Zimbabwe, Romania. "My life was already a war because I'm a woman out in the world," she said. "So why not go to war? I had to become proactive."

But after seven years she tired of the empty sex and rampant harassment. She was facedown in mud in Moscow, bullets whizzing overhead during a coup (the same one that caused Lev Sviridov to become homeless in Manhattan), when she realized she wanted out. She got married, moved to New York, and had three children. Even then she was the primary breadwinner. When her marriage failed after fifteen years, she was the one who walked. "I had reached a point where I just couldn't live in a relationship that offered no love in return for the love I was putting in." Walloped by a spate of health issues—breast cancer, a hysterectomy, heart problems—she had a May-December relationship with a young lover and parlayed her anger once more into art—photography, prose, painting.

Deb dreamed of circles—she still longed for a committed relationship—but she was, at the core, a line. "I'm picturing a piece of graph paper, there are good times and bad times, a sine wave going up and down and up."

Agency is the first, and maybe even the foremost, ingredient of a meaningful life. "At the heart of the American dream lies a belief in individual agency," writes historian Steven Mintz. Fully half of the people I interviewed chose a shape that indicated they prioritize this category. Those numbers contained a slight gender gap, with 51 percent of men and 47 percent of women.

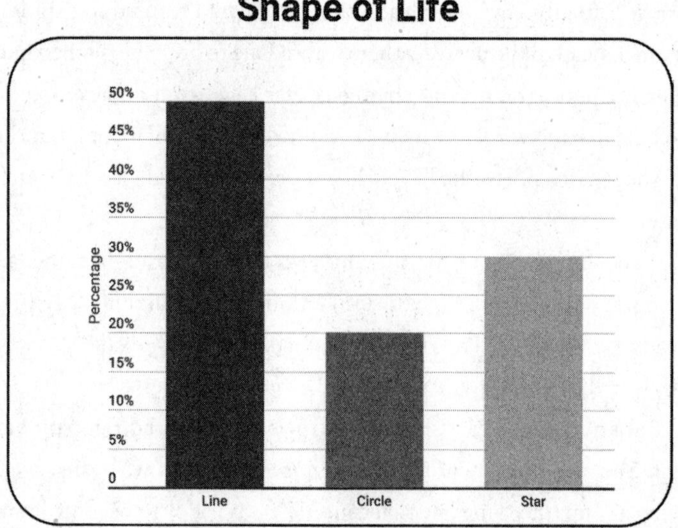

The psychologist Bessel van der Kolk defines agency as "the feeling of being in charge of your life: knowing where you stand, knowing that you have a say in what happens to you, knowing that you have some ability to shape your circumstance." People who exhibit agency have been shown to be happier and healthier, and have a higher quality of life.

Agency is so important that even deluding yourself that you have it can improve your life. Merely understanding a problem, even if you can't do anything about it, gives you a sense of control. By forcing yourself to learn what's happening to you, you come to accept it. You become an agent in your own meaning-making. As someone who falls into this category myself, I can relate. Whenever I've faced a crisis, whether my wife's high-risk pregnancy or my own high-stakes cancer, I've become the planner, the researcher, the describer.

Work is the most prominent arena in which people express agency. Like Deb, the line people I met tend to be defined by their work: they're builders, makers, doers, "people of action," as Aristotle would have said. A host of contemporary studies have reinforced this conclusion. Workers who feel they have more autonomy and control work with more zeal and focus. Workers who can decorate their own workspaces are happier and more productive. Workers who are given more freedom over their schedules are more likely to accept a job and less likely to leave.

But agency is not limited to work. General Mills found in the 1950s that making its Betty Crocker powdered cake mix too easy deflated home cooks. A team of psychologists discovered that requiring homemakers to add a *single egg* gave them a sense of accomplishment. Dan Ariely and colleagues found the same with Ikea furniture: The act of assembling the merchandise gave people a greater sense of satisfaction. Residents in nursing homes given even a modicum of personal control, like caring for a plant, are happier and healthier, and live longer.

From work to home, agency is the dominant source of meaning for those who see their lives as following some sort of up-and-down linear shape, an oscillating personal narrative.

They are people like Henry Ferris, who escaped a challenging family in Georgia, survived a kidney transplant, and became an elite book editor in New York (he edited Barack Obama's *Dreams from My Father*) before losing his job and marriage in the same year. "I look at my life narratively, as a line with peaks and valleys."

Antonio Grana, a child of gay rave culture of San Francisco, who had an abusive alcoholic lover, entered a twelve-step program, married a woman, and then started an IT company. The shape of his life: Chutes and Ladders. "You have to accept that a punctuation mark happens in your life, then slide back and take a different path."

John Evenhuis, an IBM executive in the Bay Area who, after raising children with his wife in a high-stress community, suggested they trade in their country club lifestyle and move to the outskirts of Glacier National Park in Montana, where he telecommutes and they're in nature every weekend. His life, he said, was a hockey stick. "Everything was going along fine, then, *whack!*, everything just changed and became phenomenal."

And Serena Stier, who lost her husband to suicide when she had three children under eight but went on to earn advanced degrees in psychology and law, write mystery novels, and become a mediator. "My life is like waves in an ocean. There are foamy times, there are calm times, but on the whole, it's beautiful."

The agency people are fierce and determined, and like being in control. They have a clear grasp of their *me story.* But they're not always the most focused on their relationships; that distinction belongs to the second group.

B Is for *Belonging*

Michelle Swaim never had a family. Her father left while her mother was pregnant; her mother showed very little interest in her. Growing up in Massachusetts, Michelle sometimes waited hours after school to be picked up. "I think that defined my life a lot, which caused me to jump into marriage early and not be a complete individual."

Michelle met her future husband, Dave, when she was fifteen. "I think I was just looking for a parent because I was never parented," she said. "He was definitely the hero of our relationship." They attended William and Mary together and got married when Michelle was twenty-one. "My mother didn't speak to me at my wedding because she didn't want me to leave her," Michelle said. "Also, intimacy was really hard for me. The honeymoon was miserable."

Over the next decade, Dave's career took off; he became senior pastor of a fast-growing church outside Boston. Michelle, meanwhile, spiraled into self-absorption. She became an obsessive runner and an anorexic. For nine years she barely ate. "When you have an inability to connect with people, and you feel shameful about yourself, the only power you have is over your own body. I couldn't speak up for myself, so this was the only way I could actually exert any influence over myself."

She was down to half an apple a day.

Michelle's anorexia also made her infertile. For seven years she tried and failed to get pregnant. Then one day she slipped on the ice while jogging, flew into the air, and landed on her back. In the hospital, she had a vision from God. *I did this to you*, he said. Her husband walked in the next day and said he'd had a vision from God. "He told me he did this to you for a purpose." In that moment—tearful and finally aligned—they agreed to change their lives.

The following year they adopted a boy from Korea. In the next decade, they adopted ten more children. They eventually reached eight boys and three girls. Some were American, others refugees. They were black, white, brown, Ugandan, Irish, Mexican. The girl who waited hours for her mom to pick her up after school now drives back and forth to school three hours a day.

The shape of her life: a dented minivan. It's the object that most embodies her life as a mom.

"I felt lonely as a child, and that's been a huge driver in my life. All I ever wanted was to feel loved, and all I want today is for these children to feel loved."

Belonging—the feeling that emerges from developing and maintaining close personal relationships—is the pillar of meaning that's been most reinforced by recent research. In one study of what gives us meaning, 89 percent cited an interpersonal relationship. The eighty-year Stanford study of 1,500 schoolchildren found that those with deeper social connections lived longer. George Vaillant, who led the seventy-year Harvard study of 268 men (John F. Kennedy was a participant), concluded, "The only thing that really matters in life are your relationships to other people."

In my conversations, one in five picked a shape that reflected the importance they gave to belonging. This included a wide gender gap, with 61 percent of women and 39 percent of men.

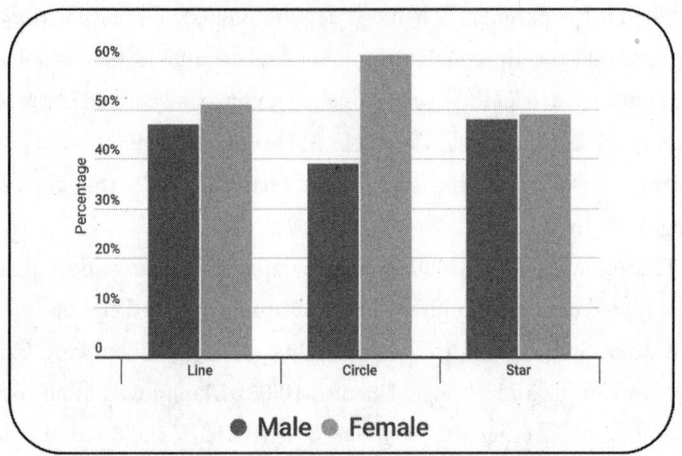

The reason belonging is so central to meaning is that our brains are cultural organs. The essence of being human is shared emotions, connections, and ideas. Findings going back decades suggest that positive social networks increase mental and physical health. Cancer patients do better in supportive communities, as do Alzheimer's caregivers, alcoholics, trauma victims, and PTSD patients. Children who experienced the Blitz in London alongside their parents fared better than those sent away from London to be with family in the countryside.

It's not just family and support groups that provide a sense of belonging—neighborhood, country, even work can provide it. People with strong connections in the workplace are more open to growth, are better colleagues, and are more resilient. They also get promoted faster. New hires who are welcomed warmly on their first day at work are more productive nine months later; employees who form trusting relationships with their managers take critical feedback more effectively. Workers who grow closer to their colleagues use *we* more than *I* in their emails; those who get fired use *we* less often.

Belonging is a defining feeling for many.

People like Ellen Shafer, who grew up on a farm in North Dakota, moved to the big city to work for Target and General Mills but, after her husband lost his job, returned to Fargo to be close to family and build community around a monthly supper club. "My life is one of those shapes you make with a Spirograph, where you put a pen in a circle and it turns into a flower. It's not a line—how boring would that be!"

Jen DeVore, a star athlete in Seattle, met her husband at Yale and became a hard-driving executive at the *Los Angeles Times* but quit to raise three boys, support her husband, and research her family ancestry. The shape of her life: a house. "I hope I've made an impact on my community and done good in the world, but ultimately I want to do good for my family."

Lisa Heffernan, the granddaughter of Russian Holocaust refugees who turned her back on her parents at seventeen, raised two boys, then worried so much about being left by them that she cofounded a popular Facebook group for empty nesters. "My entire mission has been to create a family tree. My husband and I both had undependable parents, so our focus was for our children to always be able to depend on us."

And Amber Alexander, who grew up in a tight-knit trailer park in Gary, Indiana, was pummeled by the deaths of three loved ones in her twenties, became CEO of the local Y, and then was devastated by the brain tumor of her two-year-old son. "I see my life as a heart because God has blessed me with love even through pain and trial."

Love is the dominant emotion of those who put relationships at the center of their lives. They are the most at peace of the three shapes I encountered. Their *we story* > their *me story*. But they're not the most passionate. That distinction belongs to the third group.

C Is for *Cause*

Tami Trottier was raised on the Turtle Mountain Indian Reservation on the North Dakota border with Canada. The youngest of four girls who attended Catholic schools, she was painfully shy. "The shyness was so debilitating, my face, my jaw, my mouth would open but I couldn't speak. My sisters didn't want to take me anywhere. 'She's embarrassing!'"

Tami was the only one of her siblings to opt out of the family grocery store. Instead, she enrolled at Minot State University, where she studied journalism. She also started exploring her native heritage that she felt had been stripped from her on the reservation. She went to sweat lodges, started dancing, took an Ojibwe name, Red Wind Woman. "It was all about developing relationships with other indigenous people," she said. "Our trauma is that we were attacked."

Building on that interest in trauma, she went on to get a PhD in clinical psychology. "I always wanted to be a doctor," she said. "I wanted to make our people proud." She married a fellow tribe member, had a baby, and tried for another. But problems arose. Surrounded by white men at work, she began to doubt herself. She had two failed pregnancies. "For two years I was living with angst and anxiety. I lost sixty pounds. I was a shell of a person."

Then she had a revelation. Western medicine would never cure her. She immersed herself in native health practices, studied the healing powers of animals, and emerged with a new body of knowledge she called Turtle Medicine. "I jumped up one day and announced, 'I'm going to teach people to heal themselves.'"

She moved her family back to the reservation and cofounded a clinic for women and girls. It's the first clinic on indigenous lands run entirely by women. "People questioned, 'Can you make it? Are you going to be financially okay?' I never doubted, because there's a difference between a vocation and a calling. Once I discovered what I was supposed to be doing, I knew nothing could stop me."

The shape of her life reflects her passion: It's a turtle shell.

"Like a turtle, I've learned there are times you need to retreat inside your shell to protect yourself, but you can't live inside your shell. You have to have your purpose. Mine is being mindful, living at a slow and steady pace, and taking care of my shell, but also my people."

Having a cause—a *thee story*—is the third great pillar in living a meaningful life. A cause is something you believe in that's bigger than yourself. It's serving God, being green, mentoring, marching, caretaking, canvassing. Supporting a cause gives you a sense of purpose and self-sacrifice. And it's good for you: Those who volunteer enjoy higher levels of happiness and live longer.

It's also hard. Four in ten of us say we have no cause. One reason may be that the sources of cause are changing. As fewer of us get it from religion, more of us are seeking it at work. But only a third of us say our work gives us meaning. Those who do tend to perform work that reduces suffering, improves the world, or generates delight. In a famous study, Jane

Dutton and colleagues found that even people who do the most menial jobs in a hospital, like changing bedpans, can take deep meaning from their work if they believe they are improving the lives of patients.

Caregiving is another area that gives many people their cause. Helping those in need leads to improved health and well-being, not only for those who receive the help, but also for those who give it. Patients who help new patients just diagnosed with their condition enjoy better recovery themselves.

The same even applies to those with a terminal illness. As my dad's disease progressed, he often directed attention to how difficult it was for my mom. When I got cancer, I created a Council of Dads for my daughters. Again, though I didn't know it at the time, I now see how this helped all three of the ABCs—agency ("I'm doing *something*!"), belonging ("I'm deepening bonds between my family and my friends"), and cause ("I'm helping my daughters through *their* pain").

Having a cause was the dominant source of meaning—and the dominant shape—of three out of ten of my subjects.

People like Brin Enterkin, who raised $34,000 to build a school for girls in Cambodia while still in high school, moved to Uganda in her twenties to work on malnutrition, then went on to train social entrepreneurs around the globe. The shape of her life is a Fibonacci spiral. "I see my life as a love of people that started small but is expanding to serve more and more."

Wali Ali, who was born a Jew named Melvin Meyer from Starkville, Mississippi, had a cross burned on his lawn for endorsing integration while an undergraduate at Alabama, was institutionalized after an LSD trip, and then converted to Islam and became a Sufi master. His shape is the winged heart of the Sufi order.

Daisy Khan, who was born into a traditional Muslim family in Pakistan with limited freedom for girls, attended school on Long Island, then went to Wall Street, before marrying a liberal imam and opening a nonprofit to spread equality for Muslim women. The shape of her life: boxing gloves. "I'm a fighter. I've always been pushing boundaries. And I'm going to take these gloves and pass them on to the next generation that needs them."

And Jason Doig, a Jamaican American NHL star who retired overweight and miserable, turned vegan, went through sugar detox, and became an evangelist of healthy living. The shape of his life: a torus. "It's a doughnut-shaped energy source that's constantly flowing."

A century after Viktor Frankl first placed the burden on each of us to determine what gives us meaning, we have more tools than ever to answer that call. We have three primary levers we can tug—agency, belonging, and cause. We have three principal stories we can tell—our me story, we story, and thee story. We have three prevailing life shapes we can choose—lines, circles, and stars. And every now and then, if our life takes a swerve, we can alter these priorities as we wish. I call this process *shape-shifting*, and it's a powerful way we make meaning in times of personal change.

CHAPTER 5

Shape-Shifting

How We Make Meaning in Times of Change

The meaning we make from our lives is not static or stable. It fluctuates, it oscillates, and, every now and then, it evaporates. This feeling of being directionless often happens in the wake of a lifequake. I think of these moments as meaning vacuums, when the air is sucked out of our lives and the previous balance of tendencies that give us agency, belonging, and cause is wiped clean. What follows is a series of aftershocks, ripple effects from the initial jolt that often elicit fear and confusion but can be signs of healing.

What follows is a period of shape-shifting.

"So, Um, I Got Fired"

Jamie Levine remembers his childhood in Worcester, Massachusetts, as a time of bliss. "No divorce, no relatives died. I was happy-go-lucky," he said. There were tensions, of course. His dad's mill went out of business and his father had to reinvent himself as a florist. "It scared me about money and imparted in me a general fear about wanting to have financial security,"

Jamie said. But it hardly derailed him. Tall, handsome, and ambitious, Jamie did well in school, was active in extracurriculars. He expected to go to Harvard.

He was turned down. "It was the first time I remember, emotionally, thinking, *Damn, I did not get what I wanted. I better regroup and figure out who I want to be.*" What he wanted to be was ultra-rich, he decided. He went to Brandeis, majored in economics, and took a semester at the London School of Economics.

"I wanted to be Alex P. Keaton," he said. "I was a Reagan kid, growing up with *Richie Rich* comic books. *L.A. Law* was popular—that show where everyone was rich and had great cars. I don't think I was abnormally focused on money, I think a lot of us were at that time. It was the go-go eighties. But it was very important to me."

"Were you a jerk?"

"Yes, I think so," he said. "I was very un-self-aware."

Jamie earned an MBA at the Wharton School and applied for a job in investment banking at Goldman Sachs. "Everybody in my class wanted that job," he said. "It was the top. The elite. You were the shit." He was hired. "It was my ticket," he said. "Finally I felt redemption for what happened to my dad and for getting turned down from Harvard."

He plunged in, worked around the clock, started climbing. "I totally drank the Kool-Aid," he said. "I was happy to be on the treadmill, and if somebody just pressed the button higher, I was going to run faster." He transferred to London, married a junior associate, Rebecca; they got pregnant and bought an expensive house in Chelsea. "The upward trajectory continued," he said.

Jamie was a pure line—his agency had made him who he was.

Then Jamie and Rebecca went for their eight-week scan. Their baby had a hole in its abdominal wall that allowed its intestines to escape. "It was not uncommon, and there was a high likelihood it could be cured by surgery," Jamie said. "But this turned out to be the first of many situations when if there was a 99 percent chance of something good happening, in all those cases, we ended up in the bad bucket, the 1 percent."

Scarlett was born without a third of her intestine, a condition so rare even the top doctors in London hadn't seen it. She remained in the hospital for the next ten months. From the day she was born, she could eat whatever she wanted, but it passed through her so quickly she couldn't absorb any nutrients. Every night, for the rest of her life, she would need an IV to survive.

At first, Jamie tried to keep up his pace. He went to work at dawn, was in the hospital from seven to midnight, and then did it again the next day. He made partner a few months after Scarlett was born.

But everything else was imploding. Rebecca was overwhelmed by the stress. Their marriage began falling apart. Scarlett's bilirubin number started to collapse, meaning her liver was failing. The only option was to wean her off the IV, but if they did that, she'd starve to death. "We were just waiting for her to die," Jamie said.

Then one day an email came from America. "My dad's brother's wife's brother's wife read an article in the *Boston Globe* about this doctor who had found a way to give kids intravenous nutrition without destroying their livers." A week later Jamie was in Boston meeting with the doctor; two weeks later Scarlett was on a plane to the United States.

The cocktail worked. The family moved to Boston. Jamie and Rebecca had another baby, a son. All this time, Jamie was commuting back and forth to the Goldman office in New York. Life seemed to be on the upswing. But the strain proved too great. When the company said they needed to downsize, Jamie knew what that meant.

"So, um, I got fired," he said.

Suddenly, the treadmill stopped. And with it the money, the momentum, and the meaning he took from it all.

"It really forced me to reexamine myself," he said. "To reevaluate myself."

He was out of work for a year, and when he finally took his next job, it was not on Wall Street but at a smaller biotech firm. He changed his leadership style—working closely with employees, being sensitive to their personal lives, encouraging family time. As for his own family, he and Rebecca went to counseling.

"I think the Scarlett thing really kicked us in the teeth," he said. "All of a sudden I had to strip away all the MBA stuff and become much rawer. We had to decide, were we going to separate or stay together? And staying together meant making our relationship a bigger priority. We got fucked up together, we had to get unfucked together. We had a bit of an arranged marriage; now we had to fall in love."

And they did. By the time I met Jamie, thirteen years after that eight-week scan, he and his family were living in San Diego. Scarlett had a normal life during the day—going to school, being with friends, playing sports—but every night she came home and hooked up to an IV for nine hours. Every single night.

Jamie and Rebecca adjusted their lives accordingly. She was on the board of her son's school; he was running a nutritional company. His life, once tilted toward his own achievement, was much more balanced. He was less focused on the agency part of this identity—his line—and more focused on the relationships around him—his circle. He summed up the change this way:

"Am I a jerk today? I don't think so."

In a Dark Wood

In 1302, the Italian poet Dante Alighieri was exiled from his hometown of Florence in a political feud. He wandered for years around Tuscany, heart-sick and bereft, before accepting that he would never return home. It was then that he turned back to his first love and composed one of the towering achievements of Western literature, *The Divine Comedy.* The poem opens with one of the more famous descriptions of a lifequake.

> *Midway in our life's journey, I went astray*
> *from the straight road and woke to find myself*
> *alone in a dark wood.*

The narrator goes on to lament how hard it is to describe in this thick of thickets, in a wood so dense and gnarled it evokes panic, a feeling so bitter *as death itself is bitter.*

Dante compares his state of mind to not just a crooked road, but death itself. And he's not alone. The first, and to me most chilling, aftershock of a lifequake is how many people experience their upheaval as a death. A startlingly high number of people in my conversations—I'd put the total at close to 50 percent—used expressions like *a part of me died that day, I was dead and came back to life, I was reborn.*

What could this possibly mean?

Fear of death has been a theme of storytelling since the birth of the campfire, and it's been a focus of social science since the birth of the research method. Viktor Frankl identified confronting one's mortality as the primary reason we search for meaning. Ernest Becker, the author of the Pulitzer Prize–winning *The Denial of Death* (1973), said humans are driven largely by an unconscious effort to escape and transcend mortality. Since then, scores of scholars have focused on death avoidance, death anxiety, terror management, and other ways we awkwardly confront our demise.

My conversations suggest there's something else going on that has received far less scrutiny. The language of death has become so ubiquitous that people are adopting it to characterize other critical junctures in their lives, from spiritual crises to professional setbacks. While obviously different from actual deaths, these disturbances are still so life-altering that the closest analogy people come up with is dying and being reborn. This stark comparison is further evidence of how profound the nonlinear life has become: We see our turning points as a matter of life and death.

What's more, a sizable number of people actually welcome these metaphoric deaths. They accept, even embrace, the idea that one person they used to be has *died* and another has been *born*. The deceased person may have been Catholic, while the new one is a follower of Yogananda; the dead self may have been unhappily married, while the new self is proudly single; the old you may have been unable to stand up for herself, while the new you is fierce. The discarded person may have been a drunk, a criminal, a carnivore, a workaholic—and the new one better all around.

I'm not suggesting that fearing the end of life has become less potent, but I am suggesting that accepting that life comes with periodic reincarnations is more widespread than we've understood. And that managing these reinventions is a critical part of making meaning in times of personal change.

Some people who used this language actually lost someone close to them. Nisha Zenoff, who learned from police officers at her door that her son was dead, said, "Something in me died forever in that moment, and something in me was born forever." What died, she said, was "the illusion that death couldn't touch me, that my children would live forever, that we would die in order." What was born, she said, was "the deeper belief that there is some soul or energy or spirit that lives on forever even after the physical body dies. I could never have gotten through those days, months, years, without it. I hesitate to call it God, but I know in that moment that my fear of death dissolved. I've had stage 4 cancer, and I checked myself to see if I was afraid to die, but after Victor died, I know life is short, and I want it to go on for a long time."

Others lost their bodily freedom. Travis Roy, the son of an ice rink manager in Augusta, Maine, was the number one hockey recruit in the country and a freshman on the NCAA champion Boston University Terriers when, eleven seconds into his first shift, after winning a face-off, he lost his balance and crashed against the boards, collapsing to the ice. "I was lying facedown, I could feel the cold against my face, and it was just surreal," he said. "I could see my body parts moving, but I had no sensation of that movement. I knew my life was changed forever and that everything I was would never be restored." He's spent the last twenty-five years in a wheelchair.

Others spoke of the death of a person they had become but didn't much like. Maillard Howell was born in Trinidad, earned a scholarship to Morehouse, then moved to Brooklyn and slowly inched his way into the middle class, with jobs in retail, banking, and pharmaceutical sales, each one earning slightly better benefits and slightly higher salary. But as soon as he hit $100,000 and felt secure, he realized he had become slave to the corporate slog. He quit, emptied out his 401(k), and opened a CrossFit gym. "I had to save my life," he said. "My doctor was recommending I go on antidepressants. But I used to sell that shit, I didn't want to take it. So I fucking said goodbye to that part of me that was chasing money and said I want to chase my passion."

And perhaps most important of all, nearly everyone who said they'd experienced intra-life dying mentioned that it left them less afraid of actually dying—and thus more willing to take risks to live robustly.

Kristina Wandzilak started drinking when she was thirteen and using cocaine soon after. She went through three treatment programs before she was eighteen, and within a few years was unemployable, broke, friendless, and feral, robbing homes to feed her addiction. When she was twenty-two, she was arrested for disorderly conduct and forced to spend a night in a homeless shelter. She awoke the next morning on the floor and had what she describes as a near-death experience.

"I don't talk about it much—it makes me so emotional," she said. "There aren't human words to explain what it feels like being in that light. This unequivocal, all-encompassing sense of love and peace and understanding. I remember thinking I should be afraid of this. I'm dying.

"But then the light started to dim and move away from me," she continued. "And I heard—not in words, because there are no words over there—but I heard that it wasn't my time, that I had things to do. Then I came to. I was on that floor and realized I would never be the same. The experience had changed how I lived. It brought a lot of peace around death, because I know what it's like over there. There's no longing, no suffering. There's nothing to be afraid of."

Whatever the cause of the lifequake, the first aftershock is that the devastation can feel deadly in its impact, which appears to be a backhanded way to help us find a new way to live.

An Autobiographical Occasion

The second impact is that the breach in the normal causes people to revisit their life story.

In the summer of 386, the brilliant but hedonistic North African teacher of rhetoric Augustine of Hippo was walking outdoors in Milan when he heard the voice of a child singing, "*Pick it up and read it! Pick it up and read it!*" After first thinking it was a game, he soon realized the voice must be referring to the Bible. He located a copy and opened it to a passage that warned against carousing, drunkenness, and lust. Augustine had indulged in all three, and at that moment he felt his heart flooded with light. He converted to Christianity, was baptized, and eventually became the most influential thinker in early church history.

But that may not be the most consequential thing Augustine did. Spurred by his conversion, he went on to write a detailed account of his early life of sin in a salaciously revealing memoir called *The Confessions*. Augustine, in effect, invented the modern autobiography. But why? Why would a prominent Christian leader publicly reveal everything about his inner life, from his newly sprouted pubic hair to his involuntary erections? As it happens, he addressed the question head-on in Book X. His "inward healer" compelled him to, he wrote. His conscience drove him to share his personal transformation to show that we're all capable of moving beyond our past evil deeds.

Augustine's conversion was more than just a lifequake, in other words; it was also an autobiographical occasion.

The term *autobiographical occasion* was coined by sociologist Robert Zussman to describe the moments in our lives when we are summoned, or required, to provide accounts of ourselves. He mentioned job, school, and credit applications; confessions, both religious and criminal; reunions of various sorts; therapies of various sorts; and diaries. He might have added doctor's appointments, first dates, even long plane rides with strangers. If accounts of everyday life are episodic and situational, autobiographical occasions are broader in scope and involve efforts to make sense of a wide range of occurrences. "They are not simply stories about events; they are stories about lives," Zussman writes. "They are those special occasions on which we are called on to reflect in systematic and extended ways on who we are and what we are."

This term captures what happens to most people after they experience a significant life rift. Really, any major disruption is an autobiographical occasion. In my own life, getting married was an autobiographical occasion, as was having twins and later cancer; my father was clearly having an autobiographical occasion when he lost the ability to work, walk, and bathe.

An autobiographical occasion is any moment when we are encouraged or obliged to reimagine who we are. It's a narrative event, when our existing life story is altered or redirected in some way, forcing us to revisit our preexisting identity and modify it for our life going forward.

And nearly everyone goes through such moments. In my interviews, I asked every person whether their biggest lifequake occasioned a rewriting of their life story. Three-quarters said yes. A number of these people said they didn't realize at first that the experience would trigger this kind of personal reevaluation, but that over time they did come to see it this way.

This suggests that while academics have come to understand that a big part of meaning-making is adjusting our life stories to accommodate a new life reality, that critical part of the process is still not widely known. It should be, as it's one of the primary aftershocks that is most helpful to recovery.

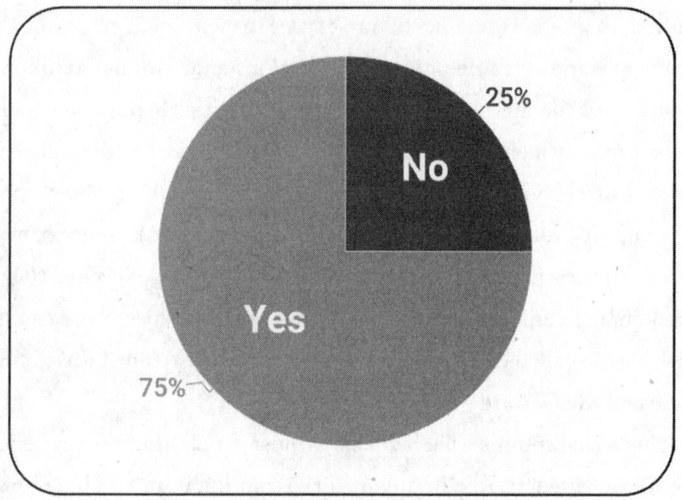

Some of the autobiographical occasions I heard about came from people who were forced to start sharing their stories publicly. Carl Bass was an early tech entrepreneur and inventor whose company in Ithaca, New York, was bought by Silicon Valley behemoth Autodesk. Carl eventually became CEO of the $30 billion software firm, a change he found challenging. "The natural thing when you become CEO of a public company is the press want to write about you," he said. "They want to know, 'Sir, who are you?' At first I just said, 'I'm just a guy who builds boats.' But I quickly found I had to have a fuller story, one that was interesting and turned heads."

Many of the autobiographical occasions mirrored the building blocks of meaning. Some of these storytelling adjustments were acts of agency. Anna Krishtal was a refugee from Tashkent who moved to Brooklyn at five and later attended high school in New Jersey. In college she fell in love with international travel, majored in Spanish, Russian, and Italian, and then moved to Israel. But when her mom got sick, she was strong-armed into returning home, where she lay in bed for a year, sulking and watching television. While doing the chair pose in yoga one day, she had a revelation. "I realized, *Holy fuck, I can change the narrative of my life by reframing it.* I saw myself as the victim of my circumstances—and I'd done that my whole life. I realized I needed to take control." She moved out of her parents' house, got a job, and restarted her life.

Some of these storytelling adjustments were acts of belonging. Naomi Clark, the Japanese American game designer who transitioned into being a woman after 9/11, struggled with how to tell her parents. She was prepared to lose them but didn't want to. So she employed a common technique in autobiographical occasions: She wrote them a letter.

"I was terrified and had all sorts of nightmare scenarios in mind," Naomi said. "I spent forever writing a serious, long handwritten letter explaining all my feelings. Then I sent it to them." How did they react? "I think they both felt very guilty, like they had screwed up, which I had to disabuse them of. But they both ended up saying, 'Oh, I don't know how we missed this for so long. Like we always knew you were different as a kid, but we thought you were just sensitive and nice.'"

Some of these storytelling adjustments were acts of cause. Melanie Krause was blessed, she said, with supercool parents in Boise, Idaho, who were hobby farmers with forty-five different varieties of grapes. Melanie studied biology at the University of Washington, moved abroad, and then moved to far western Oregon to be with her future husband, Joe. The only jobs were in nuclear reactors or vineyards, so she went to work in the wine industry. Five years later, Melanie and Joe moved back to Idaho and opened Cinder Wines. The change was more than just professional; as mom-and-pop entrepreneurs, they needed an entire narrative to sell what they were doing.

"I mean, we really had to examine ourselves and ask questions like, *Do we want our wine to be pretentious? Do we want it to be playful?* We had to figure out, *How do we take the story of our life and make it a story of our wine?* I would say before we started our own company, we never really worried about storytelling; now it's a humongous part of our lives." They elected to connect themselves to the little-known heritage of winemakers in the Snake River Valley.

The occasion of a lifequake is an occasion to reimagine your life story. It is an autobiographical occasion, the second of the major aftershocks.

Shape-Shifting

The final aftershock may be the most powerful of all. It's called *shape-shifting*.

In 1855, thirty-six-year-old, salt-and-pepper-bearded Walt Whitman published the first edition of his masterpiece, *Leaves of Grass*, in a small print shop on Cranberry Street in Brooklyn Heights, not far from where I live today. A sprawling tribute to humanity and sexuality, *Leaves of Grass* contains many notable passages, none more so than a trio of lines in section 51:

Do I contradict myself?
Very well then I contradict myself
(I am large, I contain multitudes)

Whitman's message would become a major theme of twentieth-century psychology and a central tenet of positive psychology a century after that: We contain many dimensions, and we have the power to shift among these dimensions to recalibrate what gives us meaning.

Lifequakes are a prime instigator in jolting people to reevaluate what weight they attribute to each item in the ABCs of meaning. People may dial back their emphasis on agency, ramp up their interest in belonging, pay more attention to cause for the first time, or sometimes reweight all three—all in direct response to a dramatic change in their life. In this way, humans are just like the rest of nature in how we react to the nonlinear world.

The essence of chaos is self-organizing. It's what a river current does when it eddies around a boulder and then reforms; it's what a flock of birds does when it takes off from a tree and then glides into formation; it's what a weather system does when it collides into a different system, merges, and then keeps moving; the same with sand dunes, snow squalls, clouds. In all these cases, the original entity begins in one shape, goes through a period of turbulence, a kind of mini–state of chaos, and then emerges with a new shape, both substantially similar to the prior state and wholly different at the same time. Chaos is nature's creativity in the face of constant change.

The human equivalent of this is the process of psychic adaptation. Just as the body has the ability to correct imbalances, so does the mind. Jung called this practice *counterbalancing one-sidedness.* Our lives become too tilted toward one aspect of our identity and too tilted away from others. We're all familiar with these scenarios. We become so obsessed with our work we neglect our family; we become so consumed with caring for children we overlook ourselves; we become so focused on serving others we ignore our loved ones. The more purely one thing we are, the more in danger we are of overlooking other things.

But as Whitman said, we're not just one thing: We're multitudes. Recent research confirms this observation. Scholars of core constructs originally thought that each of us has an innate slate of traits—we're introverted or extroverted, passive or assertive, open or closed. But thinking on this topic has evolved over time, and today such traits are considered partly fixed and partly in flux. In the words of leading personality researcher Brian Little, "the goggles through which you viewed life in April may no longer be helpful to you in May. . . . You revise your predictions about the world, you test new ideas, and in the process, consolidate a new set of personal constructs that work for you."

This fluidity is especially true during a searing life rupture. Your day-to-day existence simply cannot be navigated in the same way. Familiar landmarks have been overturned; faithful road maps have become obsolete. You need groundings, new passageways, new constructs.

I use the term *shape-shifting* to capture this phenomenon, because the heart of the exercise involves rebalancing the relative weight we give each of our three sources of meaning and the shapes that embody them—agency (line), belonging (circle), and cause (star). We've all experienced this in our own lives. Think of the workaholic who suffers a setback and decides to devote more time to the family, the stay-at-home parent who starts volunteering once the children are in school most of the day, the primary caregiver who burns out tending to the demanding patient and decides to take up a long-forgotten hobby.

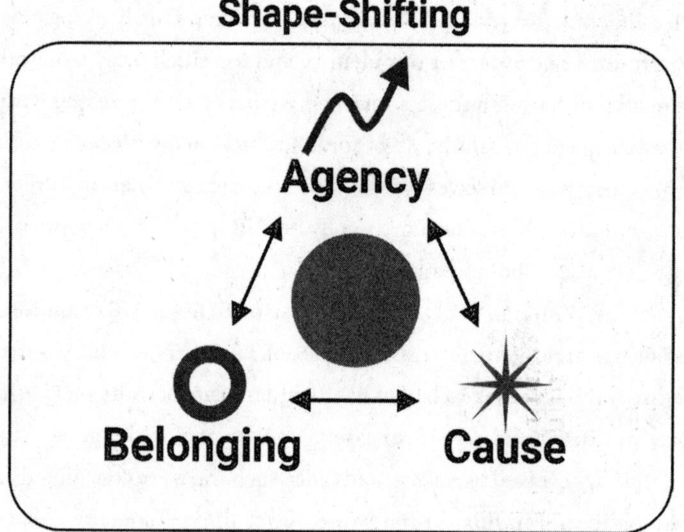

Shape-shifting is the remedy to a life out of balance. It would be nice if we had the wherewithal to do this on our own. Yet for whatever reason, it often takes a major rift to compel us to reexamine our priorities. And that reexamination takes us in surprising directions.

We've become accustomed in recent years to the language of resilience, and to the idea that after a massive interruption we revert to the norm. We *bounce back, return to our former lives, become ourselves again*. All those expressions imply that after a big life disturbance, we eventually go back to the person we were before. That kind of linear rebound does happen in some cases. But far more frequently, we actually move in new directions. Instead of going *back* to what we were before, we go *sideways, forward*, or some unforeseen place entirely. Shape-shifting, in other words, is nonlinear, just like every other aspect of the nonlinear life.

Here are some examples of how this process works in real life:

Lines

People pivoting from being primarily self-oriented to being more service- or relationship-oriented were by far the most common types of shape-shifts I heard.

Agency → Cause

Ann Marie DeAngelo had been a professional dancer since she was a teenager and rose to become leading ballerina of the Joffrey Ballet, but when she injured herself in her fifties, she became a life coach focused on helping injured dancers transition into the real world.

Darrel Ross was running an insurance company in his hometown of Grand Rapids, Michigan, but he was so shaken by the murder of a friend that he sold his company and started a nonprofit to promote affordable housing.

Agency ➞ Belonging

Jan Egberts parlayed graduate degrees in business and medicine to become CEO of a publicly traded pharmaceutical company, but after his estranged wife killed herself following an extended mental illness, he stepped down to care for his adolescent boys.

Wendi Aarons was a young screenwriter paying dues in Hollywood studios but became so turned off by the casting couch and other #MeToo-style indignities that when she and her husband relocated to Austin, Texas, she opted to become a stay-at-home mom.

Circles

Relationships are among the richest wellsprings of fulfillment, but there are limits. I heard from a number of moms in particular who reached the point where they needed to, or were forced to, look outside their children for sources of meaning.

Belonging ➞ Cause

Ann Ramer became so incensed after her dying son Brent was denied access to clinical trials because he was under eighteen that the mild-mannered mom became an outspoken advocate for pediatric cancer patients, giving fiery speeches, lobbying the vice president, badgering the FDA.

Lisa Heffernan and Mary Dell Harrington, both moms in Westchester County, New York, were so shaken when their children started going to college that they started a Facebook group called Grown and Flown to offer guidance to struggling empty nesters.

Belonging → Agency

Peggy Battin was a philosophy graduate student in Southern California who had never been that committed to what she called "husband and children and conventional country club life," so when a great job opened up in Utah, she left her children with her husband and went to pursue her career.

Shirley Eggermont was content to be the mother of seven and a supportive wife for forty-one years, but when her husband ran off with a younger girlfriend "to find happiness," she realized how manipulated and controlled she had been and became "a different person," more independent and self-confident.

Stars

Finding a calling is a great font of well-being and something many people move toward in their lives. But some who build their lives around a cause grow weary from giving too much.

Cause → Agency

John Austin spent twenty-five years in federal law enforcement, ultimately becoming an assistant special agent at the Drug Enforcement Administration, before a health scare prompted him to give up the precious job security and open a risk management firm.

Ann Imig, who built a nationwide movement of live-storytelling events for moms called "Listen to Your Mother," became so burned out by the unpaid work that she stepped down to focus on her own writing.

Cause → Belonging

Susan Pierce devoted her life to higher education and was starting her second decade as president of the University of Puget Sound when her husband had two strokes in three months, leading her to reject pleas to stay in her job and instead move to Florida to care for him.

Matt Weyandt was a young political activist in Atlanta, the only white student in his class at Emory to major in African American studies, and the head of the Democratic Party of Georgia, but when his free-spirit wife became fed up with his hours, he quit and moved with her to Costa Rica.

Shape-shifting is a powerful sense-making tool that allows us to restore balance to our lives when, for whatever reason, we become overly tilted toward one of the three pillars of meaning. This type of adjustment can happen voluntarily or involuntarily, but it often happens in response to a lifequake. Along with viewing that lifequake as a temporary death and using it as an autobiographical occasion, shape-shifting is one of the big three aftershocks of such major life disruptions.

Yet as helpful as these aftershocks can be, they're still preliminary compared to the major task of rebuilding your life. That rebuilding involves a complex, often wrenching process of transition. While that term is a familiar one, the actual mechanics of how transitions work are poorly understood. A big reason: We don't navigate transitions in the way that most people expect.

CHAPTER 6

Learning to Dance in the Rain

A New Model for Life Transitions

Let's go back for a second to our original definition of a lifequake: a forceful burst of change that leads to a period of upheaval, transition, and renewal. We've talked about the first of those issues—what causes the burst of change and what happens in the wake of the upheaval. But what about the last two points—namely, the transition and renewal? How do those happen?

The short answer: by choice. The person going through the experience has to choose to convert the change and upheaval into transition and renewal. The initial jolt can be voluntary or involuntary, but the transition *must* be voluntary. You have to make your own meaning.

Let's start with an example.

"I'm Going to Wrap My Fingers Around Your Neck"

Fraidy Reiss was the second youngest of six in an ultra-Orthodox Jewish family in Brooklyn. Her Cuban-born father was "extremely violent and abusive," she said, so her mother took the children to raise by herself. Fraidy was spunky, but not hostile toward religion. She wore knee socks under her shapeless dresses. "It was kind of lame—*Watch out, world, Fraidy is wearing socks over her tights!*—but it was still significant. I liked to push boundaries."

As a child, Fraidy had no access to television, radio, or newspapers. "I went to an all-girls school where we learned to cook and sew," she said. "I didn't know who the Beatles were and thought hamburgers were made of ham." At sixteen, she had to sign a document promising not to take the SAT.

At eighteen, Fraidy was put into the marriage pool. With parents who were separated and poor, she was not considered a good match. She started going on arranged dates on which the intendeds were not allowed to be alone or make physical contact. "You'd sit across from each other, order Coca-Cola, and talk about how many kids you'd like to have," she said. "Then you'd go home and have to decide whether to spend the rest of your lives together."

When her first match confessed he'd tried marijuana, Fraidy turned him down. Her next match was a chain-smoker who had dozens of violations for reckless driving. On two of their three dates, he got into fistfights with strangers on the street. Because Fraidy had spent her "one reject card," she agreed to marry him. Six weeks later, they were husband and wife.

"You weren't supposed to be in love," she said, "but I persuaded myself that I was happy."

He threatened to kill her on their wedding night. And not just in passing—in minute, grisly detail. "I'm going to wrap my fingers around your neck," he said. "I'm going to squeeze until you take your last breath, and I'm going to look you in the eye and watch you stop breathing." Another time he told her with graphic specificity how he would use a knife to dismember her. "He would break dishes, furniture, windows, and if we were driving in a car, he'd speed up to one hundred miles an hour, then slam on the brakes so I'd go flying." He also made her keep the bathroom door open to make sure she had nothing to hide.

Fraidy had no idea what to do. Though he never actually harmed her, the threats and menace were nonstop. She spoke to his father, who was offended that anything might be wrong with his son. She spoke to her mother, who turned and walked out of the room. She thought it might get better when they moved to New Jersey and had children; she was wrong.

"I was a twenty-year-old stay-at-home mom and housewife, and I hated my life," she said. "I hated every minute of it. I took no joy in being a mother or cooking and cleaning for this guy who would come home and, best-case scenario, not smash a window. Sometimes I would go across the street to this playground, sit on a swing, and cry for hours."

When Fraidy was twenty-seven, nearly a decade into this life, a friend slipped her the name of a therapist outside the community. In their first meeting the therapist used the expression *domestic violence* and said Fraidy might be eligible for a restraining order. "It was a mind-boggling experience," Fraidy said. "I went home and thought, *At least I'm not crazy.*"

A few days later she was caring for their newborn when her husband came home and kicked open their front door. Fraidy grabbed the baby, hopped in the car, and headed for a friend's house. He got in his truck and tailgated her, shouting, "I'm going to kill you!" Her friend's house was in a cul-de-sac, and when Fraidy parked out front, her husband blocked her in. "It was the stupidest place for me to go," she said, "but this time I had an out. I called 911."

Fraidy was the first person in the history of the Orthodox Jewish community in Lakewood, New Jersey, to get a restraining order. Her husband was removed from her home. "In any other community, this might have meant freedom," she said. "But in my community, this was a sin." The next day the rabbi sent a male lawyer to her house, and she was hauled before a judge to retract her claim. The lawyer warned that if she didn't comply, she would never see her children again. "I had no choice," she said. Then she added, "But that was the beginning of the end."

Fraidy stayed with her husband for the next five years. During that time, she secretly squirreled away cash in a Total Whole Grain cereal box in the pantry. He'd give her money for a new wig; she'd wash the old one and keep the cash. When she'd saved up $40,000, she enrolled at Rutgers University. "You're not going to college," her husband told her.

"What exactly are you going to do to stop me?" she said.

School was not easy with Fraidy's background. In her first semester, she studied Greek civilization and was stunned to learn there were other gods. Soon, she stopped wearing her wig. Appalled by her brazenness, her mother sat shiva for her, the Jewish ritual of mourning the dead. When her husband threw tantrums, Fraidy would lock herself and her children in their bedroom. One Shabbat, when he threatened to break in, she drove the children to the mall and watched a movie. The neighbors were horrified. When Fraidy and the children returned, her husband was gone. "I realized this was my chance, so I changed the locks," she said. "When he came back a week later, I told him, 'I've inhaled and tasted life without you, and it's sweet. You're not coming back.'"

Fraidy filed for divorce. She graduated from Rutgers with a 4.0 average. Her class of ten thousand students elected her valedictorian. She got a job as a reporter with the *Asbury Park Press*. (In her first assignment, she had to ask how to spell the name of the town's most famous son, Springsteen.) She bought her own house. And a few years later she founded an organization that helps women escape forced marriages. She called it Unchained at Last after what she considers the shape of her life: a broken chain.

Fraidy had clearly been through a massive shock and a stirring recovery. I asked her whether these changes were voluntary or involuntary. "It started off involuntary," she said, "in that I had no choice but to leave my marriage. My life was in danger; my kids' lives were in danger. But everything that came after was voluntary—going to school, leaving the religion, becoming an advocate for other women. I took an involuntary situation and turned it into a voluntary one."

"Since It Was My Choice, I Had to Act Like It"

Considering how ubiquitous the idea of *transitions* is in contemporary life, there's been surprisingly little academic research into how they work. The person who did more than any other to focus attention on these times of life was Arnold van Gennep. Born in Germany in 1873 to Dutch parents who never married, Van Gennep moved to France when he was six. From this cross-cultural background he developed a passion for crossing cultures. He went on to speak eighteen languages and do pioneering work in Egyptology, Aramaic, primitive religions, and folklore. His greatest contribution was to name the periodic episodes of transformation that mark a person's life, from weddings to funerals to coming-of-age ceremonies. He called them *les rites de passage*, or rites of passage (though his translators said *passage* should more accurately be rendered as *transition*).

So what exactly is a transition? Van Gennep said they're bridges that help connect the different periods of one's life. William Bridges, the business consultant and author of the influential 1979 bestseller *Transitions*, said they're the inner reorientations and redefinitions one goes through in order to incorporate change into one's life.

I like these definitions, but they miss a number of ingredients I found particularly poignant in my interviews. For starters, as I'll discuss in the second half of the book, transitions clearly involve challenging periods of bewilderment and turmoil, but they also involve vibrant periods of exploration and reconnection. Also, the standard descriptions miss the inventive nature of transitions, the way we use them to cast off habits we've grown tired of and create new ones we're proud of. Finally, the existing rubrics fail to capture the way we use these times of life to reevaluate what gives us purpose, connection, and shape.

My definition: A transition is a vital period of adjustment, creativity, and rebirth that helps one find meaning after a major life disruption.

But how do you enter this mysterious state? Does it happen inevitably or do you somehow have to decide? And if so, how do you do that?

I spent some time digging into this issue. In every interview I asked a series of questions about a major life change the person had experienced. The first question: "Was this a voluntary or involuntary transition?" The answers were remarkably consistent. Whether people chose to disrupt their lives or had their lives disrupted for them, they viewed their transition as having been their decision. They had agency over their reaction.

Kamran Pasha was a middle-class Pakistani immigrant who came to New York when he was two. He grew up poor, homeless, and filled with shame after his father was diagnosed with schizophrenia. Kamran survived in part by making up stories of heroes overcoming adversity, a passion that led him to screenwriting. But not until he was fired from his "safe" job at a Los Angeles law firm because he was too busy trying to break into Hollywood did he finally submit his first script to an agent. "The transition was involuntary, in the sense that I got pushed into the void," he said. "But once it happened, I realized I had to take the big leap. It's like that wonderful scene from *Indiana Jones and the Last Crusade* where he has to cross this canyon but there's no bridge. Once he steps into the void, he discovers there's a bridge he couldn't see."

For some the switch from involuntary disruption to voluntary transition happens over a matter of months. John Tirro was a country music songwriter in Nashville with a number one hit song to his credit when he stunned and upset his family by announcing he was called to Lutheran ministry. "I didn't want to make this change," he said. "But God wanted me to have one of those big transitions that need to happen for us to be healthy. At first I resented it, but that just destroys you. Finally I realized, since it was my choice, I had to act like it. Was it voluntary or involuntary? Ultimately, I'd say voluntary."

For others the switch takes years. Chris Shannon was a high school dropout and Titan II missile engineer when he left his air force base in

Arizona one day on his motorcycle, with his wife behind him. Within minutes they were hit by a drunk driver, breaking Chris's back and neck and severing his right leg. He was declared clinically dead, twice. (The driver left the scene but didn't get very far because Chris's femur was stuck in the radiator.) Chris spent a bitter two years sulking over his condition and tending to his wife, whose injuries were less severe but who was more traumatized, before finally electing to leave her and move on. "It took me all that time to realize the best and easiest way to get things done was to make the voluntary choice to embrace life, to wake up on a rainy day and love the smell of air."

Perhaps the best description I heard of what it feels like to go through a period of turmoil and make the affirmative decision to transition through it came from Deborah Fishman. Deborah grew up anorexic and lonely in a secular Jewish family in Connecticut. At Princeton she became Orthodox (though not as devout as Fraidy Reiss had been); after graduation she got married. At first, Deborah embraced the meaning-making aspect of being in a tight community—cooking, raising children, observing Shabbat. The shape of her life, a braid, represents stitching together a community. But over time she began to chafe at all the regulations and wanted to spend more time building a dining cooperative she founded. She and her husband agreed to divorce. "On the one hand, I think the changes that happened were brought out of me," she said. "I was coming to life. But I definitely had to flip the switch. I didn't wait for things to be resolved; I went out and resolved them. Life is not about waiting for the rain to stop; it's about learning to dance in the rain."

Why Transitions Are Nonlinear

Once you make the decision to undergo a transition, you enter into a maelstrom that often seems chaotic and out of control. But my conversations suggest there is surprising order to these times—and a substantial number of things you can do to make them go more smoothly. Let's start with the overall structure.

Van Gennep introduced a structure for transitions that quickly became the consensus view. His metaphor was place. The person going through the transition leaves one world, passes through a hinterland, and then enters a new world. He likened it to walking out of one room, proceeding down a hallway, and then entering another room. The actual crossing of thresholds is critical, he said, which is why many rites of passage involve doorways, portals, and gateways, and many thresholds are populated by dragons, ogres, and trolls. We sacralize what's scary.

Carrying through with this analogy, Van Gennep said transitions can be divided into three phases: *separation*, when you leave the comforts of the old place; *margin*, when you isolate yourself in the neutral zone; and *incorporation*, when you rejoin civilized life by entering the new space. He cited scores of examples from traditional coming-of-age ceremonies (in which teenagers are taken from home and sent into the wilderness), weddings (in which the betrothed are isolated from their families before being welcomed back as a new family), and childbirth (in which pregnant women are removed from the community, then reintegrated once they give birth).

Van Gennep's model has proven profoundly influential, being repeated virtually unchallenged for more than a century. The anthropologist Victor Turner reaffirmed the three phases in the 1960s and memorably named the middle phase *betwixt and between.* William Bridges, an English professor by training who relied on no empirical data, used the idea as the foundation of his extremely popular three-stage model. Transitions, Bridges said, begin with *endings*, continue with *the neutral zone*, and conclude with *the new beginning.*

Bridges also echoed Van Gennep in another crucial way. Reflecting the influence of the linear model of life during these years, Bridges insisted the three stages *must happen in chronological sequence.* "You need all three phases, and in that order, for a transition to work," he wrote. Endings must go first; the neutral zone must go second; the new beginning must go last.

One of the clearest findings of the Life Story Project is that this linear model of life transitions is wrong. Even worse, it is dangerous to those who believe they are expected to go through a set of emotions in a prearranged order on a predetermined timeline.

Simply put, there is no one single way to go through a life transition.

To be fair, the tripartite structure is helpful. There are absolutely different emotional steps involved in a transition that correspond to leaving the past behind, stumbling toward a fresh identity, embracing the new you. My names for these three phases are *the long goodbye*, *the messy middle*, and *the new beginning*. But the reality that came through loud and clear in my conversations is that these steps *do not happen in a straight line.*

Just as life is nonlinear, transitions themselves are nonlinear.

Just as people live life out of order, they go through transitions out of order.

While some people experience these phases sequentially, others experience them in reverse; others start in the middle and work their way out. Some finish one stage before going on to a new one; others move on to a new phase, then double back to the one they thought they had finished. Many get stuck in one phase for a very long time.

Once you stop and think about it, this varied approach makes sense. If you lose your husband in a plane crash, then remarry a few years later, that doesn't mean you stop mourning your first husband. If you're having an affair, that usually means you're starting a new relationship before saying goodbye to the old one. If you're a divorced parent who remarries, you might think you get a fresh start, but you probably spend a lot of time in the messy middle as you haggle with your former spouse over custody, money, and parenting decisions.

The point is: Stages rarely begin and end in a clean way—and that's perfectly normal. People go in and out of them in highly idiosyncratic patterns.

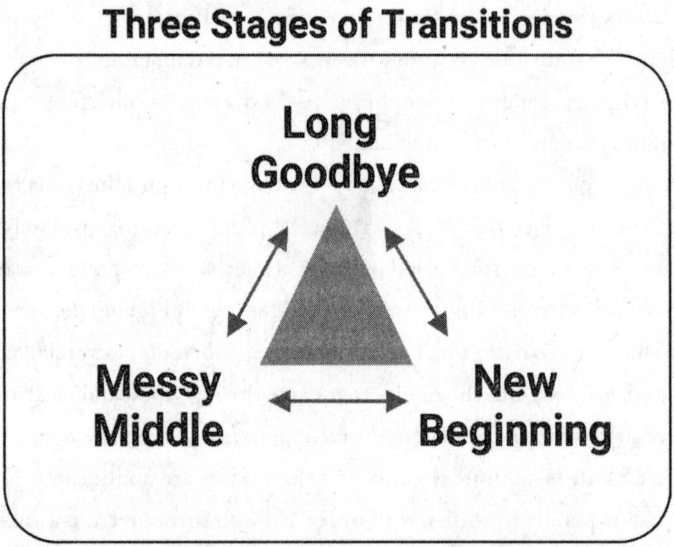

Three Stages of Transitions

What dictates the order people take?

As a rule, I found that each person is especially good at one of these three phases and especially bad at one. Each of us has a *transition superpower,* if you will, and a *transition kryptonite.* Our research suggests that people gravitate to the phase they're naturally adept at and bog down in the one they're weakest at. If you're comfortable saying goodbye, you might knock that off quickly and move on to the next challenge; but if you're conflict averse and don't like to disappoint people, you might remain in a situation that's toxic far longer than you should. The same applies to the messy middle: Some people thrive in chaos; others are paralyzed by it. As for new beginnings, some people embrace the novelty; others dread it—they like things the way they were.

The percentages of people who disliked each phase surprised me. I asked all my subjects which of the three phases they found most difficult. I expected the messy middle to be far and away the dominant. I was mistaken. The largest block, 47 percent, did say the middle was the hardest, but

39 percent—not that far off—said saying goodbye was the hardest. Fourteen percent named the new beginning.

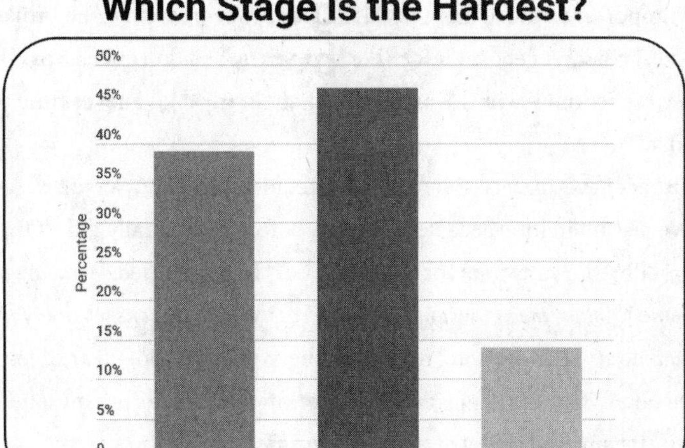

On the surface, these data are a reminder that all three of these dimensions of navigating a big life change are hard. You're not alone in finding the whole process daunting. But on a granular level, our findings point to the fact that saying goodbye remains deeply challenging for most of us, and that what comes next is even harder. If there's encouraging news, it's that most of us find starting over to be relatively easy by comparison.

Here's how these superpowers and kryptonites play out in real life.

"At Least I Know He Will Be Safe in God's Arms"

Four in ten in my study found saying goodbye to be most difficult. Psychologists have identified a host of conditions, from *loss aversion* to *the paradox of choice*, that might explain why. We found certain commonalities among those in this group.

Some are weighed down by emotional baggage from the past. Gina Bianchini, who lost her dad when she was twelve and her job as the head of the social network Ning at thirty-seven, said, "I am the worst at breakups. Every important boyfriend in my life that I broke up with or he broke up with me, I couldn't get over it for, like, two years. You don't need a psychology degree to know why. I was never sad about my dad. I never fully processed it."

Others have anxiety about what's to come. Lisa Ludovici felt the urge to leave her job in internet sales for years before she actually did. "Oh, the long goodbye is really long for me," she said. "I was terrified. *What are people gonna think of me? How am I going to eat? What happens when my mom calls and needs $800 for rent?* I've always been that person—fear of letting people down, fear of doing something for myself. I never put myself first, ever, until I quit and said, *I'm gonna live my life.*"

Some are heartbroken about what they've lost. Nisha Zenoff went into group therapy after the death of her teenage son. Frustrated by Nisha's inability to move on, the therapist threw a pillow at her one day. "Here, say goodbye to your son," he said. "I looked at him and said—I won't even tell you what, but it began with an *f*. I told him, '*Don't ever tell a parent to say goodbye to her son or daughter. That is absolutely inappropriate. I will never say goodbye. I will always say hello.*' Even then I knew what the research has come to show: Sometimes keeping continuing bonds with what's lost helps us all get on with life."

Others are simply sad to say goodbye to a time of life they cherished. Evan Walker-Wells was a star pupil at his elite Brooklyn high school, left to volunteer for the Obama campaign, and then enrolled at Yale. Halfway through his freshman year, doctors found a grapefruit-sized mass in his chest; it was stage 4 non-Hodgkin's lymphoma. He returned home for six months of chemotherapy. "About thirteen months after treatment I started having weird sensations in my chest," he said. "It turned out to be nothing, but that's when I realized, *Oh, my God, I'm just not going to escape this shit, am I?* I have to say goodbye to the idea that I'm totally invulnerable, that I can do whatever I want. I have to accept that I'm always going to be dealing with the healthcare system that my friends won't have to touch until their sixties or seventies. And I hated that."

While a plurality find saying goodbye to be their kryptonite, others find it to be their superpower. Amber Alexander had become so accustomed to burying friends and relatives after a string of losses in her early twenties that by the time her son was diagnosed with a brain tumor a few years later, she did not dwell on what she had lost. "I came to the realization when Eli was first diagnosed that I'm not in control of anything, which is kind of hard for a control freak. But I was used to it by then. As someone who is wiser than me said, 'At the end of the day, my belief is that Eli is a son of God.' I love being his earthly mother, but if he does transition from this life to the next, then at least I know he will be safe in God's arms."

Nina Collins was always precocious. Born in New York City to mixed-race, hippie parents, she got her first job at thirteen, graduated from high school at sixteen, moved to Europe at eighteen, and then returned home at nineteen in order to raise her younger brother when her mother died of cancer. Nina went on to have multiple careers, multiple marriages, and multiple homes. "I'm very decisive in saying goodbye," she said. "I remember my mother dying. I was like, 'Okay, this is happening, now I have to deal.' It's the same with moving or opening and closing businesses. I do it all the time, and I really enjoy it. My therapist once said I underattach to things. I think it's because my mother died young, but I have a strong sense of how short life is, so I want new experiences."

"The First Thing I Did Was Drop an F-Bomb"

The messy middle is messy for many, though everyone seems to find a different aspect of it messy.

For some the most difficult part is being thrust into a situation you fear you're not ready for. Jenny Wynn is a native of rural Oklahoma who survived two near-death experiences—one when she was six and went into respiratory arrest from asthma, the other when she was twenty and with four family members who ate poisoned frogs' legs they caught while noodling catfish. (Doctors were so concerned that they gathered the family and told them to say goodbye to one another.) Jenny went on to become associate minister at a church in Oklahoma City, but when her boss dropped dead, she suddenly faced a barrage of challenges all at once, including whether to seek his job.

"The first thing I did was drop an F-bomb," she said. "Then I told the congregation, 'I can't lead right now. I'm trying to grieve myself.' But they needed me to lead, so I found myself going from associate to senior pastor—and the first female one at that. The whole process took two years. Right before I took the job, I was scared shitless, so I took a two-month sabbatical. I needed time to transition my own thinking, and I needed the congregation to transition how they thought of me."

For others, the messy middle is filled with perilous emotional lurches. Kirsty Spraggon grew up in the outback of Western Australia, where she was bullied for being skinny. Ambitious and eager to escape, she became a real estate agent, moved to Sydney, and rose to become one of RE/MAX's top one hundred agents worldwide. But all the time she was hiding a shameful secret: She got a sexually transmitted disease when she was nineteen, which decimated her confidence, prevented her from getting close to men, and drove her into a series of unhealthy relationships. So she quit and moved to Los Angeles to pursue a career in corporate speaking and finally confront her past.

"You go through this dark night of the soul," she said. "I had no friends when I moved to America, I had no mentors, you can't pick up the phone and be like, *Oprah, can you give me advice?* And what happens if AT&T or Pfizer found out? I mean, I get that the chrysalis is important for making a butterfly, but it's no fun for the caterpillar."

But a shocking number of people told me they thrived in the messy middle. Rosemary Daniell, a scarlet-haired poet from Atlanta whom we met briefly in chapter 2, was the daughter of an alcoholic father and a mother who died by suicide. Married at sixteen, Rosemary divorced her first two husbands but was divorced by her third, a lefty intellectual from New York. She was so devastated she responded by dating only manly men—cops, cowboys, teamsters—working on an oil rig, and writing a steamy kiss-and-tell called *Sleeping with Soldiers*.

When I asked Rosemary about that muddled period when she was searching for Mr. Wrong (she eventually married the winner of that search, an army paratrooper, and they've been together for three decades), she looked at me with bemused scorn. "You can call it muddled, I call it a vacation from life. And I loved it!"

She cackled and went on, "I see it as a period of fun, new experiences, creativity, and meeting all kinds of people I had never met before. There's a paragraph in *Sleeping with Soldiers* about a dream I had during that period. It was about how sex with all those different people was good for me. I mean, there were a few scary moments when I thought I might be raped, but overall I would say it was exciting. I felt independent for the first time and like I didn't have to follow the rules I'd been brought up with."

Rob Adams also found the messy middle exhilarating. Rob was born into an all-American family in Cincinnati, lived in Mexico City and Geneva for spells as a child, and then went to Dartmouth and on to Northwestern's Kellogg School of Management. He held a series of lucrative consulting jobs in Chicago before moving his wife and children back to New England to become the president of the family-owned Simon Pearce glassware company. He started work ten days before the Great Recession hit. Sales dropped by a third the first month. After a protracted negotiation, he was asked to step down.

"Saying goodbye was hard for me," he said. "I loved the people, the mentoring, the coaching. The whole parting of ways probably took longer than it should have. But once that was done, I relished the messy middle. I loved the analysis, the research, the thinking it through. I talked to forty different people about what I should do next. I'm a consultant; fixing problems is my expertise."

He and his wife decided to move their family to Africa for a few years, where he ran a soccer nonprofit and they adopted a third child. The messiness led him to revisit a part of his childhood he most appreciated and give his children exposure to another side of the world.

"I Was Glad I Was Sober, but What the Hell Do I Do Now?"

After the marathon of the long goodbye and the messy middle, you might think the new beginning would be a welcome relief. But one in six finds this stage the hardest.

Peggy Fletcher Stack was a reporter at the *Salt Lake Tribune* ("Not bad, considering my mother told me I was the second dumbest in the family") and married to Mike, the "very handsome man with wildly curly hair" she hired at her first job. They had two children under two and were "happy, happy, happy."

Then Peggy got pregnant with twin girls, one of whom, Camille, had a heart condition and was not expected to live a week. Mike quit his job and for the next two years navigated tubes, tests, and prayer, until early one morning Camille stopped breathing. "I heard this little voice in my head say, *Mom, do I have to be superbaby? Please let me go, please, please.* Mike let out the scream, like a wounded animal, and I was in shock. It was horrifying, agonizing, but also kind of peaceful. We turned the oxygen off and sat there watching the sun come up."

Surely that time would be the low point of their lives, right?

"Basically, we still look at those years as the best years of our marriage," Peggy said, "which is weird because they were also the hardest. We never got a full night's sleep; we never took a vacation; I had no sick days." But what happened, she continued, "is that our best selves emerged. We were our very, very best marriage partners. We were our best at parenting. We were not grumpy or crabby or snapping or fighting."

But when that messy middle ended, she said, they were lost. "We had to figure out, *Now what kind of people do we want to be?* We've fallen out of sacred space and time. We're just another couple with three kids. We're judgmental and fighting and have $60,000 in unpaid bills. We're still together, but we're very different in how we process emotion. Now what?"

Janelle Hanchett also found meaning in the chaos and emptiness and was somewhat lost when it was over. Janelle grew up in central California as the daughter of an absent alcoholic dad and a Mormon mom who sold knives and art. Janelle was "Captain Responsible" until she started drinking and using cocaine, acid, and mushrooms in college. She got pregnant at twenty-one, married the nineteen-year-old father, sank into depression, and then had another baby. "By twenty-eight I was unemployed, addicted to cocaine, on seven different psychotropic meds, and suffering from schizophrenia." Her mother had to take her children, her husband left her, and she spent time in a mental institution.

"Finally, on a Sunday two weeks before my thirtieth birthday, I rolled over one morning after a three-day binge, shaking and body aches, and realized I didn't want to be a slave to alcohol anymore. I wanted to live as a free person on this planet."

She went to an AA meeting that afternoon. A year later she moved back in with her mom and children. She reunited with her husband. They bought a house and resumed being a family. But as messy as that period was, again there was structure—the twelve steps, the goal to stay sober a day, another day, a week, a month. Like Peggy, and all of us who have faced issues of life and death, there is an odd safety in this time. There is purpose. There is meaning.

And then, suddenly, there is none.

"That new beginning was by far the hardest for me," Janelle said. "I was glad I was sober, but what the hell do I do now? I had another kid by then. I was feeling incredibly bored by motherhood, unfulfilled, erased every day by the monotony, the brainless rhythm. And now, I don't have alcohol, so I had no choice but to figure out my life sober, and that was tough."

Transitions are not simple or smooth. They are not straightforward or straight ahead. They are not predictable.

Transitions Take Longer Than You Think

And one more surprise: They take longer than you think.

I followed my question about which stage was hardest by asking how long the transition took. The answers were consistent—and not what I expected. A few people were on the margins. Eight percent, for example, said they were done in a year; 9 percent said their transition was ongoing. One in five said their transition took two to three years, a similar number

How Long Do Transitions Take?

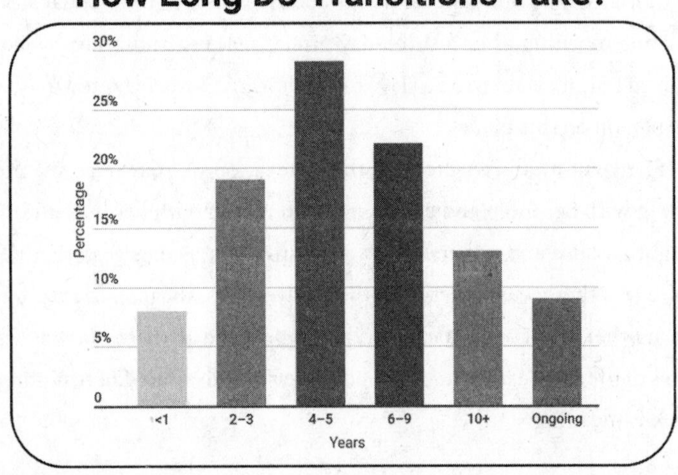

said six to nine. But the most common answer—and the average answer—was four to five years.

These data, I should say, are somewhat cloudy. Sometimes the person I was speaking with was not five years removed from the original disruption. As for those who said "ongoing," some did so because they believed "life is one long transition," others because they had yet to reach the end. But the larger message of these exchanges was undeniable.

The life span of a transition is around five years.

My initial reaction was *Whoa, that's intimidating!* I would not like to be the person to tell a loved one who just went through a major life change, *Don't worry, you'll be over it in half a decade.* But on reflection, I began to see a different message in these numbers.

First, our lack of general discussion about life transitions has left a lot of us unprepared for what they mean. The simple fact is, *three-quarters* of the hundreds of people I spoke with said their life transition took four years or longer. And many people used these figures apologetically, as if to suggest they were somehow outliers. The opposite is true. Also, once they learned that they were in good company, they felt relieved. To me, the issue is not how long transitions take, it's how long we expect them to take. The burden is on us to adjust our expectations.

Second, we spend a huge percentage of our lives in transition. If you consider that we go through three to five lifequakes in our adult lives, and each one lasts four, five, six years, or longer, that could be thirty-plus years we spend in a state of change. That's half a lifetime! To my larger point that we need to make the most of our transitions, this may be the best argument yet. If you view transitions as times to resent and resist, you're throwing away far more of your years than you realize. Better make the most of these times before they make the least of you.

That leads to the final lesson. The poet Robert Graves once wrote of life in the trenches of World War I that "noise never stopped for one moment—ever." That's what it feels like to go through a massive personal change. Life becomes noisy, cacophonous, confusing, confounding—and it doesn't stop.

The transition is what helps quiet the din. It's the slow, nonlinear, effortful process of turning the noise back into music. Lisa Porter, the professor of stage-managing who gave birth to Daisy, a daughter with special needs, made a beautiful analogy between life transitions and theatrical transitions. The transitions are like the mortar between bricks, she said. "The bricks are the building blocks of a show or your life; the mortar is what holds them together. If the mortar doesn't work, the building comes crumbling down."

A transition is an adhesive and a healer. It takes something broken and begins to repair it. It takes something shaken and helps to steady it. It takes something shapeless and starts to give it shape. That process, as intimidating as it seems, actually can be broken down into a series of tools that help make the transition easier to navigate and more likely to succeed. The second half of this book explores in detail what those tools are and how to use them most effectively.

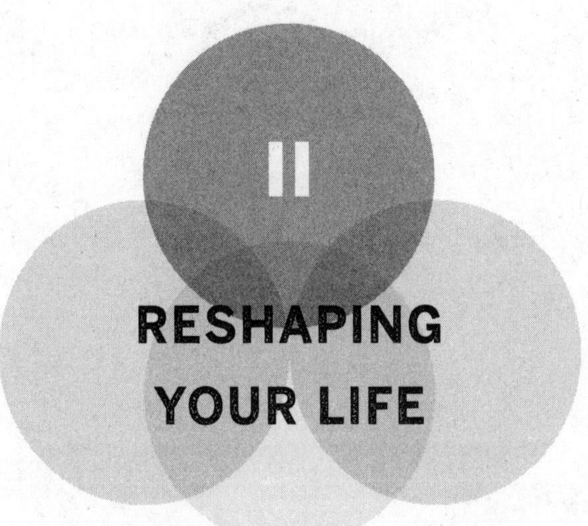

II

RESHAPING YOUR LIFE

CHAPTER 7

Accept It

Identify Your Emotions

The iconic expression *in the beginning*, from the King James translation of Genesis 1:1, is among the most recognizable phrases ever rendered into English. But there's a phrase in Genesis 1:2 that gets far less attention that may be even more relevant to the periodic disruptions of our nonlinear lives. That expression is *tohu va-vohu*, which describes the unformed void—the disorder and emptiness—that covered the world before creation. The Hebrew Bible is not alone in this idea. Religions from Mesopotamia to Africa to China all describe a state of disarray in the world before there was order.

Long before there was chaos in science, there was chaos in religion.

And these religions all share another idea, too. At various times in our lives, we return to that chaos, we touch back on a state of disorder and confusion. And we do so *in order to create ourselves again*. As the great scholar of religion Mircea Eliade wrote, "The symbolic return to chaos is indispensable to any new creation."

A lifequake represents that period of chaos.

A life transition represents the way forward.

The bulk of every conversation I had in the Life Story Project—all 225 of them—focused on how people navigate these life transitions. As I soon discovered, the chief side effect of the nonlinear life is that these transitions are becoming more plentiful. Half of our lives are spent in a state of in between.

But I also discovered something else: Life transitions are a skill. Specifically, they're a skill we can, and must, master. Research into everything from habits to happiness has found that if you break familiar processes down into their components, you can engage with these components to achieve a better outcome. Understanding each element is a precursor to performing it better.

The same applies to transitions.

So what are the elements? In my conversations, fascinating clues began to appear. A woman who left a strict religious order told me a stranger in a Shake Shack gave her a piece of advice that changed her life; a former alcoholic told me a stranger in a coffee shop gave her a job when no one else would. A cancer survivor described getting a tattoo to mark the end of her treatment; a divorcé described going to a sweat lodge to mark the end of his marriage. Dozens of people told me that in the nadir of their transitions they took up singing or quilting or dancing or cooking. They turned to creativity to help create themselves anew.

Ultimately, I found, there are seven groupings of tools for navigating life transitions. Collectively they form the transition tool kit. I prefer *tool kit* to *road map*, *blueprint*, or some other example, because there is no single way through a transition.

The seven tools are:

- *Accept It: Identify Your Emotions*
- *Mark It: Ritualize the Change*
- *Shed It: Give Up Old Mind-Sets*
- *Create It: Try New Things*
- *Share It: Seek Wisdom from Others*

- *Launch It: Unveil Your New Self*
- *Tell It: Compose a Fresh Story*

Before we dig into this process, a few observations:

First, most people use a number of these tools, either instinctually or because they've worked on them; no one uses all seven. Everyone has room to grow.

Second, the tools are rarely used in sequence. The first two—identifying your emotions and ritualizing the change—are broadly associated with the long goodbye. The next two—giving up old mind-sets and trying new things—generally happen in the messy middle. The final two—unveiling your new self and composing a fresh story—usually happen during the new beginning. The fifth tool—seeking wisdom from others—tends to float. Still, even this sequence is not rigid. Like every other aspect of the nonlinear life, the transition tool kit gets employed out of order.

Finally, only you can decide which tools you most need to work on. In the chapters to come, we're going to explore these tools one at a time, but keep in mind, there is no single formula. My goal is not to cajole you into doing one thing or another, but to share with you how other people in similar situations have navigated their unsettled times, and then let you find the approaches that are more helpful to you or your loved ones. By the end, I'm almost prepared to guarantee you'll find some ideas that will make your transition easier.

Now, let's get started. For simplicity's sake, we'll begin with the first tool, *accept it.*

"I Had Been Tumbling Down a Cliff, and Now, for the First Time, I Stopped"

Charles Gosset was born in Oklahoma City into a close-knit family that was also filled with anger, rage, and what he called isms, including alcoholism. "I loved school," he said. "I loved learning. I was consistently in the top 1 percent of nationally standardized tests." But he also felt disconnected from the world. "I remember feeling from the age of five that something was off. There was either something out of place with me or the world itself."

As he entered adolescence, Charles became depressed and aggressive. He turned to psychiatrists and preachers for help, to little avail. He started dabbling in gangs. "Mostly I was just trouble looking for a place to happen," he said. "Then I found alcohol at fifteen and the clouds parted. Everything was possible. I could forget myself with the bottle, and I thought that was the answer."

Charles drifted in and out of relationships and at nineteen, while at Oklahoma State, he swallowed a bottle of pills in an attempt to end his life. Just before he passed out, he visited the dorm room of a classmate he had a crush on. She called for help. Several years later, they were married. Christy became an elementary school music teacher; Charles became a city forester. They had two daughters.

But Charles continued to drink, downing a pint of whiskey every afternoon between work and home. He tried various ways to get sober, but it never lasted more than a week or two. Finally, Christy took the children and moved out. This time he checked into a facility.

"While I was there a word came up on the screen during one of the sessions," he said. "The word was *acceptance*. I'd heard the word so many times in meetings before, but this time I really thought about it. I had been tumbling down a cliff, and now, for the first time, I stopped. I had to accept, at that moment, that my life had become unmanageable. That I was an alcoholic, and, lo and behold, that an alcoholic can't drink successfully. Alcohol was not my solution; it was my problem."

Charles completed the program, but Christy remained skeptical, so he was banned from seeing his children. "Rightfully so," he said. He lived in a sober house, mowed lawns, and started the painful process of finding his true self.

"I was looking for an authentic connection to who I am," he said. "I'm very much a poet, a seer, a hearer of reality. I wanted to serve." He made a classic shape-shift: from agency to cause. He started volunteering with at-risk youth, counseling people in recovery, helping schools identify budding addicts. He became a certified life coach.

"I was sick and tired of doing jobs I didn't want to be doing," he said. "I wanted to be a positive influence on the world."

The shape of his life, he said, was a bonsai tree: He likes helping people who feel damaged and small discover their inner beauty and pride.

As for his home life, Christy eventually forgave Charles and welcomed him back to their family. He became an active father. He went on church missions. When I asked for the high point of his life, he mentioned the births of his daughters. The low point was missing his younger daughter's first birthday because he was in treatment. The turning point: when the counselor projected that word *acceptance* onto the screen.

"I would love to be able to explain how I resisted making this change for so long," he said. "I was in denial. I was an escape artist, always finding a way to escape responsibility.

"But in that moment," he went on, "I began to crumble away that fabric of resistance. I began to accept that there are ways to navigate pain, loss, and sorrow with more effectiveness."

To do that, he said, he needed the inherent architecture of a transition—the pain of bottoming out, the bracing reality of being alone, the gratitude of returning home.

"For me, at least, that disruption was required, because once I had that moment of clarity, I began to think, *I'm at the bottom of the cliff looking up, and, you know, maybe there is a foothold here and I can finally start to climb.*"

The Moses Moment

The simple fact is: Most people resist transitions. We deny, avoid, wallow, resent. Perhaps we like the way things were or are afraid of what might come; maybe we just don't like change. Whatever the reason, faced with a defining moment, we balk. I think of this reaction as the Moses moment, because in the book of Exodus, when God appears to Moses in the burning bush and recruits him to free the Israelites, Moses's reaction is *Who, me?!* Offered the chance to make history, he hesitates.

Moses is hardly the last to have this reaction. Many people have a hard time accepting what Jean-Paul Sartre called the *facticity* of their situation. When Beethoven first learned that he was going deaf, he resisted mightily. "I will seize Fate by the throat," he wrote a confidant. "It shall certainly not bend and crush me completely." Sure enough, a few years later, he succumbed to the inevitable. "*Resignation*, what a wretched resource! Yet is all that is left to me."

The food writer M. F. K. Fisher was years into battling Parkinson's when she realized she had to give up her lifetime joy of sleeping naked because she could no longer stand the image of the "strange, uncouth, ugly, kind of toadlike woman" staring back at her in the mirror every morning. She broke down and bought some nightgowns. "I don't think I'm a compromising person, but I certainly do know that there are certain facts of life that you've got to accept. I know some women who refuse to be old and they are like zombies walking around."

Moving from resistance to acceptance is the first tool of a life transition. How do we do that?

Twelve-step programs have long stressed that the key is giving up any illusion of control—to admit that we're wrong, weak, or full of it, and then relinquish authority to a higher power. Many religions make a similar point. We can't understand everything that happens to us, so we must accept the mysteries of the divine. Lots of people find this approach helpful.

But my conversations point to another approach that many find more self-affirming. Instead of turning to a higher power, they turn inward. Even if they didn't cause the situation they're in, they assume the burden for making it better. They take agency over their own transition.

In what I found to be an unexpected twist, many people described how this act of agency meant acknowledging that their bodies understood change was coming before their minds did. Charles Gosset knew something was wrong with his life long before he started drinking and knew something was wrong with drinking long before he was able to quit. Naomi Clark perceived something was askew in her body for years before she even heard the concept of transgender. Nisha Zenoff felt sick and started dry heaving over lunch at what she later learned was the exact hour her son fell off a mountain in Yosemite.

The Nobel laureate Pearl Buck describes a similar sequence in her memoir about her husband's death. "Years ago I had learned the technique of acceptance. The first step is simply to yield one's self to the situation. It is a process of the spirit but it begins with the body." Psychologists call this the *James-Lange theory*, after William James and Carl Lange, who stumbled upon it independently in the 1880s. They found that in matters of emotion, the body acts before the mind fully identifies what's happening. James came upon this insight while hiking in Alaska. His aha moment: "I am running from this bear; therefore, I must be afraid."

Recently, this body-first mentality has gained currency as scientists have been able to show how the body becomes both a vessel for registering crises and a starting point for overcoming them. A number of people I spoke with described feeling they were undergoing a massive change even before they had vocalized it to themselves. They had a *gut feeling*, heard an *inner voice*, felt something in their *heart of hearts*. *Somehow, I just knew.* The neuroscientist Antonio Damasio says such feelings are our wake-up to a problem "that the body has already begun to solve." The point is: We may already have entered the transition before our mind even realizes it.

Here are some ways people overcame their resistance and accepted their new reality:

For some the switch was instant, like an epiphany. David Figura, a sportswriter from Syracuse, had grown so unhappy in his marriage that he was in the middle of driving to a nearby hotel to sleep with an old flame when he realized he was about to destroy his life. "I actually broke down in tears," he said. "I started thinking, *What am I going to tell my son when I get home?* That was the moment when I said, *I cannot do this*, and turned the car toward home." Lisa Rae Rosenberg, who struggled with addiction, was confronted by her sponsor, who said, "Look down at your feet. See where you are. And start there." "There was something about the specificity of the language that made the difference," Lisa said. "*Those are my feet, these are the shoes I happen to be wearing, this is the floor I'm on.*" She hasn't used drugs or alcohol since.

For others, acceptance comes in the form of a mental calculation. When I first learned I had a malignant tumor in my left femur, I quickly created a formula in part to put myself at ease: I'd have a lost limb, a lost year, or a lost life. Karen Peterson-Matchinga, a model and psychic in California, did the same thing when she got a phone call that her husband, an art director, had fallen off a ladder on a film set. "*Is he alive?*" she asked the producer. "Yes. *Can you move his toes?* Yes. *Can he move his fingers?* Yes. *Okay, I can work with this.*"

Psychologists call this *negative visualization*, where you imagine situations that are worse in order to help you accept the otherwise awful situation you're in. In *Option B*, Sheryl Sandberg relates that after the sudden death of her husband, Dave Goldberg, her friend Adam Grant asked Sandberg how the situation might have been worse. "Worse?" she asked. "Are you kidding? How could this be worse?" His answer: "Dave could have had the same cardiac arrhythmia driving your children." Sandberg says she found his answer helpful in reframing.

Loretta Parham, whom we met briefly in chapter 2, told me that when her daughter, Leah, was killed in a car crash just minutes after leaving Loretta's home in Atlanta (Leah's older daughter, who was also in the car, was injured but survived), Loretta had a hard time accepting what the police were telling her. "I said, '*No, no, no. Not my Leah!*'" Loretta insisted on going to the morgue. "Two things in that visit helped me," she said. "I was able to be grateful that, one, Leah's younger daughter had not also been in the car and, two, that Leah had not been lying in a hospital dying by herself. She died immediately, and that gave me a lot of peace."

Even people whose life changes are positive sometimes have a hard time accepting them. When Carl Bass learned he was about to be asked to become the CEO of Autodesk, he "hid in the bathroom for five days." "I thought, *This is not for me. I don't want to do it. I don't have the skills to do it.*" When Carol Berz, an attorney in Chattanooga, Tennessee, was pressed to run for city council, she was mortified when she won. "Like many women, I suffer from imposter syndrome," Carol said. How did she get over it? Her answer was the same as Carl Bass's: "I hope I never get over it. It drove me to work harder and learn more than everybody else."

Acceptance is difficult precisely because it involves drawing a line we usually don't want to draw and entering a realm we usually don't want to enter. But it's also difficult for another reason: It never happens in isolation. It's part of a larger stew of emotions that leaves us feeling inert when we go through times of change.

The Only Thing We Have to Fear

I asked everyone I interviewed, "What was the greatest emotion you struggled with during your transition?" The answers ran a wide gamut. At 27 percent, fear was clearly the most popular reaction, followed by sadness at 19 percent, and shame at 15 percent. Others that made the list included guilt, anger, and loneliness.

I then asked how people coped with or overcame these emotions.

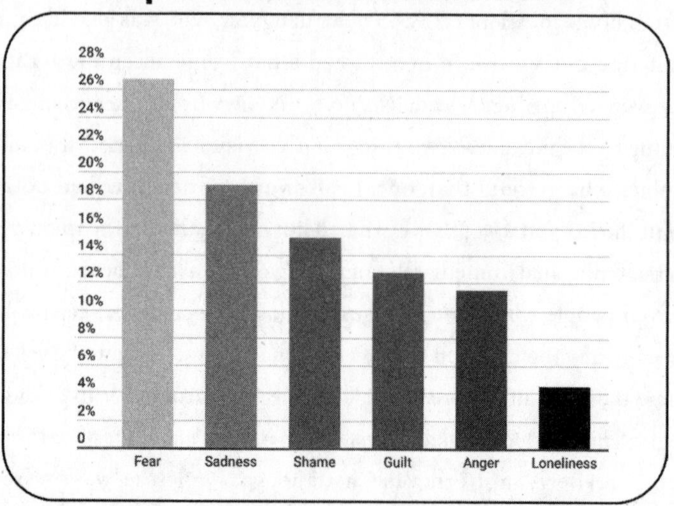

Their answers were practical, poignant, and quite inventive. Let's examine the top three.

Fear clearly terrorizes people—and paralyzes them with indecision. Fraidy Reiss told me that after living with her abusive husband for fifteen years, and finally escaping with her children, she was overcome with fear. "It wasn't fear of failure," she said. "It was fear of the unknown. I just didn't understand this world, and now I had to raise two kids in it." On top of that, she was diagnosed with breast cancer. "When I went into the hospital for surgery, I had to list my next of kin. 'Can I name my eleven-year-old daughter?' I asked. 'No, it needs to be an adult,' they said. That's when I realized I didn't have a single person who would help me out in a crisis."

At its root, fear is positive. Being afraid triggers a series of physical reactions—rapid heartbeat, flushed skin, adrenaline—that help save us from peril. Face-to-face with a lion, we know we must fight or flee. "Fear is good," said the screenwriter Steven Pressfield. "Fear is an indicator. Fear tells us what we have to do."

But not all fearful situations are as clear cut as staring into the eyes of a four-hundred-pound predator. Many involve emotional adjustments, financial insecurities, or just plain dread about facing an ordeal with no guarantee of success. Fear escalates during transitions precisely because it nags at these kinds of doubts. In 1986, the psychologists Hazel Markus and Paula Nurius introduced the idea that all of us keep a running catalog of *possible selves.* These imaginary selves represent our hopes for what we'd like to become, our *dream selves,* and our worries for what we're afraid of becoming, our *feared selves.* In times of change, our dream selves retreat and our feared selves become more looming.

And yet, humans are remarkably adaptive. As fear has metastasized in our nonlinear age, our coping mechanisms have grown. I heard a wide array of ways people push back against their fears.

Compare Down

The most frequent tactic is that people create a mental equation under which fear of the future, as great as it may be, is still less than fear of the present. The equation looks like this:

Fear of the Unknown < Fear of the Known

This is how Brian Wecht justified leaving his physics job in London for his YouTube comedy band ("I'd rather live with fear and failure than safety and regret"), how Lisa Ludovici described giving up her ad exec lifestyle to become a hypnotherapist ("The fear of staying was greater than the fear of leaving"), how Katrina Alcorn described leaving her husband for her boss ("The unpleasantness of doing the normal was so great, I was prepared to do the non-normal"). We tame our fears of the future by making them milder than our knowledge of the present.

Write Down

The next most popular explanation is to write down your fears. A number of people described actually listing out their anxieties—and their corresponding hopes—as a way of taking some control over them. Gena Zak was so fearful of leaving her corporate job and starting her own business in Maine that she made a list of everything she wanted out of life ("have more friends, be closer to family, spend more time in nature"), then put it by her bed so she'd see it first thing every morning. Travis Roy was so directionless after becoming a paraplegic and ending his lifelong dream of joining the NHL that he wrote out everything he could still hope to get out of life ("graduate in four years, take classes in public speaking, start a foundation to raise disability awareness"); when he achieved everything on the list, he made another, and has continued the practice for decades.

Buckle Down

Many people took an approach I often use when I feel myself succumbing to career stress: *Shut up and go to work.* John Austin told me he felt gripped by fear upon leaving the DEA after twenty-five years and opening his own security firm. The antidote? "Diving right in." Eric Maddox was petrified when as a rookie army interrogator trained in Mandarin he was sent to Iraq to help find high-value targets. "My biggest fear was being sent home, so I thought, *I can be scared, or I can go to work, keep my head down, and get to stay another day.*" Eric soon realized he needed to scrap the browbeating techniques he'd been taught and just start listening to the captives. His new technique eventually led him to identify the hiding place of the highest-value target of all, Saddam Hussein. When Eric's joint task force used his information to unearth the former dictator, Eric earned a Legion of Merit, a Bronze Star, and a personal invitation from then secretary of defense Donald Rumsfeld to help retrain the entire army in listening skills.

Face Down

The final way people overcome their fears is by confronting them head-on. The renowned Buddhist nun Pema Chödrön observes that we think the brave have no fear, but they actually push through their fear. "When I was first married," she writes, "my husband said I was one of the bravest people he knew. When I asked him why, he said because I was a complete coward but went ahead and did things anyway."

When Richard Sarvate moved to Hollywood from Silicon Valley to break into stand-up, he had to get over a lifetime fear of talking to strangers. "My entire life has been about avoiding social interaction," he said. "Just the other day, I got up the nerve to message a comedic idol that I wanted to see his show. 'Come on in,' he said. As soon as his set was over, I got in my car and drove away, then I was like, *What are you doing? No.* So I drove back and forced myself to stand at the bar and have a conversation with another struggling comic. We had a lot to talk about."

When Susan Keappock graduated from Texas A&M and moved to New York to try to get into theater, she was intimidated and full of fear. "Having just lost my dad, I had a fear of losing my mom," she said. "I had a fear of the big city. I had a fear of walking off a curb and being hit by a bus. I realized I just had to face all of them. You have to pretend you don't feel it—fake it till you make it. Then, without even realizing it, you just learn to be fearless."

The moral of these stories: Fear is innate; fearlessness can be learned.

Hopelessness Is a Thing with Feathers

Sadness was the second most common emotion, with nearly one in five saying it was their primary source of struggle.

Nancy Davis Kho believes she won the jackpot with her family in Rochester, New York, with loving parents and a dad who taught her to horseback ride every summer in the Adirondacks. Eager to see the world, she earned a degree in international business, moved to Germany, and married an Indonesian American. They settled in the Bay Area; she got a job in tech and had two children. Her life was linear.

But in her forties Nancy ricocheted through an obstacle course of change. Bored and burned out, she quit her high-voltage career and started a music blog. The move unnerved her husband and strained their marriage. Then, in a stretch of twelve months, her beloved German shorthaired pointer died, her first child went to college, and her father succumbed within weeks to a brain tumor.

"It was a giant hole of grief," she said. "I hate to compare my dad to my dog, but these two presences in my life were just so steady and reliable. You don't even know—until you start going through loss—how lucky you are. You value things you didn't have the experience to value before. There's beauty in that, but boy was it hard to live through."

If fear is the feeling that stalks you in times of change, sadness is what weighs you down. Fear is relentless; sadness is enervating.

As its core, sadness is the emotion that occurs when we've lost someone or something that we know is not coming back. That someone might be a friend, a loved one, a pet; that something might be a home, a job, a time in our life that is past. The downside of sadness is that it's heavy, physical, wearying, isolating. Pearl Buck wrote on learning of her husband's death, "How quickly, in one instant, years of happy life become only memories! . . . The day I had dreaded had come. The final loneliness was here."

That loss often leads to longing. In *The Fault in Our Stars*, John Green captures the yearning this way: "The pleasure of remembering had been taken from me, because there was no longer anyone to remember with. It felt like losing your co-rememberer meant losing the memory itself, as if the things we'd done were less real and important than they had been hours before."

But I was surprised to learn that there is an array of positive side effects of sadness. George Bonanno, the resilience researcher who did so much to debunk the five stages of grief, has found that sadness compels us to turn our attention inward, which is exactly what we need in times of grief. We become more reflective and self-protective. We double- and triple-check that we're doing okay. We focus more on details.

In this way, sadness is almost the opposite of anger. While anger prepares us to fight, sadness prepares us to protect. Anger speeds the world up; sadness slows it down. "Sometimes bereaved people even say that living with the sadness of loss is like living in slow motion," Bonanno writes. "There seems to be less need to pay attention to the world around us, so we are able to put aside normal, everyday concerns and turn our attention inward."

I found three primary ways people describe coping with sadness.

Resignation

The first is a slow, gradual surrender. This begrudging acceptance, like so much of life today, is not linear, and returns at the most unexpected times.

Oscar Emmet, a genderqueer medical student in New York whose traditionally religious family in California rejected his decision to no longer live as a girl, to take male hormones, and to grow a beard, grieved the road not taken. "Sometimes I feel sad that I lost a certain path," Oscar said. "I'm jealous of the people whose lives seem easy and laid out. Like my best friends growing up: They got married to the man they were set up with; they have children who are good and successful; their husbands come home, sing songs, and put the children to bed. As much as I like who I am now, there are times when I long to be one of those people who don't have to deal with a real world that's messy and scary."

Leo Eaton, a British filmmaker who fell madly in love with an American debutante and had to work hard (including concealing a stint writing pornography) to earn her trust, described the uncontrollable grief he felt at her passing from breast cancer after forty-five years of marriage. "I would often talk to Jeri in my mind," he said. "I remember standing on the deck of a ferry and just telling her what I was going through. She is always the voice in my head. Everything she ever was and is was downloaded into me." He wasn't always sad, he said. "There were moments of absolute joy in remembering her with friends. But then the grief returns, like waves. Last week I was watching a silly romance on television and a wave of grief swept over me just as strong as any tide. It passes, but in that moment it was just stunning in its power."

Relationships

Many people turn to others in times of sadness. After Elisa Korentayer moved from New York City to rural Minnesota to be with her canoeing guide, she felt "the sadness of a loss, the sadness of not fitting in, the sadness of doubt that I had made the right choice." The corrective? "Making connections. When I would feel down or lonely, I'd go to the local coffee shop. People would smile at me or talk to me; the owners became my friends. I'd go to the post office and be recognized. The cure was feeling like I became part of the community."

After Sarah Holbrooke found herself divorced with a newborn, her friends nurtured her back to life. "I hate being alone, and suddenly I was *very* alone. That made me so very sad. But I wasn't really alone because I had so many friends who would come over and spend time with me. Relationships got me through the relationship trauma."

Radical Honesty

The last way people deal with sadness is to finally, fully admit their feelings—to themselves and to others. Sasha Cohen was born in Los Angeles to a Russian mom and American dad, started gymnastics and ice skating as a toddler, and by sixteen made the US figure skating team at the Salt Lake City Olympics. But she fell in the long program and finished a disappointing fourth. Four years later, in Turin, she was first after the short program, but again fell in the long, ending with a silver.

Her sadness dogged her for years. “I tried not to burst into tears in every conversation.” Until one day, a friend forced her to watch the tape. “It was just tears, more tears, and more sadness. I think I finally just allowed myself to feel the tragedy and pain instead of just trying to shut it down.”

After Sean Collins was fired from his job as a top producer at NPR, he returned to his hometown of Saint Louis and to his roots as a parish preacher. While his instinct was to conceal what happened to him, he eventually learned to share it. “I think of that Emily Dickinson line ‘Truth is such a rare thing it is delightful to tell it.’ Part of my experience was learning to be truthful, to tell that story. I made a living asking other people to be truthful, yet some of the hardest stuff was to do it for me personally.”

You on Shame

The third most common emotion was the most surprising for me: shame. One in six chose this as their toughest struggle. Unlike fear and sadness, the shame stories were somehow more visceral, more painful, in part because there was an element of personal responsibility.

When Kristina Wandzilak, whom we met in chapter 5, woke up in a homeless shelter in California after ten years of drinking, homelessness, and crime, she was deeply ashamed. Born in Indiana to a stay-at-home mom and an alcoholic father, Kristina was largely estranged from her family. After Kristina had run away from three treatment programs, her mother greeted her at the door when she was eighteen and said, “You are no longer welcome in my home or in my life until you’re living a life of recovery. If I never see you alive again, I want you to know how much I love you.” Then she shut the door in Kristina’s face.

It took Kristina three years and twenty-two house burglaries to finally commit to that life of recovery. By then she had another problem: her inconsolable shame about her criminal behavior.

"I just couldn't look people in the face," she said. "I felt like I had to live small, because if anybody found out what I had done, I would lose everything. People wouldn't love me."

Then, in the middle of the night, the answer came to her. "I had to do a turnabout and walk right into it," she said. "I'd be more free in jail or paying financial restitution than I was living like this. So I went to each of the twenty-two homes I robbed, knocked on the door, and when the person answered, I said, 'My name is Kristina. I want you to know that I robbed your home in the last six or nine months. I'm willing to pay restitution, legally or financially, however I can make this right. I also want you to know how sorry I am.'"

Most people were shocked to see her, she said. "I think they expected someone of a different color or a different sex." Most said, "Fuck you, don't come near my property again." No one said, "Thank you." One woman said, "You've taken something that can never be replaced. It was a gold ring that was my great-great-grandfather's wedding band. Also, you took my sense of security."

"But she also said she wasn't going to call the police," Kristina said, "that she didn't feel being in jail would be useful to me, that I was clearly trying to make this right. So she asked me to write her a twenty-five-dollar check, every month, for a year—and never bother her again."

Kristina did as she was asked, except she didn't have a checking account, so she asked her mother to send the money for her, which in turn helped with that reconciliation. Years later, after Kristina opened an international program to help former addicts reconcile with their families, she was asked to be on *The Oprah Winfrey Show*. The producers requested that she contact the woman and invite her to tell her side of that story. "I was eager to make them happy," Kristina said, "but I had made a commitment that day to never bother her again, so I politely declined."

Shame is the intensely painful feeling of believing we are flawed and therefore unworthy of love. Shame is so powerful it undercuts all three of the ABCs of meaning. It saps our sense of agency by making us feel impotent; it destroys our sense of belonging by making us doubt our ability to connect with others; it weakens our sense of cause by making us self-absorbed and incapable of serving others. Shame is even more pernicious than its evil twin, guilt. Brené Brown, the bestselling author and researcher, offers this convenient formula: Guilt is *I did something bad*; shame is *I am bad*. Some have proposed that women are more prone to shame than men, but my interviews suggest otherwise. Shame is equal opportunity in its ability to make us feel like failures, quitters, or weaklings.

What's the remedy to this toxic gnaw? My conversations point to responses that best address the area of identity most weakened. Those feeling devoid of agency are most effective when they step forward, verbalize their vulnerabilities, even go public with them. Those feeling disconnected feel greatest relief when they share their true feelings with others. Those feeling like they have nothing to give do best when they find ways to help those in similar situations. The common ingredient is actively taking steps to evict the shame from your head.

Here's how this plays out in real life.

Agency

Carolyn Graham got over her shame of her two failed suicide attempts by writing about the incidents, having her writing group respond with compassion, and then feeling free to share even more of her pain. "I had to first hear the voice in my head, then get it on paper. There were times I was so uncomfortable sitting at my desk that I was overwhelmed."

Kirsty Spraggon, who had panic attacks for two decades over her shame of having a sexually transmitted disease, finally built up the courage to write the word *herpes* in her diary. That simple step produced a cascade of reactions, led her to give a TEDx Talk on learning to share your secrets, and finally resulted in her having the phrase *truth teller* tattooed on her arm.

Belonging

When Christian Picciolini left the neo-Nazis, he descended into depression and drug use for five years; when he finally emerged and began telling his story, he was gutted by "toxic shame." His response: "I had to be much more genuine than I was prepared to be. I had to stand on the stage and say, *This is my ugly inside I'm struggling with.* Then I had to find a similar pain in others and connect with it. The solution to shame is empathy."

When Erik Smith, the young Virginia preacher, felt embarrassed that his faith and mental health were wavering after multiple family deaths, he found renourishment in his special-needs students. "They taught me the key is being honest," he said. "My impulse is always to hide. I have to resist that—admit my brokenness, admit my neediness, admit my suffering. They have no artifice—when they like a food, they shove it in their mouths—so they became my teacher."

Cause

Allen Peake, the Republican state legislator from Georgia, was so humiliated that his extramarital dalliances on AshleyMadison.com became public that he considered resigning. But he had just taken on the crusade to legalize medical marijuana on behalf of a five-year-old cerebral palsy patient, so "my wife and I made the conscious decision to endure whatever public shame we needed to in order to get the legislation passed." He succeeded; the legislation was signed into law.

John Smitha, who harbored shame for fifty years over his killing of forty civilians in Libya, finally turned his life over to God, became ordained as a Christian lay leader, and started volunteering as a counselor. "I made my life an open book. I tell anybody that wants to hear what I did and my regrets. And I do four meetings a week with veterans; I can't get enough of it."

From shame to sadness to fear, from overcoming your resistance to embracing the brutal facts of your situation, the first tool of transitions is to identify the circumstances you're in and accept the emotions that come with this new state. The next tool may seem even harder to master, yet it's the one approach people seem to crave more than any other.

CHAPTER 8

Mark It

Ritualize the Change

One unavoidable consequence of the nonlinear life is that life is, well, nonlinear. That means it's unstructured, impermanent, volatile, variable. That kind of freedom can be great when you're feeling stuck or unhappy, overwhelmed or beaten down. You can simply pull back, pivot, and reboot.

But sometimes, especially when you're in the midst of some massive life change, that kind of fluidity can be downright overwhelming. *Enough with all this unpredictability; give me something concrete to hold on to!* When that happens, people turn out to have a remarkable ability to generate their own concrete. They invent novel techniques to calm themselves down, assemble keepsakes to remind them of what's lost, hold ceremonies to mourn the past.

They create rituals.

Ritual is something of an old-fashioned word. It's associated with stuffy institutions, outmoded customs, uncomfortable clothes. *Oh, God, not another prayer circle.* But one consistent finding of the Life Story Project is that when people feel most adrift, they often turn to ritualistic solutions, many of them homemade. They sing, dance, hug, purge, tattoo, turpentine, skydive, schvitz. In a world with no boundaries, rituals create demarcation. In moments of deluge, rituals provide containers.

In periods of shape-shifting, rituals give shape.

"I've Been Thinking About This for Ten Years"

Margaret Patton was born into a life of undeniable privilege and inescapable prestige. Her great-great-grandfather was George S. Patton Sr., a Confederate colonel during the Civil War. Her grandfather was George S. Patton Jr., the iconic World War II general who spearheaded the invasions of North Africa and Sicily and led the Third Army across France and Germany after D-day. Her father was George S. Patton IV, a major general who served in the Korean War, the Vietnam War, and the Cold War.

"I always thought I would marry into the army, have a bunch of kids, and travel," she said.

But Margaret had a rebel streak. When her family flew first class, she "refused to sit there and went to the back of the plane where the real people were." When her parents set her up with an eligible officer at the Kentucky Derby, she "fled to the infield to be with the masses." She got kicked out of high school for smoking pot.

"I was kind of leading a double life," she said. "I was wrestling with the money my family had. With the motto we all grew up with, 'To whom much has been given, much shall be required.' With the implications of our involvement in Vietnam. But whenever I said I wanted to run, I was always told, '*You're a goddam Patton. Your blood won't let you.*'"

When Margaret was eighteen, her freshman roommate at Bennington College started Catholic instruction with a community of Benedictine nuns in Bethlehem, Connecticut, called the Abbey of Regina Laudis. One weekend, Margaret tagged along. A half-hearted Episcopalian, Margaret was intrigued by the isolation, the spirituality, the commitment.

She returned over the summer for a longer stay. One night, the foundress, Lady Abbess Benedict Duss, asked to see her. Mother Benedict explained that the nuns were having a ceremony the next day, August 27, to commemorate the liberation of the parent abbey in Jouarre, France, from the Nazis in 1944. It was that event, the abbess explained, that had inspired her to open the facility in Connecticut out of appreciation for American troops. Mother Benedict asked Margaret if she would raise the American flag in the ceremony.

Thinking of her ambivalence toward the American military, Margaret demurred. "I don't think you have the right person," she said.

"I really do have the right person," the abbess said. "You don't know this, but our foundation owes its life to your family. Your grandfather led the soldiers that liberated our parent abbey. We wouldn't be here without him."

Margaret was flabbergasted. "I remember the day as kind of riveting," she said. "Here was this abbey I responded to and my family was in its history."

Even more, here was the place, the peace of mind, and the self-sacrifice she had been seeking her entire life. She asked if she could join the order.

The abbess turned her down. Margaret was too young, too naive, too restless. Too angry. "If you don't want it badly enough," the foundress said, "then you're not ready." Margaret spent the next ten years wrestling with her desire to be a person of the world and her attachment to this mysterious stone cloister in the Connecticut woods. She traveled, dated, started a school, fell in love. And all that time she kept coming back for retreats and extended stays.

"I got the counseling I needed," Margaret said. "I straightened out certain things. Then, on one of my visits, the foundress said to me, 'You know you could lose it.' And I'll never forget that moment. It went through me like a sword. And I said to myself, *Okay, I don't want to lose it.* There was a mutuality I felt when I was here. There was someone on the other side, and I wanted that someone to be the center of my life."

"Is that someone God?" I asked.

"That someone is God."

Margaret informed her family she was joining the abbey. It would mean almost a complete separation. No shared holidays, minimal communication, a new identity. She had finally figured out how to outrun her *goddam blood*.

She would give her life over to God.

Her parents were devastated. Her mother was so upset she refused to attend Margaret's entry ceremony. Her father, though, fell back on the family's military training: He viewed supporting her as his duty. On New Year's Eve 1982, the general escorted his daughter to dinner at the nearby Mayflower Inn. "We sat down, and my father said, 'I want the best wine in the house! My daughter's going in the convent.' And I'm like, '*Da-aad!*' On my way to the salad bar, the maître d' stopped me and goes, 'You're too young. Don't do it.' And I say, 'I've been thinking about this for ten years. It's home for me.'"

After dinner, General Patton drove his daughter to the abbey. Margaret went to a changing room and put on a black tunic with a white scarf. When she came out, her father was reading the Bible. "He looked me up and down and says, 'So that's the uniform, huh?'"

They entered the sanctuary; everyone else remained outside. "The foundress invited my dad to say one of the prayers and bless me, which was kind of an exception. Unbeknownst to me, one of the nuns had been taking target practice from a retired policeman for self-defense. She happened to be Dolores Hart, the former actress who made her screen debut with Elvis Presley. She has a feel for drama and wanted to do something for my dad. So right after the prayer, she shot a rifle into the sky.

"And you know," Margaret continued, "a soldier knows the sound of a gun. My dad goes, 'What's that?!'"

The nuns took Margaret inside the private walls. "Then they closed this great, huge gate behind me. Dad yells, 'Good luck, Margaret!' And I yell back, 'Thanks, Dad. I'll need it!'"

The transition from living a life of personal freedom, earthly love, and sexual experimentation to one of personal asceticism, lordly devotion, and chastity is extreme by any measure. No part of a nun's daily existence is unaltered from her prior life. Stability, obedience, and conversion are the highest values. But how do you execute such a profound transformation? What have orders like the Benedictines learned from millennia of guiding people through one of the more profound life transitions imaginable?

The answer: Go slow; insist on deep, personal reflection; mark each stage of the journey with carefully constructed rituals that delineate and demarcate the new status achieved.

In the case of Margaret, this process lasted *ten more years* before she became a full member of the community. First, there was the *ritual of searching*. Margaret, like all postulants, spent her first year exploring her genealogy so she knew exactly what family history she was bringing to her new role. The year ended with the *ritual of clothing*. The postulant is given a black tunic and head scarf, her hair is cut and covered with a white veil, and then she announces her name. Margaret chose Sister Margaret Georgina, thereby honoring the four generations of George Pattons she'd spent her whole life trying to outrun.

Next is the *ritual of language*. The newly anointed sister studies Latin, liturgy, and song, and learns to express herself through parable and prayer. That's followed by the *ritual of commitment*. The sister embarks on a course of study to identify what gifts she already possesses and which arena of God's service—from cheese making to bookkeeping—she'd like to embrace. Margaret chose plants, so she studied agriculture and assumed responsibility for the flower and vegetable gardens.

The final step is the *ritual of consecration*. "You say to the church, 'I am yours,' and the church says the same to you. Then you lie on the ground while the community chants the litany of the saints. It's like a wedding day; you wear a crown of flowers. Mine were from all parts of the abbey's land."

But why exactly do they do all this? Why take ten years, require each of these elaborate discourses, perform all of these antiquated ceremonies?

"Because people need it," Margaret said. "They help the community understand where we're at in the process. They help us think differently about ourselves. You need a certain stability in order to grow. What these rituals provide is that stability."

A Light in the Window

In my interviews, I asked everybody whether they marked the moment they entered a life transition. I was pretty open-ended about what might qualify as such an indicator. They could be rituals, gestures, tributes, or commemorations of any kind.

Seventy-eight percent of people said yes; 22 percent said no.

The answers themselves showed remarkable inventiveness and revealed a consistent, almost instinctual need people have to reassure themselves in times of upheaval that they're not going to be swept away by the turmoil. I found four broad categories of ritual. In order of popularity, they are:

- *Personal* (getting a tattoo, building an altar)
- *Collective* (throwing a party, hosting a ceremony)
- *Name change* (adding or subtracting a married name, adopting a religious name)
- *Cleansing* (going on a diet, shaving)

For simplicity's sake, the term *ritual* is a catchall for these different activities. A ritual is a symbolic act, gesture, or ceremony that helps add meaning in times of transition.

What explains their popularity?

At their heart, rituals are acts of meaning. They help restore a sense of

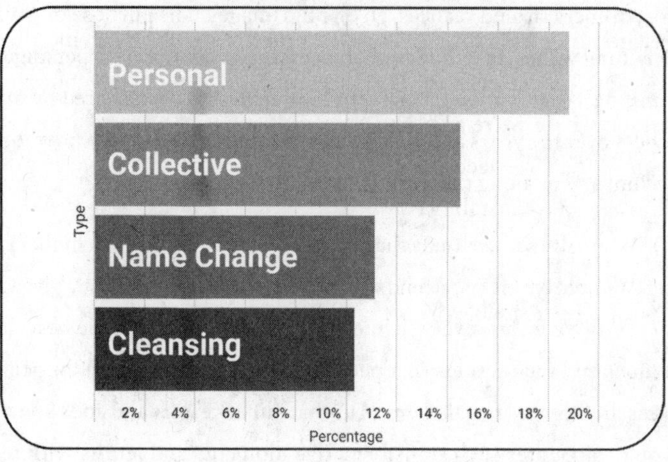

agency, belonging, and cause in those times of life when we feel stripped of all three. The author and feminist scholar Christine Downing captures the anxiety we feel upon entering such a time in her memoir *A Journey Through Menopause*. "I felt alone, uninformed, somewhat afraid—and yet also curious and expectant," she writes. "I was at the brink of a centrally important life-change and had no knowledge of the myths or rituals that had helped women throughout history live this transition with hope, dignity, and depth."

As in other meaning vacuums, our responses to these moments reflect the ABCs of meaning.

> A) We are drawn to rituals that reassure us we still have some control over the world. We start tinkering with our bodies, lighting candles, erecting memorials. Rituals, in this way, are like punctuation marks, writes psychologist Jeltje Gordon-Lennox. Sometimes the punctuation you need is a full stop, like a funeral or farewell party. Sometimes it's a comma, like a sabbatical or fast. Other times it's an exclamation point, like a wedding or commencement.

B) We are drawn to rituals that deepen our relationships with others. We host dinners, attend séances, go on pilgrimages. The purpose of rituals, Downing writes, is to integrate the personal with the transpersonal, to remind us that our deeply personal suffering has been shared by many others over the years and to help us assemble a tribe *right now* who can accompany us along the way.

C) We are drawn to rituals that connect our pain or joy to a higher calling. We hold baptisms, attend wakes, don masks, join protests, give valedictions. We feel so overwhelmed by our own emotions, the best thing to do is embrace actions that people have found comfort in for generations. In this way, rituals remind us that our ancestors and gods knew we would encounter such transformative moments and left us with techniques that can contextualize our fears.

Here are some of the many rituals I heard about in my conversations:

Personal

- After Maillard Howell left his job in big pharma to start his own CrossFit gym, he got the words *breathe* and *think* tattooed on the middle fingers of his right hand, and *successful* and *happy* on the middle fingers of his left hand. "I knew I couldn't go back to pharma with that shit on my hands. I was done. I told my friends, 'I'm going to tattoo my face like Mike Tyson.'"
- The first thing Oscar Emmet did after leaving Orthodox Judaism was eat a ceremonial cheeseburger, buy a symbolic pair of jeans, and enjoy a forbidden first kiss.
- Following a brutal year in which she lost her job as a Hollywood producer, had a blowup with her mother, and went on fifty-two first dates,

Lisa Rae Rosenberg jumped out of an airplane. "I had a terrible fear of heights, and I thought, *If I can figure this out, I can figure anything out.*" A year later she was married with a child.

- When Nancy Davis Kho lost her father, she built an altar on her mantel with his photo, a Genesee Cream Ale, a golf ball, and a teacup filled with rice. Alongside the teacup, she propped up the prayer card from his funeral. "I was just waiting for a sign from my dad, but I knew he'd say, 'Oh, please.' He and I are very pragmatic like that. But one day I went to the mantel and there was a thumbprint in the rice. My kids were too young to reach it, and I thought, *Yeah, that's how he would do it, just to tweak me.*"

Collective

- After Fred Schloemer left his wife of thirty years and came out as gay, the Kentucky psychologist attended a Native American sweat lodge in New Mexico where small groups of practitioners gathered stones and hawks' wings and did piercings, a practice involving cutting the breast above the nipple, inserting a twig, and stretching the skin while others whoop and chant.
- Naomi Clark hosted a "hormone party" for friends at a chic Manhattan bar when she first began the process of transitioning to a woman after 9/11.
- Deborah Fishman, as she was preparing to leave her Orthodox husband, exiled him from the house one night over Passover and hosted a women's empowerment seder, in which she wrote a series of prayers and observances that celebrated spring, focused on wellness and renewal, and stressed not the liberation of the Israelites from Egypt but women from men. She's done it every year since.

Name Change

- Sarah Pinneo made millions as the rare female derivatives trader on Wall Street but gave it up to move to New Hampshire and pursue a career self-publishing steamy romance novels. To protect herself from ridicule, she adopted the pseudonym Sarina Bowen. "It felt almost ritualistic," she said, "like assuming a new persona. I had this other side of me, but I didn't want other people to see that part."
- After Sarah Siskind published an article about race relations at Harvard that made her persona non grata in liberal circles and ultimately sent her to Fox News, she had a change of heart, renounced her conservative views, and wanted to become a comedy writer. In order to distance herself from her former persona and give her some freedom to develop a new brand not haunted by the internet shaming she had experienced in the past, she added her middle name, Rose, to her professional identity.
- Sasha Cohen was so eager to escape the long shadow of her stage persona as an Olympic figure skater that she went back to her birth name, Alexandra, in order to have a more "normal" life.
- Courtney Rogmans, a lifelong seeker (Christianity, Hinduism, Hare Krishna) and builder of alternative communities from California to Oregon, went through a bitter divorce that led her to embrace Sufi teachings and change her name to Khaliqa Baqi, a variation of the Arabic for "creating and forming your own expression of the divine."

Cleansing

- After Jason Doig left the NHL, he grew lazy and gained weight, so when a new girlfriend inspired him to go vegan and embrace a healthy lifestyle, he went on what he called a turpentine purge, taking controlled dosages of a Native American elixir made from pine spirits to help wean himself off sugar, leading to violent, sweat-filled withdrawals.

- When Allen Peake confessed in an open letter to friends that he had been having extramarital affairs in Atlanta while serving as a state legislator, he sold the condo he'd been using as his love nest and committed to driving two hours home every evening from the capitol to be with his family in central Georgia.
- Christian Picciolini faced a secondary problem after leaving the skinheads; his entire body was covered in Nazi tattoos. Erasing them was challenging, so he chose to cover them with other tattoos. "I had an eagle holding a swastika on the back of my neck. The only thing wide enough to cover it was Jesus on the crucifix. It became a symbol of my rebirth."

Death Be Not Proud

Not all rituals or ways of marking transitions involve physical expressions; some are purely emotional. None more so than mourning. But for whatever reason, no aspect of going through a life transition is more misunderstood than what *Eat, Pray, Love* author Elizabeth Gilbert calls the "sweet time of grieving." My conversations suggest we misjudge the causes, the solutions, even the form this process takes.

Larry Moldo wears a black cowboy hat in his professional headshot, which is not surprising, considering he lives in Cheyenne, Wyoming, but somewhat surprising, considering he's the rabbi of Mt. Sinai Congregation, the oldest synagogue in the "cowboy state."

Larry was born in Minneapolis to a father who was a sheet metal worker. A reader and introvert, Larry hated the outdoors. "I believe that God allowed us to create walls so we could be inside of them." A math whiz and autodidact, he was asked by his second-grade teacher, "'Do me a favor, don't learn any more math until your class catches up.' Six years later, they caught up, but by that time I had moved on to history."

Uncomfortable around others, Larry lived at home for college, took a job in Jewish education in Peoria, Illinois, and then became director of ritual at a synagogue in Omaha. He got married, worked for his father-in-law in a pawnshop, and then became a licensed gun dealer.

"I did it because my father-in-law asked me to," he said. "Turns out you can sell things you don't use. I was selling jewelry even though I don't wear much jewelry. Out here, even grandmothers have handguns because twice a year they bring them onto the street and shoot them in the air. That's how you celebrate New Year's Eve and the Fourth of July."

After Larry was held up by gunpoint, though, he quit and decided to become a rabbi. "A friend said to me, 'You already have the knowledge and the experience, but people don't hire based on knowledge. You need the title.'"

During much of this time, Larry and his wife were trying unsuccessfully to have a child. She finally became pregnant, but the baby was stillborn, having stopped developing around six months. "It was very complicated emotionally," he said. "Also, nobody in my wife's family had told us about the high-risk nature of first pregnancies in that family. For six generations, the first child was stillborn. The deaths were caused by cord wrapping every single time."

A traditionalist by nature, Larry was particularly upset to discover that his branch of Judaism had no rituals or other practices to help families cope after having a stillbirth. He and his wife couldn't even hold a funeral because the hospital refused to release the remains. "My wife continues to be angry over this," he said.

So the autodidact in him kicked in. Larry spent the next dozen years doing an in-depth study of miscarriage, stillbirth, and other neonatal fatalities in Jewish literature, from the Torah to the Talmud. "There wasn't anything that felt comforting," he said. He eventually wrote his rabbinic thesis on the topic, "Unsuccessful Pregnancies and Neonatal Deaths: Pastoral Care for the Rabbinate and Cantorate."

What did he learn?

"Grief is what you feel," he said. "Mourning is what you do. If you don't have any way to express your grief, it bottles up inside you and incapacitates you. With neonatal deaths, the community had not allowed rituals to happen so the grief had nowhere to go."

Armed with his knowledge, Larry and his wife developed their own ways to mourn. They named the child and asked loved ones to acknowledge the loss of the baby's potential life. They lit a candle on the anniversary of the stillbirth. And when they later adopted a son, they shared memories of his unmet sibling.

"One of the things I found in my research is that even if you don't mark what happened to you, the body does it for you. There will be times when you feel miserable and you have no idea why, but fifteen years earlier the event was happening, and your body remembers year after year. The purpose of mourning is to get these feelings out into the open—even sharing them with the community—because if you don't, they'll just bite you later on."

Mourning is something people tend to think they understand: It applies mostly to deaths; it takes a long time; it unfolds in stages. None of these truisms is exactly true. Let's look at them one at a time.

For starters, grief is not just for death anymore. People grieve all sorts of things, from the loss of a home to the departure of children for college, from the job that went to someone else to the naive expectation that everything would work out in the end. In my conversations, sadness was the second most common emotion people felt during a transition—and much of this sadness was not for things that had been lost but for things that never came about. The happiness never achieved, the dream never realized. As John Greenleaf Whittier wrote, "For all sad words of tongue or pen, / The saddest are these: 'It might have been!'"

As for the second myth, mourning need not take a long time. As recently as a century ago, people thought mourning lasted forever. Former first lady Sarah Polk, who was forty-five when her husband, former president James Polk, died in 1849, wore black mourning clothes for the rest of her life—more than four decades. Today, mourning is understood to be far more contained. George Bonanno, the grief researcher at Columbia, has found that up to 60 percent of mourners show no symptoms of grief a month following a loss. Some overcome their sadness in days. On the opposite extreme, up to 15 percent of bereaved people struggle with grief for years.

Finally, grief is nonlinear. Like many areas of human psychology, grief went through a period in the twentieth century of being reduced to a progressive timeline of tasks, steps, and stages. What's more, those who failed to tick off each box in the prescribed order were deemed to be deluding themselves and in need of corrective counseling. Now we know each person follows their own path and their own timeline. "One of the most consistent findings," writes Bonanno, "is that bereavement is not a one-dimensional experience."

What Bonanno and others have found is that grief passes more quickly if those experiencing the loss take concrete steps to mourn what's gone. Mourning has the added benefit of helping those around the person who has experienced the loss. Especially when the mourner mixes in what might be considered positive, even public experiences—laughing, sharing stories, holding gatherings, building memorials—the act of mourning becomes an act of connecting and by extension an act of rebuilding. It's no wonder that in my conversations, two-thirds of people said they mourned in some way during their transition.

Here are some of the more effective mourning techniques I heard about:

- *A personal anniversary.* Davon Goodwin created a special holiday on the anniversary of his traumatic brain injury in Afghanistan. "Every

August 31, I don't do anything. I don't work. I just sit and think and call my friend Kelly who was in the back seat, see how she's doing. There's not a single time the day has not affected me."

- *A family observance.* Dwayne Hayes, a onetime hyper-macho husband in Michigan, was emotionally ripped open when his wife, having already had two failed pregnancies, had a placental abruption and delivered twin daughters, both dead. "We created a lot of rituals around the girls," he said. "We celebrate their birth every year with their siblings, who were born later. We get cupcakes and visit the cemetery. We bring wreaths in winter."
- *A fond send-off.* Lisa Heffernan, the mom who feared being an empty nester so much she cofounded a Facebook group for moms of young adults, carefully managed how she transitioned her kids to college. "I created all sorts of rituals that have to do with how I put them in their dorm room, the restaurants we go to, the shops we visit. I ritualized how we would communicate, by setting up a special group text. I call it the digital dinner table. I eventually realized I wasn't grieving their leaving. I was grieving knowing them less. I just didn't want them to become strangers."
- *A private reflection.* Helen Kim, a Korean American biophysics professor in Alabama, got late-stage gastric cancer, which led to the loss of two-thirds of her stomach and then to the end of her marriage, as she was no longer able to devote herself fully to her husband and he was unwilling to care for her. Helen's trauma kept being reignited every time she went out to eat with colleagues. "I invariably had to disappear into the bathroom with diarrhea. I would sit there and think, *Why do I have to be different?* I would do a little mourning, then I'd go back to the table and nobody would know the difference."
- *A sense of perspective.* Seth Mnookin, the Harvard graduate who spent most of his twenties as a heroin addict, said twenty-five years later he still mourns experiences he can't have. "I mourn things like going to a

concert and smoking pot, which I used to enjoy. I mourn being able to try psychedelics, which I'm curious about. I mourn being an outlaw, a cowboy, which is much more romantic than me in a Subaru Forester, taking animals to the vet, and going to see my GI doctor. I mourn all those things, but I'd still rather be who I am today than who I was then."

These Boots Were Made for Talking

Some of the patterns I uncovered I went looking for; others came looking for me. The latter is what happened in the case of the last way people tend to mark the end of an emotional time of their lives: They single out a memento that links them to their prior life and becomes a vessel to carry forward otherwise raw emotions into the future.

One of the earliest interviews I did was with Dawan Williams. Dawan was the fatherless son of inner-city Philadelphia who was imprisoned for armed robbery at twenty-two. Already the father of multiple children, Dawan went through a program for incarcerated dads, then was released and went to work for the program. He told me he still has his prison boots by the back door of his house, so they're the last thing he sees every day when he leaves home. "They're a constant reminder that *this is not what you want, sir. You've come a long way and you have everywhere to go.*"

Not long after that interview I was speaking with Eric Haney, the descendant of seven generations of white Appalachian hillbillies in north Georgia who went on to become a member of the first class of Delta Force, the elite army counterterrorism unit. On April 25, 1980, Eric was in the lead airplane that landed in the desert of central Iran as part of Operation Eagle Claw to rescue American hostages held in Tehran. The mission encountered an unexpected weather phenomenon called a *haboob*, an enormous opaque cloud of dust. In the darkness that followed, an American Sea Stallion helicopter hit the plane Eric was in, causing a huge explosion.

"I have a personal horror of burning to death," Eric said, "but once the blades hit the gas, the fuel just poured through the cut in the plane and all down the interior." The team leapt to safety, and Eric was the last man dragged aboard one of the surviving planes as it fled the aborted mission.

Today, in the office where he writes, Eric has the boots he was wearing that night. "I'm not trying to relive that period," he said. "I find meaning in this new phase of life. But I want to remember that's part of who I am."

Even Davon Goodwin has by the door in his bedroom the blood-stained boots he was wearing in Afghanistan when he drove over the IED. "I look at them every day. I need to. It makes me think, *I made it*, and reminds me to be humble."

Three different lives. One object. The same story. What's going on?

I incorporated a question about mementos or other symbolic objects into my interviews. Eighty-five percent of people said they relied on such keepsakes; 15 percent did not.

The idea that possessions contribute to our identity is hardly new. Scholars for two generations have observed that belongings play a role in creating and preserving our ongoing selves. "Things tell us who we are," Mihaly Csikszentmihalyi and Eugene Rochberg-Halton wrote in the early 1980s.

But I began to feel there's something more urgent going on. Beyond their symbolic value, these bloodied shoes, faded photographs, unworn jewelry, and facial scars become agents of change themselves. For starters, they serve as vessels for many of the unruly emotions that bubble forth in moments of upheaval. Assigning these otherwise amorphous feelings to a specific object somehow makes them more contained and less threatening.

Even more critical, the object becomes a means of emotional time travel. *I touch this necklace and remember my mother. I look at that picture and remember what I was feeling before I got that awful call.* The memento, in this way, not only manages to disappear into the background of our lives—it sits on the back of a shelf, after all, or lies tucked away in a drawer—but also stands ready to awaken in an instant and teleport us to the past. The memento thus becomes a stand-in for the original experience itself, gradually becoming part of the overall story of our lives, even as it occupies a less and less prominent place in our everyday routine.

Some of the meaningful mementos I heard about are visual:

- Amy Murphy keeps a photo on her phone of her joyfully holding her newborn son at two weeks old, before he was diagnosed with the mental disorder that would dominate their lives for the next eighteen years.
- After Jan Egberts's wife took her own life, he gathered dozens of photos of their shared life over the years onto a digital picture frame. "I was very angry at the time," he said, "but seeing the progression from all the happy pictures when we just met, or were traveling to China, Afghanistan, and Iran, to her mental health deteriorating, to the point where she wasn't smiling at all and there were no more happy pictures, I had never noticed the progression before and it helped me."

Others memorialize medical traumas:

- Peggy Fletcher Stack keeps the stethoscope she used to listen to the heart of her daughter Camille, who died of a congenital illness, along with a packet of bills. "Each one is a physical thing that reminds me of that era. I just finger through the bills and remember, *This is when I took her to the cardiologist. This is when I took her to the hospital.*"
- Adam Foss, who was hospitalized in a mental institution in Boston after a drinking binge that followed a bad breakup, carries a piece of paper in his wallet with his blood pressure and pulse at the time he was admitted. "Basically there was no pressure because my blood was so thin. It was all liquor. That's how much I consumed. I keep this paper

as a reminder: *This is what you did to yourself. This is how close you were to dying.*"

Some involve clothing:

- Jen Leary wanted to be a firefighter her whole life. She was one of only two women in her class of one hundred at the Philadelphia Fire Department, and she later started an organization to save pets that the department rescued from fires. But when a pit bull she was temporarily housing attacked her girlfriend, Jen went to intervene and the dog shredded her wrists, forcing Jen to retire at thirty-one. A friend in the safety office took pity on her and allowed Jen to break regulations and retain her helmet, which she keeps at home.
- Vivienne Ming, who played football in high school when she was still male-bodied, dropped out of college, lived in a car, and nearly died by suicide, before returning to school, earning a PhD in cognitive neuroscience, and transitioning to a woman. "I still own the tuxedo I crazily bought to take my first girlfriend to the prom. When I married my wife, I was already taking hormones and losing weight, so I wore that tux to my wedding. It felt like a costume, but nobody knew except me and her."

Others we carry around on our bodies:

- Eric Johnson, who worked for a mob boss for years in Brooklyn running numbers, watched his girlfriend get murdered, became a cocaine addict, then got clean, opened a plumbing company, and became a church deacon, said his memento was track marks. "They're needle marks on my arm. I'm not ashamed of my story, because it's what got me here, but I look at those and remember I don't want to go back."

- Doc Shannon shaved his mustache when he was deployed to Vietnam in 1968, but when two buddies were killed, he regrew it to honor them. "Every day for the rest of my life, when I shave, I see my mustache and think about those guys. It's been fifty years, and I still have my mustache. When each of my five grandchildren turned thirteen, I shared this story with them and asked them to share it with their grandchildren, so they can remember my friends, too."

Ceremonial occasions and objects—from rituals to mourning exercises to mementos—are all ways of helping to contain and give shape to emotional times in our lives.

They are especially effective in the long goodbye part of a transition, as they help us acknowledge that the past is, indeed, past. They both embody—and keep in check—our uncertainties and fears. And they are statements—to ourselves and to others—that we've gone through a critical life change and are ready, however tentatively, for what comes next.

CHAPTER 9

Shed It

Give Up Old Mind-Sets

It's called the messy middle because it's messy. It's disorientating, disheartening, liberating for some, infuriating for others. Habits we've been attached to forever collapse; identities we've cultivated for years melt away. Personal stories we thought we'd be telling for a lifetime come to an abrupt end.

Now what?

My conversations show that people do two overriding things in this critical period of a life transition. They don't necessarily do these in order, they don't do them quickly or even consciously. But they do do them.

First, they shed things: mind-sets, routines, ways of being, delusions, dreams.

Second, they create things: new attitudes, aptitudes, skills, talents, means of expression.

We're going to explore the first one in this chapter and the second one in the next chapter. Let's begin with an example that has a bit of both.

"My Bullshit Was Going Out of My Backside"

Mark Lakeman was born in Portland, Oregon. "I was the Frankenstein child of two heroic, modernist designers, architects, and planners," he said. "I was cultivated in their creative household, then sent forth to do their bidding." Mark's father was the founder of the City of Portland's Urban Design Division; his mother was a scholar of early urban villages who dragged her son around the world, studying Neolithic communities.

"I got exposed to so much interesting content," Mark said. "Plus, throw in the sixties, John F. Kennedy asking us to consider what we could do for our country, I was just hardwired to think there was something we could do about it."

In high school, Mark channeled his zeal into creating a giant comic book, two feet by three feet, in which he repurposed Marvel superheroes and villains into space characters feuding over Western expansionism. "I think I was trying to compensate for my teenage angst."

Following a gap year renovating houses, Mark studied architecture for five years at the University of Oregon, then went to work at a local design firm.

"Fortunately, at exactly the point when I was questioning my career, there was a huge toxic waste cover-up," he said. "My firm was designing a Bank of America building in downtown Portland, right at the edge of the river, and it turns out our contractor was paying the government inspectors to ignore the fact that there was a high concentration of contaminated material in huge storage tanks that were buried on the site.

"The way this was disclosed," he continued, "was in a joking way. Everyone laughed as if it were no big deal and we weren't breaking the law."

Mark's response was to turn it into a big deal—and least for himself. "I did this beautiful job of quitting," he said. "I brought all six of my bosses into the conference room and lovingly harangued them about how we all had common aspirations when we went into design but now had abandoned them. I basically said, *I'm leaving but I still believe in you*. Years later, one of my bosses told me the speech had helped the firm to make some changes. It was nice to hear."

Mark then did what many people do in the wake of a lifequake. He drifted, he wandered, he got lost.

"I started traveling. It wasn't with much intention at first, I just knew I needed to go out and look around. I went to Europe, around the Mediterranean, then down in North Africa. I started asking people, 'What's wrong with me? What's wrong with my community?' And people said, 'You know, Americans aren't really interesting. You tend to talk a lot about how much things cost, and you don't listen very well.'"

But those people also asked him to hang around. For the next seven years, Mark lived on the road. He'd pitch up in a place, make some friends, they'd give him some work, and he'd live there for a while, then move on. All during this time, he was going through a process of jettisoning layers of his identity, peeling back, one after another, his pretensions, his Ugly American–ness, his tendency to talk too much. He felt raw and defenseless. "At one point I was dreaming of walking down to the bridge about six blocks away and jumping off."

But slowly he worked to unearth his core beliefs. He shed his attachment to money. "I had to simplify my life, liberate my need for comfort, stop trying to be a consumer." He dialed back his fixation with career. "I had to recalibrate, figure out how to work with alternative capital, stop thinking in terms of budget and accomplishment." He reduced his attachment to civilized comforts. "Finally I realized that in order to fully experience human patterns I would have to visit a pre-industrial people who had never been impacted by colonialism."

So he did. Mark traveled deep into the remote jungles of southeastern Mexico, where he was invited to live among the Lacandon Maya people, one of the most isolated tribes in the world, who reside in the Zapatista war zone on the border with Guatemala. "It was kind of like trying to find the Garden of Eden."

There, after months of building trust, Mark had an experience that would only have been possible, he believes, after all of the purging he'd put himself through. "There was this moment I never talk about but that I could pretty much call holy," he said. "I was sitting with this young man on the edge of a Mayan sacred house. The whole community was having a gathering. Everyone was wearing the same clothing. Except for some facial hair, they could have been androgynous. This man, whose name was Mario, had been my guide for months."

As the two of them were sitting cross-legged, a butterfly alighted on Mario's shoulder. "Then, with a wave of his hand, the butterfly leaves his shoulder and starts to fly above his hand. The butterfly begins tracing arcs of horizontal circles just above his open palm but not landing on it. Mario leans forward into a squat, puts out his other palm, and the butterfly hops onto that wrist, then goes back and forth in a kind of dance, I would say six times.

"Then, how can I describe this?" Mark continued. "The butterfly lands on his right index finger. Mario leans forward, as if he's offering the butterfly to me, and says, 'Put your finger up.' I put my finger up, and the butterfly clearly wasn't interested in jumping on me. So Mario leans in and seems to be trying to compel the butterfly with some urgency. Eventually the butterfly jumps from his finger onto mine. And, you know, I'm not really interested in Steven Spielberg effects, space aliens, planets exploding, but in that moment, watching the subtle dance between a butterfly and a human, I felt like there was a ten-year-old boy inside my body that was still alive and that there was more to life than I would ever have thought possible.

"And I remember feeling," he went on, "that something inside of me was melting away, like my bullshit was going out of my backside or something, I felt so affirmed, and that I had to recover that sense of doing something for the world that I had first felt when I was a boy."

Mark returned to Portland determined to carry with him the idea that humanity had lost communal gathering places like the one he had experienced that day. We had succumbed to the urban grid of industrial streets, closed front doors, minimal human contact. He started a guerilla design community called the City Repair Project. Their first initiative was to build a mobile teahouse, constructed out of doors and windows that could open and close, along with giant extending canopies that were modeled after butterfly wings. A team would set up this teahouse on Monday evenings in busy residential intersections and invite neighbors to bring desserts and enjoy music.

"It was a kind of fusion of a Mayan gathering place and a shop where you'd have afternoon tea in Oxford, England," he said. "We were saying we should repurpose intersections. My God, there are twenty-two thousand in this city."

The residents loved it; soon other neighborhoods started inviting the team to take over their intersections. But city officials balked. Mark harked back to the bedtime stories his father would tell him about battling corrupt local officials. Finally, when the public outcry grew loud enough, the mayor and city council passed a law to make the neighborhood gatherings legal. Mark's movement was underway. In the next quarter century, his organization would grow to incorporate "placemaking" activities from barn raising to painting over ugly crossroads in communities around the world.

The genesis, he says, was that butterfly moment. "I mean, to lose your job, you can sit there and bemoan, or you can see it as an opportunity for personal reinvention. I went into the cocoon of that world, felt safe and sacred, and became consumed with this desire to transform. I don't need it to be mystical, but I'm not closed off to the idea that I'm, like, inhabited by a butterfly or something. I returned to a primal state, became vulnerable, and came out again with wings."

The Lost Art of Getting Lost

The messy middle is all about what happens when we're in the state of in between. It involves a complicated alchemy of giving up old ways and experimenting with new ones, moving beyond what's past and beginning to define what's coming. In butterfly-speak, it's cocooning; in hero-speak, it's getting lost.

Before we delve into the question of how people handle getting lost—even take advantage of it on occasion—it's worth pausing to remember that getting lost is an unavoidable part of the process. And it's been that way since the dawn of storytelling.

Most major religions include the idea that significant human breakthroughs include periods of disconnection and disorientation. Hindus call this phase *forest dwelling*; the Abrahamic faiths liken it to desert dwelling. Abraham goes forth into the unknown; Moses leads the Israelites into the wilderness; the Israelites are exiled to Babylon; Jonah disappears into the whale; Jesus goes into the desert; Paul ventures on the road to Damascus; Muhammad retreats to the mountaintop.

Ancient myths have the same trope: Oedipus heads into the unknown, as do Hercules, Jason, Perseus, Achilles, and Odysseus. The same happens later on with Benedict, Antony, Buddha, Machiavelli, and Dante. Classic fairy tales have a similar theme: Little Red Riding Hood scampers into the scariness, as do Jack and Jill, Snow White, Sleeping Beauty, and Jack up his beanstalk. Joseph Campbell called this leg of the hero's journey *crossing the threshold*, when the hero leaves the ordinary world and embarks on an adventure.

That characterization perhaps makes this step more romantic than it feels. Margaret Atwood may have captured the sensation of disorientation better when she observed, "When you're in the middle of a story it isn't a story at all, but only a confusion; a dark roaring, a blindness, a wreckage of shattered glass and splintered wood; like a house in a whirlwind, or else a boat crushed by the icebergs or swept over the rapids, and all aboard powerless to stop it."

Now that's what it feels like to be lost!

And while it's small consolation when you're going through it, that is what you're supposed to feel. As André Gide said, "One doesn't discover new lands without consenting to lose sight of the shore for a very long time." The counterintuitive thing I learned from my conversations is how many people recognize, even welcome, this sensation of anguish. Of *hitting bottom* in the language of addiction. Because bottom means there's no place left to go but up. J. K. Rowling said of the moment, seven years after graduating from university, when she was a divorced, jobless, single mom, "as poor as it is possible to be in modern Britain, without being homeless" and "by every usual standard, the biggest failure I knew": Rock bottom "became the solid foundation on which I rebuilt my life."

Bruno Bettelheim famously titled his book on the hidden value of fairy tales *The Uses of Enchantment*. Maybe it's time to consider the inverse, *The Uses of Disenchantment*. There's plenty of spiritual evidence for this: "I once was lost, but now am found," goes the most famous hymn of all time, "Amazing Grace." There's plenty of psychology evidence, too: For decades researchers have found that people who experience identity crises—and manage to resolve them—are superior to others in achievement, intimacy, and adaptability.

But the best evidence of all may be in those fairy tales. The wolf is invariably the one who brings out the best in the hero. Without the wolf, the whole thing's merely a walk in the woods.

Here are some examples of how people embrace the meaning vacuum that comes in the midst of a life transition:

- Gina Bianchini said she still remembers exactly what she did after getting fired from her CEO job in Silicon Valley: "What I did that night, and essentially for weeks afterward, was drink red wine and eat french fries. Actually, the french fries were more important to me than the red wine. I just really wanted to eat french fries, especially with friends."

- Anna Krishtal found that after moving back home from Israel to be with her infirm mom, she had to acknowledge that she was flailing and directionless. "I think the experience I had with binge-watching, lying on my bed in yoga pants, my legs out, my laptop propped on my stomach, zoning out, gorging on episode after episode of *Parks and Recreation*, finally got to me. I remember thinking, *This is absurd. If a caveman walked in here right now, he would think this wasn't even human.* Like, *I'm fucking here, I could spend another three months wishing for a change or I have to make the change.*"
- Bob Hall returned home to Nebraska in his fifties after his stint writing *Batman* ended, his marriage failed, and he learned he was adopted—a three-car pileup that left him completely adrift. "I had no story," he said. "It felt like I didn't exist. It was as if the *Titanic* had suddenly shifted in the other direction. Everything was being reset, but I didn't know what it was being reset to."
- Brad Corrodi was devastated after being passed over to become partner at Booz Allen and then rebounding into a promising job at a startup that sputtered, too. He christened the experience *being in the quiet room*. "The quiet room is when you're sitting there in the spare bedroom, no one is calling, and you're wondering, *Can I muster up the confidence, and the conviction, and the motivation, to go back to my spreadsheet of potential investors and just start picking up the phone, trying another four calls, having small talk with secretaries, listening to the same lame excuses as to why someone can't talk to you or didn't call you back last week.* Anytime you're in one of those situations, the room goes quiet again, and you don't believe you can go on."

- Deb Copaken was so ambushed by four years of personal, professional, and health crises, she decided the only way to respond was by owning the conflagration. "I call these the chaos years. I look at these years of tumult and change as the most painful of my life—*Oh, my God, am I going to survive until tomorrow?*—but also the most beautiful. I think we all fear tremendously the lack of structure, the lack of care, the lack of love, the lack of everything we understand. I'm not saying I don't have dark moments. I'm saying that when I do, I'm able to say, *I'm having a dark moment right now.* I get through it by sitting in the back side of my feelings for a while, come out of it, and then I'm fine."

Three Paths Through the Woods

One common feature of these accounts is that people describe their messy middles with phrases like *the dark period, the chaos years, the wandering, the walkabout*. There's a sense of aimlessness, blindness, vagrancy, nomadism. We become exiles from the normal boundaries of life. Refugees from the routines of everyone around us.

How do we respond? We draw our own boundaries. We devise our own routines. We conjure up fresh ways to structure the otherwise structureless time we're in.

I hadn't been particularly focused on how we organize our time during transitions until I met Ida Benedetto. Ida grew up as a free-range kid in New York's Hudson Valley. "When I think back on my childhood, there are all these moments of me just going and exploring, usually solo, and finding great joy in doing that."

She also attended all-girls Catholic schools, which gave her an overlay of guilt. "While I loved wandering off, there was a level of danger I never wanted to expose myself to. I didn't experiment with drugs, I never had careless sex."

Ida bounced between college and travel, until a friend recommended she study game design. "I took a course and was like, *Whoa, what have I been doing my whole life?*"

After graduating, Ida and a boyfriend started organizing "trespass adventures" around New York City. These included a photo safari in a defunct sugar refinery, a concert on an abandoned observation deck, and a speakeasy in a water tower. Their signature event happened after the couple stopped off at a resort in the Poconos. "We pulled in and realized it was abandoned," she said. "We let ourselves in. There were all these cabins, a wedding-bell-shaped swimming pool, what seemed like the ghosts of honeymooners past."

They invited guests on a secret adventure. "We didn't tell them where they were going; we didn't tell them what to do when they got there. Over half the couples had sex."

The company grew; paid commissions started to roll in; Ida and her boyfriend were onto something big. But the romantic relationship that undergirded it started to fray. Her boyfriend had a wandering eye, Ida became needy and untrusting, and soon the partnership collapsed. "I guess we were one of those tumultuous, ugly relationships that produce brilliant, creative work."

Ida was a wreck. Her response, though, was instructive. She turned to what she knew best—game design—and its insights on how to create structured play. Specifically, Ida started going to sex parties, communal gatherings where singles, couples, gays, straights, and bis come together to play. She began using ayahuasca, a hallucinogenic drug made from an Amazonian vine that participants consume in controlled settings. She went on wilderness expeditions.

Ida went on to write a master's thesis on these kinds of danger-tinged activities called "Patterns of Transformation: Designing Sex, Death, and Survival in the 21st Century." She then parlayed her interest into designing group experiences for corporations. Her takeaway: "When your life is falling apart, you need anchors. If you approach transformation through designed experiences, the transition is more likely to succeed."

My conversation with Ida and other gamers taught me a valuable lesson about the need for structure—what gamers call *designed experiences*—in life transitions. There are three primary types of games. The first is a *sandbox.* These are games with strict boundaries and radical freedom within. Examples include *Minecraft*, *Farmville*, and the more exploratory version of *Fortnite*. The second is a *quest.* These are games with the goal of achieving a certain end and earning a specific reward. Examples include *Pokémon*, *World of Warcraft*, and scavenger hunts. The third is a *cycle.* These are games with a series of loops in which the goal is to perform better each time. Examples include *Mario Bros.*, *Candy Crush*, and *Pac-Man*.

These categories, with their differing approaches to routine, risk, and reassurance, struck me as a perfect analogy for how people organize their lives during periods of instability. So I added a question to my interviews: "How did you structure your time during your transition?"

Sure enough, a similar pattern emerged. Some people gravitate toward a more exploratory approach, akin to a sandbox: They sleep around, experiment with drugs, tinker with their appearance, redecorate. Others adopt a more linear, quest-like path: They join a twelve-step program, go on a pilgrimage, enroll in classes, open a bed-and-breakfast. Others choose a cyclical model: They attend religious services, meditate, garden, journal.

Of the scores of responses we coded, all but two fit this rubric. The cyclical model was the most popular, suggesting that people prefer regularity. The sandbox approach was second, a reminder that many people do stretch themselves in these times and test their limits. The quest type was third. A number of people did mention using a combination of the three.

Here are some examples of how people structured their most unstructured times:

Cycle

Eric Johnson started attending church every Sunday.

Helen Churko joined a monthly writing group.

Chavie Weisberger went into therapy.

John Smitha volunteered with veterans' groups three times a week.

Melanie Krause planted vegetables.

Margaret Klein embraced the life cycle events of the Jewish sacred calendar.

Quest

Barbara Prestigiacomo, a former perfumer, enrolled in pest control school.

Bob Hall set out to find his biological parents.

Ed Conant made a multistate road trip with his third wife to find a retirement home.

Michael Angelo made a cross-country trip to save his failing marriage.

Leo Eaton went on a walkabout to all the places he'd lived with his wife, before he finally arrived on the Greek island they had called home, where he sprinkled her ashes in a garden.

Bret Parker set out after being diagnosed with Parkinson's to run seven marathons on seven continents in seven days. He succeeded.

Sandbox

> Matt Weyandt quit his job and moved to a hut on the beach in Costa Rica with his wife and newborn baby.
>
> Doc Shannon experimented with drugs.
>
> Serena Stier, having dated only her husband before their marriage, went through a period following his suicide when she experimented with men and "had to find out about myself sexually."
>
> Jason Doig, after retiring from the NHL, dabbled in real estate, stocks, and carbon offsetting.
>
> Ann Imig went on more than a dozen twenty-minute informational interviews in all different fields after giving up on acting and having a miscarriage. Her opening line: "I'm trying to figure out what I'm doing with myself. I want to hear why you love what you do."
>
> Sarah Holbrooke dated indiscriminately. "My husband had just cheated on me while I was pregnant with his baby. I'd just gotten divorced. I lost the baby fat right away. I had big boobs because I was nursing. I wasn't forty and wrinkled or fifty and sagging. My clock wasn't ticking. I wasn't looking for Mr. Future, I was looking for Mr. Meantime. And I was really clear with everyone: 'I'm not looking for a serious relationship. If you are, don't spend time with me.' And you know what, that's not so hard to find! It was a little bit crazy and a little bit wild and that suited me at the time."

Sarah eventually fell in love again; she's been happily married for twenty years and has two more children. Her story is a reminder: Many of the people who choose a cycle, quest, or sandbox do so because it's their natural rhythm. But for others, the structure they adopt might be a temporary fix that gives them the structure they need at the moment, even allows them to test out a different life shape, before they resume the rest of their life.

A Field Guide to Shedding

Acknowledging that you're lost and finding a way to structure your time, as critical as those steps are to persevering through the messy middle, still pale next to the real work of entering this pivotal period: We have to let go of old ways. How exactly do people do that?

The same way animals do.

The biological process of molting is how animals routinely cast off their horns, hair, skin, fur, feathers, wool, even gonads. Snakes shed their skin, birds shed their feathers, crabs shed their shells, grasshoppers shed their entire exoskeletons. They do this because they're growing. They're undergoing a change in size, shape, season, or maturity. They can't achieve the new state without first casting off remnants of the old.

Humans undergo a similar process when we pass through a life transition. We molt mind-sets, convictions, routines, dreams. Psychologists have found that up to half of the actions we perform every day are not because of decisions but because of habits. And guess what? We shuck those, too. The process isn't always easy. Habits are "not to be flung out of the window," wrote Mark Twain, "but coaxed down-stairs a step at a time." But my conversations suggest this isn't always true: People often embrace the opportunity for change.

The idea that people can grow in times of change is another significant distinction between today's whenever life crises and the old "midlife crisis" model. The traditional view had been that people confronting their mortality were somehow reluctant to accept their limitations. *Oh, well, guess I'm not going to play center field for the Yankees, make vice president, or retire to that private island. Guess I'll cheat on my spouse—or buy a sports car—instead.*

Now that view has changed. Many of the qualities people shed are ones they *didn't* admire, like people pleasing, overeating, or drinking to excess. Sure, some of what people shed are treasured pleasures, like wearing a bikini, riding a motorcycle, or playing pickup soccer. But just as many were vices, sins, or vanities we're just as happy to cast off.

The bottom line: Giving up identities, whether painful or pleasurable, is a necessary precondition for making way for the new identities waiting to onboard. It might even be a source of satisfaction.

The biggest category of things people relinquished in their transitions was parts of their personality.

Carol Berz had to abandon her sense of inadequacy after being elected to city council in Chattanooga. Christian Picciolini had to forfeit his intoxication with power after he left the neo-Nazis. Deborah Fishman ditched being obedient to men when she stepped away from Orthodox Judaism. Michael Mitchell had to dispense with the idea that he should always be doing something constructive after he retired from four decades as a doctor. Ellen Shafer had to give up wearing sexy clothes when she returned to North Dakota from Minneapolis, after a colleague told her she could no longer show so much cleavage at work. Karen Peterson-Matchinga stopped trying to make everyone around her happy following the year she spent nursing her injured husband back to health. "I don't have time anymore. My life is too precious to me, and I want all my sacred space to myself."

The next largest bloc was letting go of an emotion.

Mary-Denise Roberts was so scarred from a childhood history of sexual abuse that she struggled to move beyond the fear that the man she was dating would strike out at her at any moment. Eric Haney made a conscious effort to dispense with his need for discipline, orderliness, and control after he retired from his military career and his paramilitary security business to become a full-time writer. Tiffany Grimes had to let go of her attraction to her wife's body when Dade transitioned to a man. Loretta Parham loved being a grandmother, but when she was forced to raise her granddaughters, she had to pass up merely indulging them and instead become more of a disciplinarian.

Many people spoke of abandoning certain aspects of their lifestyle.

Coco Papy had to abandon walking everywhere when she moved from Brooklyn back to her hometown of Savannah. Amber Alexander had to abstain from date nights with her husband after her son was diagnosed with a brain tumor. Ann Ramer sacrificed time with friends during the years she was caring for her two children with multiple cancers. Leigh Wintz had to abolish her habit of walking into the house and immediately opening the fridge when she finally committed to losing sixty pounds. And in one of the more remarkable cases I heard, Randy Riley had to give up the idea that she knew her own body after completing her liver transplant, because suddenly she craved guacamole when she never liked it before, started loving spaghetti when she never ate pasta before, and had blond pubic hair when before she had dark. “I know that’s total TMI,” she said, “but it took some getting used to!”

A number of people said they had to jettison certain beliefs.

Lester Johnson had to give up celebrating Christmas and eating ham when he converted to Islam. Jenny Wynn had to scrap being a follower when she became senior pastor of her church. Kate Hogue, after surviving the tornado, had to discard her view that God would solve every problem and begin to see God as being present and relying on humans to be his hands. Janelle Hanchett, after getting sober, had to “stop walking into every situation asking what I could get out of it and say what can I give to others.” John Austin, upon stepping down from a quarter century in law enforcement, had to get used to not having a gun and to playing by the same rules as civilians. “Wait, now I have to stand in line when I fly? Now I have to stop for that traffic light? Now I have to persuade people to listen to me? I used to be able to compel them.”

Finally, a lot of people were forced to abandon certain attitudes toward money.

Jeffrey Sparr had to drop his need for a regular paycheck when he quit his family's textile business to start a nonprofit around mental health. In order to leave her corporate job to start her own business, Gena Zak had to abandon her childish need to prove to her mother that she was successful. Vivienne Ming had to give up the status (and income) of a job at Stanford after she was fired while transitioning from male to female. Melanie Krause had to do away with going to her favorite Chinese restaurant, seeing movies, or any other night out after she and her husband poured all their savings into starting their winery in Boise. "It was really annoying and stressful to say, 'Okay, it's Friday night. What should we do? Well, we don't have any money, should we just stay home and have sex?' I'm not sure you want to write that down, but that's what it was really like!"

Like many aspects of life transitions, the act of shedding is fundamentally an act of adjusting your personal story. It's a narrative event. It involves closing certain chapters in your life story in order to open a new one. That new chapter, as it happens, is built around one of the more exciting things I heard about: a period of breathtaking creativity.

CHAPTER 10

Create It

Try New Things

A lot of going through a life transition can feel like a slog. There's accepting the uncertain situation, ritualizing your change in status, shedding your old impulses. But somewhere along the way, something unexpected happens: The process starts to get inventive, imaginative, even buoyant. You experiment with a fresh diversion; you pick up a long-forgotten interest; you start to revisit your story.

You try. Something. Anything. In a way that didn't seem possible even a few days earlier.

And in a pattern I didn't see coming, a remarkable number of people described how at this otherwise dreary juncture—at the bottom of their massive life shift—they turn to creativity. And not just *creativity* in the abstract sense of a fresh approach to a familiar problem, but in the actual sense of creating something new. They start to dance, cook, sing, paint; they write poems, letters, thank-you notes, diary entries; they pick up banjos, tap shoes, juggling balls, garden shears.

At the moment of greatest chaos, they respond with creation.

"What I Really Enjoyed Was Exploding Paint on the Canvas"

Zachary Herrick was the premature child of African American crack addicts in Kansas City who was adopted by white parents who had two other black children. "Even in the eighties, people would look at us at the pool, a white couple with a bunch of black kids, and say, 'Why?'" He was mocked as "funky monkey"; someone spray-painted *NEGRO* on his sister's car.

With various learning issues from his birth, Zach found school difficult and unappealing. He played sports, had a job, was popular, but grades were never his strength. "My parents really pushed that you can't let external forces shape who you are, so that's something I took and ran with." After graduation he went to work in a cabinet factory, then in construction, until his father, a Vietnam veteran, suggested he join the army.

"I loved it from the very first day," he said. "I made the most friends I'd ever had." He breezed through infantry training in Fort Benning and was transferred to Hawaii. "I'm thinking, *That's nice: beaches and women!*" But it was the mountains the army was after, as the Hawaiian high terrain is similar to that in Afghanistan. Soon enough, Zach and his battalion were in Kandahar Province.

Three months into their deployment, in the third week of June, Zach was on a mission to hunt down the Taliban in the Arghandab valley just north of Pakistan. "We land at two o'clock in the morning and start going down the mountain toward the town. We were about a mile away from the village, when we stopped to assess the situation. Then we were ambushed."

Zach was dressed in full gear that day—helmet, rifle, ammunition mags, grenades. Now, for the first time, he was also carrying something else: fear.

"We started to engage the enemy. They were about thirty meters away. There was this one guy, sitting outside a mud hut. I could look into his eyes. I mean, it was a close fight. *Boom!* Then I got hit by a sniper rifle—or an

AK—I'm not sure. It felt like a firecracker going off in my mouth. It was daylight, I remember, because I went back into the hut where my buddies were. I said, 'I got shot.' They said, 'Yeah, we know.'"

Zach lay down on the floor, while the firefight continued around him. "I didn't think it was that bad," he said. "I could still see, I could feel that my jawbone was hurt, I was swallowing teeth and bones. I couldn't breathe through my nose but I could through my mouth."

The medic came in and called out, "Hey, Black Curly!" "That was my nickname," Zach said. "I put my thumb up. He runs over and his eyes get soooo big. And for a split second he kind of looked at me, like, *Holy crap*. Then he gets his bag and starts pushing the gauze on me. He starts shoving my face full of it, here, there, wherever. 'Just keep awake,' he says. I thought to myself, *If I die right now, that's okay, because at least I'm dying surrounded by the best friends I've ever had*. Just then my squad leader comes in. He also got shot in the face. He sits down and we kind of look at each other like, *Man, this is a bad day*."

In rapid order, Zach was shoved into a Chinook helicopter, airlifted to Germany, and then transported to the Walter Reed medical center outside Washington, DC. "When we took off on that last flight, the pain started coming—in my arms, my legs, my chest. It felt like forever. I started choking on my blood, I could feel my jagged teeth, I couldn't breathe. But I said to myself, *There's no way I'm dying on this plane*. I woke up to a beautiful blond nurse with these big, beautiful smiling eyes, and I said to myself, *I'm alive*."

It was Zach's sister who first brought a mirror and showed him what no one had dared say out loud: His face had been shot off. There was virtually nothing left of his oral cavity, lips, nostrils, and mandible. In the coming years, Zach would have thirty surgeries from the tip of his nose to the tip of his chin, including sewing his tongue back on, inserting a new jawbone, and reconstructing his face. He ate exclusively by feeding tube. He was confined to a wheelchair from losing so much weight. "It was a long road," he said. "Not only physical, but emotional. I basically couldn't function."

He made a plan to take his life.

But then something unexpected happened. Zach had been transferred to solo living by this point, the tubes had been removed, his weight had begun to come back. His mother had moved next door. But he had to give up many of the foods he'd once enjoyed. "Spicy foods were out. My mouth couldn't handle them," he said.

So one day he decided to take up cooking. "My mom encouraged me," he said. "'You like eating,' she said, 'you should make your own food.' It was also a trick I started to use when dating." He learned to make lamb chops, baked chicken, grilled salmon. "I like barbecuing," he said. "And breakfast. I just made pancakes today. Panini sandwiches are my specialty. I love it all, I love experimenting, I love creating things."

And cooking wasn't the only thing he embraced.

"Writing really helped me," he said. "I started at Walter Reed. Then I took a writing class at USO. Now I'm in my third one. You can create a whole different world, you can write your feelings down. That really helped me. I learned how to identify things that were difficult for me to say or get out of my head, but I could put them on paper." He wrote poetry, stories, essays. "Instead of saying to someone, 'I had a bad dream,' I can write about it and feel better."

Then he started to paint.

"Flowers, trees, stuff like that," he said. "But I'm an infantryman, what I really enjoyed was exploding paint on the canvas. That was exciting! It was aggressive in a way that wasn't damaging another human being, which I enjoyed."

"Wait, you started splattering paint on the canvas?" I asked.

"Yeah, you know that guy? Jackson Pollock. Like him."

Whoa. I asked Zachary what his sixteen-year-old self would have thought of the idea that his twenty-five-year-old self was making pancakes, writing poetry, and painting like Jackson Pollock.

"I probably would have said it was stupid," he said.

So what happened? What made tough-guy rifleman Zachary Herrick, a onetime anti-student who barely graduated from high school, turn to cooking, writing, and abstract expressionist painting in such a way that it would renew his confidence, help him court a woman who looked beyond his disfigurement and married him, and finally allow him to get to the point, not of killing himself, but of opening his own solar energy company?

"I think of it as a different way of expressing yourself," he said. "Instead of taking down the enemy with a gun, now I take down the enemy with a strong vocabulary or a strong voice. It helped me transcend to a different realm. I'm still Zach, but now I'm Zach, the creative guy. I'm Zach who can splatter paint on the canvas and make it beautiful. I'm Zach who can connect through poetry. I'm still strong physically, but now I can shift to other ways of being. I'm the full 360."

The Matisse Rule: Experiment

In January 1941, the seventy-one-year-old French master Henri Matisse, already heralded as perhaps the greatest painter of the twentieth century, was lying in a hospital room in Nice preparing to die. Doctors had discovered a tumor in his colon that they deemed untreatable. Pushed by his daughter Marguerite, Matisse undertook a treacherous twelve-hour journey toward German-occupied Lyon, where doctors performed an experimental surgery to remove fourteen inches of his intestine. The procedure took four days and brought him even closer to death.

"In those little moments of calm, between two pangs, I imagined the inside of a tomb," Matisse recalled, "a little space, completely enclosed, with no doors. And I told myself, 'No, I prefer still being around even if it does mean suffering!'"

And he suffered. For three months the great painter remained indoors; he received only a handful of visitors, and to them he was gruff. When Matisse finally ventured out to a nearby park, the nuns nicknamed him *Le Ressuscité*, "the man who rose from the dead." The artist picked up the theme himself that May in a letter to his son: "I was resigned to the idea that I would never get off the operating table alive. So now I feel as if I had come back from the dead. It changes everything. Time present and time future are an unexpected bonus."

What he did with that bonus was reinvent the history of art. Matisse would go on to live another fourteen years, but he was an invalid, confined to bed, and unable to stand up, hold a paintbrush, or even see that well. His response was to devise an entirely new way to create images that he called "drawing with scissors." He would take painted sheets of paper, in saturated blues, yellows, and reds so vivid he had to wear sunglasses to protect his eyes, cut them in bold, graphic shapes, and then have his assistant place them on the wall. As he was unable to accrue new experiences, the worlds he brought to life in these cutouts—circuses, gardens, dancers, women—were "crystallizations" drawn from memories of his youth.

It was a life story project of its own, and critics have called Matisse's cutouts the most prodigious work of his already magnificent career. From the shadows of the valley of death, he created the vibrant signature of what it means to have a "second life."

And he's in good company. Creativity may seem like an unexpected response to a life transition (it did to me), but it turns out to be quite common. History is filled with stories of people who reacted to setbacks with flurries of imagination. Michelangelo responded to torquing his back to paint the Sistine Chapel by making images that were groundbreaking in their anatomical fluidity; Monet adjusted to blurry vision from cataracts by making his water lilies less detailed but even more evanescent and ethereal; Frida Kahlo rebounded from a traffic accident at eighteen that confined her to a wheelchair by switching her career from science to art; Beethoven answered his worsening deafness with an unrivaled burst of originality. "Thanks to [virtue] and to my art, I did not end my life by suicide," he wrote.

Sure, these are among the more creative minds in history. Easy for them to make art out of misery! But the reasons why they responded to their setbacks with leaps of imagination prove remarkably applicable to the rest of us.

First, creativity thrives on isolation and disconnection. Studies of creativity for two decades have found a consistent pattern: Those facing adversity often suffer from social exclusion, a sense of being ostracized from society, and a feeling of being out of sync or out of touch with those around them. These attitudes, in turn, give these individuals more freedom to take risks, to experiment, to explore means of expression outside the social mainstream. A study of people living with long-term illness who turned to art found that their experience facing hardship sharpened their perceptions, increased their sensitivity, and stoked their desire to address deep issues around life. They craved creative outlets.

Second, creativity flourishes in marginal spaces and liminal times. Henri Poincaré, the nineteenth-century mathematician, offered a memorable description of how ideas get born in moments of betwixt and between. One evening, he reported, contrary to his custom, he drank black coffee and couldn't sleep. "Ideas rose in crowds. I felt them collide until pairs interlocked." He likened these ideas to gnats, swarming in every direction, crashing into one another, dancing. Such moments often follow periods of intense concentration, he found, when you're least expecting them, half-asleep, or focused on something else entirely. Going through a life transition is a never-ending stream of such moments. No wonder we let the gnats dance in these periods and find ourselves embracing unexpected ideas.

Finally, creativity feeds on chaos. A common theme in stories of creativity is how bursts of novelty or invention emerge in moments of rupture or upheaval. Just think of any artistic breakthrough of the last century—jazz, rock and roll, cubism, abstract expressionism—all were born in some way of major breaches in the world. What applies to societies also applies to individuals. When we go through disruptions, sprigs of innovation start to appear. As my conversations showed, sometimes these fragile sprigs blossom into new versions of ourselves.

Here are some examples of the breadth of creative pursuits people began in their transitions:

- Gayla Paschall started building hand-painted birdhouses after getting caught up in a faculty scandal at Emory and losing her research position. Soon she was selling her creations at a gallery.
- Hal Eastman, a Stanford MBA whose thirty-year career included stints at Boeing and Ford, helming two public companies, and starting two companies of his own, abruptly stopped working at age fifty-five. Seeking a change, he spotted a dancer one day in a restaurant near his home in Idaho and asked if he could photograph her in nature. "It's not sexual," he said, "bring your boyfriend if it would make you feel more comfortable." He went on to publish five books of fine art photography, including one of time-lapse images of dancers in the outdoors, another of bareback horse riders in dreamlike states, another of rhythmic forms in nature.
- Sarah Rose Siskind learned to play the ukulele while going through a depression after leaving Fox News and renouncing her conservative views. "It's a great instrument to get you through a transition because even when you fuck up, it sounds beautiful."
- Evan Walker-Wells taught himself to cook and play guitar while he was going through chemo. "I was learning how to dice onions and having these fever dreams at night. The two had nothing to do with each other, except I really wanted to do the onions right, and it became a vessel for my anxiety."

- Jenny Wynn began drawing visual representations of her prayers after being elevated to senior pastor. "I'm normally so focused on language; this felt like the spirit interceding with signs that were too deep for words."
- Khaliqa Baqi set up a sewing room in her home after leaving her husband and "started making beautiful creations with fabric."
- Jeffrey Sparr, the Ohio State tennis player who was debilitated by OCD, left his family's business, and opened a nonprofit using art therapy to help people with mental illness, was petrified about giving his first speech. What if he had an episode? "I'm down in the basement practicing. I come up to the kitchen and say to my wife, 'Hon, I got an idea. I'm going to paint live?' She says, 'You're fucking nuts.' I said, 'Watch this.' I put on a fedora, a splattered white painter's smock, and create this whole persona. Then I started painting. She said, 'Okay, you can do it.'" He later used this technique in two TED Talks.
- And in one of the more inventive acts of creativity I heard, Vivienne Ming created an entirely new voice. After transitioning into a woman, Vivienne, who holds a doctorate in theoretical neuroscience, read research papers, consulted doctors, and concluded that the biggest challenge transgender women face is the resonance of their voice. So she designed a series of exercises to lengthen her vocal tract, giving her pitch a more female range. "Now, even when I'm anonymous on the phone, people say *ma'am*, which gives me the undying pleasure of being able to respond with, 'I think you mean *doctor*,' because, really, I'm a pain in the ass."

The Baldwin Rule: Write

In early November of my freshman year at college, I went to a large lecture hall at the Yale University Art Gallery to hear a talk by James Baldwin. I can't remember what motivated me; I think I went alone. Baldwin, the storied novelist, essayist, and activist, was fifty-nine at the time. And though I didn't know it, he had already earned a reputation as the giver of blistering bons mots about writing.

> Talent is insignificant. I know a lot of talented ruins. Beyond talent lie all the usual words: discipline, love, luck, but, most of all, endurance.

> If you are going to be a writer there is nothing I can say to stop you; if you're not going to be a writer nothing I can say will help you. What you need at the beginning is somebody to let you know that the effort is real.

> The whole language of writing for me is finding out what you don't want to know, what you don't want to find out. But something forces you to anyway.

Sure enough, at the end of the lecture, someone stood up and asked Baldwin if he had any advice for budding writers. Even though I had no inkling at the time of trying to become a writer myself, I can still remember every syllable of his answer.

> The only thing you need to become a writer is a table, a chair, a piece of paper, and a pencil.

While today that answer seems a tad quaint, with its "Lincoln-in-the-log-cabin-by-candlelight" old-fashionedness, at the time it struck me with epic, Mount Rushmore–like authority.

Wanna be a writer, kid? Shut up and write.

I thought of his answer repeatedly while doing the Life Story Project.

I was flabbergasted by the sheer volume of people who told me that out of the blue, in the midst of their life transition, they started to write. Just as the world seemed to be its most volatile and the ground underneath their feet the most fluid, they found a table, a chair, a piece of paper, and a pencil, and started to write themselves back to life.

There's good evidence suggesting why. In 1986, the inventive psychologist James Pennebaker of the University of Texas at Austin conducted an experiment in which he asked a group of students to write their thoughts and feelings about a traumatic life experience. A control group was asked to write about superficial topics. For logistical reasons of classroom availability, the students were instructed to do this for fifteen minutes a day, four days in a row.

What Pennebaker found was dramatic. Many students cried while writing; they poured out long, heartfelt descriptions of challenging moments in their childhoods; they described dreaming of their challenging experiences over the course of the four days. The immediate aftermath of the experiment was an *increase* in sadness and anxiety. But then something profound happened. When Pennebaker followed up with the students months later, he found a marked *decrease* in visits to the student health center for illness and a greater sense of value and meaning. Seventy percent said they understood themselves better.

Since that initial experiment, hundreds of follow-ups have been conducted around the world. The results are stunning. People who write about their most stressful life experiences develop greater insight into their emotions, can express themselves more fully, even show evidence of a strengthened immune system. People who've been laid off from their jobs who write about their feelings not only cope with their resulting marital, medical, and money woes more easily, they also get hired more quickly. Within three months, 27 percent of *freewriters*, as Pennebaker calls them, landed new jobs, compared with 5 percent in the control group. By seven months,

57 percent of those who wrote about their layoffs had jobs, three times the control.

Pennebaker says he can't isolate one reason why writing works. Participants say they come to a new understanding of their problems; situations that once seemed overwhelming become easier to resolve; once these circumstances are resolved, there's less reason to worry about them anymore. Central to the act of writing is a process of growth, of slowly gaining control of their narrative. On day one, participants tend to describe the event; by the last day, they give shape, context, and purpose to it. The act of writing speeds up the act of meaning-making.

That last explanation—writing as a meaning accelerator—resonates most deeply with the stories I heard. Writing is a supercharged form of the storytelling we already do in our heads. It forces us to take ideas that are abstract and unstructured, sometimes even in the back of our minds, and put them into some form that's both concrete and structured. Along the way, the ideas become sharper, the emotions crisper, and the meaning clearer. And what once seemed like a solitary source of suffering begins to feel both safer and more universal. Also, by converting our thoughts into words, we participate, just for a moment, in the act of creation.

Here are some examples people shared with me of how writing helped ease their transitions:

- Karen Peterson-Matchinga, following a brutal year spent tending her husband after his fall and donating her bone marrow to her brother, turned for comfort to an unusual kind of self-expression: joke writing. She started doing stand-up comedy in clubs around LA. "I had come out of a situation where the only relief we had for two years was to laugh. And I thought, *I should put myself in a show.* I would show up at open mic night and there's all these angry young dudes who only wanted to make dick jokes. They got very uncomfortable because, at fifty-one, I represented their mom."

- Dwayne Hayes started a magazine about fatherhood—*STAND: For Men Who Give a Damn*—after his wife gave birth to stillborn twin girls.
- Ivy Woolf Turk, after being imprisoned for participating in a $27 million real estate Ponzi scheme, began penning long handwritten letters to her children that sustained her until she was released and opened a support group for formerly incarcerated women.
- Leigh Wintz kept a weight loss journal in which she wrote down how much she weighed, how she was feeling about her diet, and how she learned to reward herself in ways other than food. "One of the recurring themes was *How can I be unhappy?* I had plenty of money, I had education, my kids were healthy. It was like I had survivor's guilt."
- Ed Conant, a retired Cold War submarine officer turned defense contractor, started writing op-eds about the dysfunction in Washington for his local newspaper in Georgia.
- Carol Berz overcame her imposter syndrome upon being elected city council member by learning to slap back at the constituents who wrote her obnoxious emails. "People would write me letters that began, *You're a real piece of shit.* Usually men. I used to write back, *Thank you very much for your note. I respect your opinion.* Finally, I decided, screw this. I started writing these fuck-you emails. *Don't you ever threaten me again, and if you do, I'm going to the police.* It was part of learning to be myself."
- Rosemary Daniell began writing poetry after suffering postpartum depression. "I was twenty-four years old, I saw a flyer for a modern poetry class at the continuing ed program at Emory. I had never heard of Emily Dickinson or any of those people, so it was like being evangelized. Everybody in the class thought I was real funny because I would say things like, *I put an ejaculation point at the end of the line*, and I couldn't pronounce *Oedipus Rex*. But my life suddenly changed." She's been a professional poet for sixty years.

The Tharp Rule: Dig

Twyla Tharp is one of the most forward-looking artists of the last sixty years. Since forming her own dance company in 1965, she has choreographed one hundred twenty-nine dances, twelve television specials, six Hollywood movies, four Broadway shows, and two figure skating routines. She received a Tony, two Emmys, the National Medal of Arts, the Kennedy Center Honor, and a MacArthur "genius" award. She's known for breaking barriers, stretching boundaries, and pushing herself and her dancers to the very limits of the cutting edge. And yet, in her book *The Creative Habit*, Tharp makes the unexpected point that sometimes the most effective way to work through a difficult life situation is not to look forward for inspiration, but backward.

Tharp relates that "one of the more successful executives I know" once told her that when he's stuck, he reads through some of his company's four- or five-year-old files. The seemingly tedious task never fails to bring back a torrent of memories and spark a host of fresh ideas. "Look, it's very rare to come across something truly original in a corporate environment," the man said. Most of the good ideas are locked away in file cabinets or in people's minds. The executive is onto something, Tharp concludes. "While most people in the workplace—and in the arts—think they have to be constantly looking forward to be edgy and creative, this man found that the real secret of creativity is to *go back and remember.*"

Tharp's description of her personal process helped me understand something I had been hearing in my conversations. When she's in a rut, instead of performing science fiction and transporting herself to the future, she performs archaeology and transports herself to the past. She digs out old photos, listens to old music, channels old mentors, and, most of all, recovers old memories. "Once you realize the power of memory, you begin to see how much is at your disposal in previously underappreciated places."

A clear theme of the Life Story Project is that when people are remaking themselves in their transitions, they find comfort—and renourishment—in their past. They resuscitate former passions, reignite childhood fantasies, revive long-dormant dreams. Remember that paint set, tennis racket, or trumpet you packed away under the bed? How about that desire to build a boat, open a wine shop, or grow perfect tomatoes? *Oh, right, now it's coming back to me, I used to want to tap-dance, sing in the choir, sauté my way through* Mastering the Art of French Cooking. For many people, the worst of times in their lives turn out to be the best of times to excavate a former interest and turn it into a rejuvenating task.

Here are some examples of how people dug into their past to jump-start their present:

- Janay Brower, who grew up in poverty in Grand Rapids, rose to become head of the homeless coalition, then left in an ugly shake-up, and found herself returning to poetry. "I would drop my kid off at school, go to Starbucks, and write these little poems and reflections. That's when I realized I had forgotten what I used to love. I kept thinking, *It's like I get amnesia about these things that grounded me.*"
- Helen Kim, in the wake of her stomach cancer and retirement from teaching college biology, picked up a continuing ed brochure one day and noticed a class called Adult Ballet. "As a little girl, I had seen a performance of *Swan Lake* by the Bolshoi Ballet and thought, *Wow, this is so cool.* But I got turned off by the idea of being on your toes in these funny little shoes. This time I thought, *I'm going to be a ballerina.* I went to the class, and all the other ladies were so far ahead of me. A few weeks later I went to the teacher and said I had to quit. He said, 'No, no no, you've got the form.' I think he wanted the money. But then the other ladies, said, 'No, no, no,' so I decided to continue."
- John Ruskey, a Colorado native, read a copy of *Huckleberry Finn* in boarding school, and with a classmate built a raft after graduation and

floated five months down the Mississippi River, before crashing into an electrical tower south of Memphis. Nearly twenty years later, going through a difficult time after leaving work at the Delta Blues Museum in Mississippi, he returned to his first love, the Big River. "I bought a canoe and started paddling, and exploring, and reconnecting with the great wild spirit of the outdoors. I began drawing and then painting what I was seeing out there. And every time I went onto the water, the river seemed to reward me with something that made me go back the next day." He soon opened a company that led guided canoe trips down the Mississippi.

- Laura Deitchler, an elementary school teacher and mom in Lincoln, Nebraska, learned from her husband that he planned to start selling pot vaporizers. After kicking him out and spiraling into depression, she rekindled a childhood dream of being a novelist. "The divorce ended up being a chance to hit refresh, to try and re-create the person that I was meant to be and the life I was meant to have. That person kind of went dormant for many years; she just needed some tending." One Saturday afternoon Laura drove to Barnes & Noble and bought a stack of Moleskine journals, which she filled with accounts of her dating life, which in turn became the basis for an amusing autobiographical book.

The Feldenkrais Rule: Sweat

Moshe Feldenkrais had one of those colorful lives that fill twentieth century spy novels and twenty-first-century biopics. Born Jewish in present-day Ukraine in 1904, he moved to Belarus when he was eight. In the winter of 1918, at age fourteen, Feldenkrais walked from Belarus to Palestine to flee persecution, with no passport and only a pistol in his boot and a math text in his knapsack. The temperature reached well below zero. To survive, he briefly joined a traveling circus, where the acrobats taught him to fall safely. By the time he reached Krakow, two hundred people had joined his march, including fifty children.

Feldenkrais settled in Palestine, where he worked as a laborer and quickly learned to defend himself from widespread knife attacks. Others were interested, so he wrote a book called *Jiu-Jitsu and Self-Defense*, which became required reading in the fledgling Jewish defense forces. When he learned the founder of judo, Jigoro Kano, was coming to Paris, Feldenkrais went to meet him and hand over his book. Impressed, Kano asked where he'd gotten it. "I wrote it," he said. "I don't believe you," Kano replied. "Attack me with a knife," Feldenkrais responded. Soon the knife went flying, and Kano hired Feldenkrais to popularize judo in Europe.

Feldenkrais moved to Paris, earned a PhD in physics, and worked in a laboratory of two Nobel physicists, where he built a device that helped split the atom. In 1940, his biographer recounts, Feldenkrais fled the approaching Gestapo, carrying two suitcases containing military secrets and two liters of heavy water, which could be used to make a nuclear weapon. His task was to keep them out of the hands of the Nazis. Unable to find a ship to England, Feldenkrais again started walking, this time with his wife. They finally joined an Allied naval evacuation, which was organized by a British officer named Ian Fleming, who went on to write the James Bond novels.

During the journey, Feldenkrais began to notice that his knee was flaring up. With his subtle knowledge of anatomy, he traced how the injury affected other parts of his body—his feet, his back, his shoulders. These, in turn, shaped his gait, which in turn affected his entire mood. Feldenkrais began the process of breaking down every movement into its microcomponents, which he realized were influenced not just by physical stress but by emotional stress, too.

After the war, Feldenkrais began a practice that combined mind-body healing to improve mobility and increase quality of life that came to be called the Feldenkrais Method. His core insight: When we go through periods of turmoil, our bodies share the brunt. To create new selves, we have to create new ways of moving. We have to tweak how we walk, sit, stand, lie, dance, even have sex. We have to rewrite the story not just of our lives, but of our bodies.

I love this story, in part, because in the wake of my seventeen-hour cancer surgery, I was left with a medical miracle of a left leg, but also one that's more than an inch shorter than my right, missing half a quad, and with a fibula that's located in my thigh, not my calf. In the years since, I've done more than a lifetime's worth of physical therapy and have had to rethink dressing, climbing, writing, and sleeping, along with every recreational activity you can think of.

So it wasn't exactly a surprise in my conversations when person after person described how during their transitions they sought changes involving their bodies. They adopted extreme workout routines, enrolled in hot yoga, signed up for Tough Mudder, took up ballroom dancing, tried swinging, went vegan. What *was* surprising was the conviction so many had that these small adjustments in their physical routines opened the door to larger adjustments in their identity. Changing their body became a stepping-stone for changing their mind. In this way, going biking in the park can be every bit as creative as journaling, cooking, or painting because it's equally an act of imagination. You imagine a new life for yourself, and that simple glimmer of fantasy becomes a reassuring sign that you're starting to conjure up the future and are no longer just padlocked to the past.

Here are some examples of how people bring physicality into their lives during their messy middle:

- Erik Smith plunged into kickboxing during the year he lost multiple relatives, got addicted to painkillers, and started working with special-needs students. "My wife would make me go. I'd come home and be so upset and she'd point to the door. I would go in the middle of the night, do ten rounds on the heavy bags, and come back a different man. By day I was caring for students who were significantly disabled, I was compassionate, loving, and gentle; and by night, I was beating people up in the gym."

- Chris Howard moved to San Francisco from the East Coast after a failed marriage (to a woman) and a toxic rebound relationship (with an older man). Once on the West Coast, he fell into a group of circus artists, burlesque performers, and dominatrices and began performing aerial acrobatic routines.
- John Evenhuis traded in his golf clubs for serious physical training once he left the Bay Area for Glacier National Park. "It wasn't just losing weight. It's like your feet need to get in shape because you're going to get blisters, you have to be able to hike up a friggin' mountain. So you get in shape not to look good in a bathing suit but because your life depends on it."
- Susan Keappock began tap-dancing to show tunes to get over the loss of her dad and her brain tumor. "It gives you a chance to get outside yourself a little. Whether you're painting or singing or dancing, it's not like you're watching a movie on the screen; it's like you're in the movie. You're also physically changing something, so it gives you a sense of being able to impact the world."
- And while it may or may not qualify as exercise, Sarah Holbrooke joined the curling team when her husband relocated their family from Brooklyn to Telluride, because, she said, "That's where all my friends were on Monday nights, I was lonely, and I wanted to hang out with them. Also, I did the Whole30 program, because my friends were doing that, too. And to make up for all the weight I gained going to the coffee shop every morning, because that's where you run into everybody in town."

Creativity need not be isolating, stuffy, or overly grand. It need not follow any template at all. What people seem to crave from it is what creation has represented in mythology since the dawn of time: a fresh start. It echoes the timeless cycle of creation, followed by destruction; followed by re-creation. In turning to creativity, we tap into the part of us that's most human: the ability to generate new life.

CHAPTER 11

Share It

Seek Wisdom from Others

Many of the tools for navigating transitions have an element of time built into them. They involve letting go of the past, marking the end of a life phase, beginning fresh initiatives, introducing your new story. This time component is what broadly aligns these activities to one of the three stages: the long goodbye, the messy middle, or the new beginning.

But one of the tools has no temporal element at all: it floats; it reoccurs; it happens all the time and sometimes only once; it's both time-sensitive and timeless. It's sharing your story with others. It's connecting with a friend, a loved one, a colleague, a stranger, a co-sufferer, a neighbor, or a mentor, and receiving, at exactly the moment you need it most, the feedback you most need.

One bright, flashing pattern of my conversations is that we crave different types of support from these outsiders. Each of us appears to have a phenotype of feedback just as we have a default way of structuring our time or making meaning in our lives. We like being consoled, pushed, inspired, called out, or, for some of us, even provoked. Whatever the type of advice we crave, the role it serves in our transition is the same.

We need help.

"I Think We All Have People in Our Lives Like Mike Shane"

Rockie Lynne Rash began life about as helpless as you can be. "I was found in a garbage dumpster, somewhere near Troutman, North Carolina, on November the fourteenth, 1964, abandoned and left to die. I was taken to Barium Springs Home for Children, which is where I grew up." Around the time Rockie was two, Fred and Ethel Rash, an older couple unable to have children, came to the orphanage, looking to adopt a child.

"My first memory was the African American lady who ran the orphanage pointing at me and saying, 'Well, you don't want that one. He's got a flat head.'" Rockie's head is still flat, he said, which he believes may have come from his time in the orphanage. "That's why I have long hair to this day, so you can't notice it."

From the start, the adoption was challenged. Rockie's mother had only a third-grade education, was illiterate and clueless how to raise a child, Rockie said. Rockie's dad, a Korean War veteran who also couldn't read, was a primitive Baptist who was skeptical of doctors' offices, banks, schools, and other civic institutions. The family had almost no money.

"The first time I was taken to the doctor, they called the police, because they thought I was being abused," Rockie said.

In one sense, he was. The Rashes chose the name Rockie because they wanted someone solid and strong, who liked hunting and sports, but Rockie from the start was more interested in the arts. "I was everything my dad did not want," Rockie said. "He locked me in my room at night and put a padlock on the door so I couldn't get out."

Around sixth grade, Rockie went to a yard sale at a local church and saw a turntable with a speaker and two albums, Jimi Hendrix Experience's *Axis: Bold as Love* and Kiss's *Alive!* "They wanted seventy-five cents for the whole shebang. I went to my mom, and I said, 'Can I have this?' She gave me a dollar. I bought the stereo and hid it in my closet, because I knew if Dad found it, it'd be gone."

Rockie threw himself into the world of music. He mowed lawns to buy a guitar from JCPenney. By eighth grade he was in a band with grown men. He circled an ad in *Guitar World* magazine for the Guitar Institute of Technology in Los Angeles. "My entire goal in life was to figure out how to get to this school. I had no idea how I was going to do it. I lived on a dirt road in North Carolina. I was trapped."

And this is when magical outsiders—Good Samaritans, perfect strangers, lucky angels—began showing up in Rockie's life. Exactly when he was most adrift, someone would appear and direct him through the woods.

A military recruiter came to his high school and offered money for college. "My father had said he would kick me out the day I graduated. He had put in his time, he had raised this little faggot, you're out. So Uncle Sam became my ticket."

Rockie joined the army and became a paratrooper with the Eighty-Second Airborne Division. "Everybody else hated it, but I had never had three meals a day in my life. Plus, all the drill sergeants were these hard-core infantry fighting men from Vietnam. They took no shit. But it was the first time any grown men had ever said anything positive to me, ever. There was this great big black guy, a staff sergeant, who was six foot five. I was afraid of him, and he was tough on me. But when I graduated jump school, right before they slam those wings on my chest, he said, 'If you can do this, son, you can do anything.'"

Rockie served for the next three years, and when he got out, he took the money he earned from the GI Bill, moved to California, and enrolled in the Guitar Institute of Technology. "I was going to be Eddie Van Halen; it was just going to happen." But he was an awkward fit. "I was dependable, I could play. But I didn't drink, I didn't smoke, I didn't do drugs, I wasn't fun to hang out with."

He earned his certification and, again at a loss, got in his car and drove east until the road ended in a seedy beach town in the Carolinas. He joined a dinner-club jazz trio ("mostly Ipanema stuff") and slept in a sleeping bag in the back of an abandoned video store, with only a cooler and an amp by his side. He was at another dead end.

One night he went to the nearby town of Calabash to hear a singer named Mike Shane. In the break, Rockie introduced himself. "You that kid over at the Islander that everyone's talking about?" Shane asked. "I hope so!" Rockie replied. "You can start with me tomorrow night," Shane said and handed him a cassette. "Go home and learn these songs." Rockie came back the next day, having learned every one. "I didn't mean in one night," Shane said.

The two played together all summer. Shane coached Rockie on how to perform, how to use his body more when he played, how to charm an audience. When fall rolled around, Shane announced he was going to Nashville to do a recording and wanted Rockie to come with him. "Bring your bag, we're gonna be there awhile. Bring your amp, bring everything." They drove to Nashville and stayed at the Hall of Fame Hotel near Music Row.

"I should have known something was weird, because we got two rooms," Rockie said. "Whenever we went on the road, we always shared a room to save money. I didn't get a good night's sleep, and when I woke up, there was a note under the door.

This is where you belong. I'll have your truck sent.
I paid your room for two weeks.

Mike Shane was the opposite of a wolf.

He was a fairy godfather.

Rockie went to work. He got gigs, he wrote songs. He hit the road, played cruise ships. He got married, got divorced, had a daughter. And finally, though it took a number of years, another magical outsider came into his life and got him a thirty-minute audition with the head of Universal Music in Manhattan. "They told me I could sing two or three songs. When I got to three and they didn't kick me out, I sang another, then another. When I was done, he signed me to a record deal that day and moved me to a really fancy hotel overlooking Central Park and put me in the presidential suite."

The boy who was left for dead in a dumpster in North Carolina had reached the pinnacle of American entertainment. He used the fame from his first album release to build an organization he founded called Tribute to the Troops, which has since raised hundreds of thousands of dollars to provide college tuition for children who lost a parent in active duty. Having benefited from surrogate parents his entire life, he now is one to thousands of children he will never know. He traces his sense of obligation to the man who changed his life.

"I think we all have people in our lives like Mike Shane," Rockie said. "Symbolically, I think he's God. He's the one that got me where I was supposed to be. If you listen to my album *Faith*, the first song is called 'Right Where I Belong.' It's about being lost and being found, about making mistakes and doing things wrong, but being brave enough to walk through the door when the right person comes along and opens it up for you."

The Wisdom of Grannies

A number of years ago, a friend asked me to speak to a friend of hers who was having some difficulty with a big media company with whom I had tangled. My friend's friend gave me a call; he was English, as I recall. I related at some length my experience; he described, in even more length, his experience. Then he thanked me for the call. "But I don't feel like I've been very helpful," I said. "Oh, the quite opposite," he replied. "This was perfect. My granny always said, 'A problem shared is a problem halved.'"

His granny was right.

People going through life transitions often feel apart from those around them. It's one of the more painful aspects of the process—the aching feeling of being separate, isolated, abandoned. People between jobs can't answer that most common of questions, "What do you do?" People whose children are struggling with addiction or mental illness blanch at the most innocent of inquiries: "How are the kids?" I felt this acutely when I was sick. Lying in chemo fatigue in my bed, unable to walk because of my leg or leave the house because of my immune system, I would sometimes stare out of my window, observe people strolling effortlessly down the street, and mutter to myself, *You don't know what it's like. You don't what it's like.*

Being in a state of in between means being in some state of loneliness. Being neither here nor there often feels like being nowhere.

Which is why connecting with others is so central to getting through one of these times. Human beings like to share. Researchers at Harvard found that people devote between 30 and 40 percent of their speech output solely to informing others of their own subjective experiences. They do so because self-disclosure is extremely rewarding. Personal revelation releases soothing chemicals in our brains and activates special systems in our bodies that help us relate better to others. When people relate their most traumatic experiences, their blood pressure, heart rate, and other physiological functions rise in the short term, but afterward fall to below where they were before their confessions—*and remain there for weeks afterward.* People are even prepared to give up money in order to be able to share more of their troubles. This desire to talk about yourself extends to strangers. In group therapy, the more people talk, the more they like the group. The more they themselves talk, the more they claim to have learned from the group.

Granny wasn't just perceptive; she was a neuroscientist.

One takeaway from all this research is that talking is not a solo sport. The reason we seek out others, or go to group therapy to begin with, is the power of having listeners. And those listeners, in turn, shape the stories we tell. Our audience becomes our co-narrators. Beginning in adolescence, which narrative psychologists have identified as the first time we attempt to create coherent life stories, we rely heavily on co-narrators, many of them adults—parents, teachers, preachers, coaches. Even as we age, we still crave wise elders. Think of all the gurus, grannies, Yodas, uncles, oracles, mahatmas, mentors, and sages that dot the history of mythology. We need what philosopher George Herbert Mead called *significant others*, people who reflect at us the significance of our actions, and, in doing so, help us create meaning from events we're often too close to see.

But what kind of significant others do we value most? Anyone who's ever shared their struggles with another person knows the feedback can range from pure affirmation to gentle criticism to harsh attacks. Which is most helpful? I asked everyone I interviewed this question. The answers ran a wider gamut than I would have anticipated. We coded people's answers and found that they sorted into four types: *comforters*, *nudgers*, *slappers*, and *modelers*. A fifth category came up often enough that I decided to include it, even though this person wasn't exactly encouraging. It's a *naysayer*.

The percentages were as follows: Comforters (*I love you; I trust you; you can do it*) came out on top, with just over a third choosing this category; nudgers (*I love you, but maybe you should try this*) came in second, with around a quarter; slappers (*I love you, but get over yourself*) came in third, with one in six choosing this option; modelers (*You may not know me, but follow my lead*) came in fourth. The final category, naysayers, are people who tell us we're fools, we're crazy, or we'll never succeed. For some of us, that's all the motivation we need.

Let's examine how these figures shape us in real life.

Comforters: "I Will Buy You a Bus Ticket, I Will Buy You a Plane Ticket"

Loretta Parham was bereft and aimless after the car accident that took the life of her daughter and left her the primary caretaker of her two granddaughters. She felt she couldn't show her grief at work, where she was director of the library at a consortium of historically black colleges in Atlanta. At home, she needed to be strong for her granddaughters. "All kinds of friends call me," she said. "But I don't take any calls, I don't talk to anybody. I am happy to withdraw."

But there was one person for whom she made an exception. "It wasn't a close friend at all," Loretta said. "She's our library director in Baton Rouge, Louisiana, who lost her son—I think it was to AIDS—when he was college-age. She called me a lot during this time, and I will call her when I have a moment. I will literally pull over to the side of the road, she'll let me cry, and she'll talk me through."

What role did she serve? "She comforted me," Loretta said. "She was the one to let me know that it's okay to feel the way you do. She would tell me, 'You know, you'll get better, but you don't have to be better now.' And she said, 'Don't let anybody tell you how to grieve.' Because my husband is the kind that he wants to distract you, he don't want you to think about it a lot. But she would say, 'Don't let anyone tell you what to do. This is yours.'"

Humans, like all mammals, crave companionship. Gorillas travel in bands, hyenas in cackles, porcupines in prickles, hippopotamuses in bloats. We travel in families, teams, congregations, workplaces. Researchers have found that in times of crisis, people's self-esteem tends to be maintained by those around them. The more friends you have, the healthier you are, though this effect is directly connected to how much you speak with your friends about your problems. Those who've been laid off suffer less if they share their stories with loved ones, the same with returning veterans and HIV patients. Children who overcome a hard-knock life have what researchers call *adoptability*, or a knack for being taken in by others. Like Rockie, they're likable, easy to be around, and skilled at inspiring others to help them out.

One of the more vivid examples I know of how the comfort of others can help people triumph over hardship involves a onetime abandoned child, a shy, depressive World War I veteran and failed businessman named William Griffith Wilson. During a trip to Akron, Ohio, in November 1934, to visit an old drinking buddy, Wilson was rattled to find his friend had become sober under the guidance of missionaries. *I need a drink!* Wilson thought. Pacing the lobby of the Mayflower Hotel, getting agitated from the laughter and tinkling glasses wafting from the bar, Wilson had a revelation: "No, I don't need a drink—I *need* another alcoholic!"

Wilson turned his back on the bar, headed toward the telephone booths, and eventually found his way to fellow alcoholic Dr. Robert Smith. The two cofounded Alcoholics Anonymous. From that very first meeting, the idea of sharing your struggle for sobriety with a fellow sufferer was central to the organization's success. "You see, our talk was a completely *mutual* thing," Wilson wrote. "I knew I needed this alcoholic as much as he needed me." This "mutual give-and-take," as he called it, became the backbone of AA.

Nearly a century later, it's become second nature that unconditional support, from either someone who's been in the same shoes or even someone who hasn't, can be lifesaving. Sometimes we seek out such comfort; other times it falls in our laps. However the connection happens, it's the preferred type of support of a plurality of people, a third in my study.

People like Chris Howard, the game designer who was going through an acrimonious divorce from his wife, starting to date men, and out of work, when he hit a wall. "I was living off beans and rice for months, seeing a therapist, going to the gym four days a week, and as part of my mental health regime, I started reaching out to close friends and saying, 'I'm going through a lot of stuff right now. I'm emotionally bankrupt. I don't have the capacity to show up for you in the way that I would love, but right now I need you to love me.'

"I was overwhelmed by those who not only told me they would show up for me, but actually did," he continued. "They cried with me, they came to see me, they said, 'You're not that far away. I will buy you a bus ticket, I will buy you a plane ticket, take a week, take however long, just come and stay with me and we'll rebuild together.'"

People like Sarah Cooper, a Jamaican web designer who managed to get one of the most coveted jobs in Silicon Valley, at Google, then quit to chase her dream of becoming a humor writer. "I was losing sleep because you feel like if you can't be happy at Google, maybe you'll never be happy. A week before my last day, I considered telling the company I had changed my mind. But then I found a former colleague who said everybody who leaves Google goes through something like this. Then my boss introduced me to someone who also left to pursue writing. And people wrote me through my blog and said, 'I just want to help you.'" She never went back.

People like Dwayne Hayes, who was working in publishing in Michigan when his wife gave birth to stillborn twin girls, sinking him into depression and almost cratering their marriage. "There was this Pakistani developer on the technology side of our company," he said. "He was very large, with a long beard, a very devout Muslim—his wife was pregnant at the same time as mine. By the time I got back to work, I hadn't seen him in weeks, and of course I'm avoiding people. I stuck to my cubicle. And I walked out one day and hear his voice. I turn around and he comes up to me, puts his arms around me, hugs me, and says, 'I am praying that Allah grants you a thousand times more joy than the pain you are experiencing.' It was exactly what I needed."

Nudgers: "It Made Me Think Back on What My Dad Told Me the Day He Died"

Amy Cunningham, the freelance journalist in Brooklyn who became a mortician in her fifties, has a particular person she turns to in moments of insecurity. Her name is Shelley Ackerman, and she's an astrologer. "I don't know that I believe in astrology," Amy said, "but I call her every time I do something big. She helps me reframe things."

After Amy's dad died in South Carolina, Amy was deeply moved by the funeral. "There was something about the South that I didn't recognize in New York, the connection people have with the funeral director through the chamber of commerce or Rotary Club. And the light bulb just went off over my head." Amy chatted with friends, consulted her family, and was ready to enroll in undertaker classes.

Then she called Shelley. "Amy, I love you, but I think you need to go deeper," she said. "This comes off as a little shallow." Amy was stung but absorbed the feedback. "That's when I began to remember that my brother died before I was born," she said. "My father's brother died; their father died early, too. There was a lot of death in our house, and I spent a lot of time lifting sad people up. I shared this with Shelley, and she thought that was significant."

After Amy got her degree in mortuary science and was starting her new website, the Inspired Funeral, it was Shelley who came up with the name and told her to launch it at 12:28 p.m. on a Sunday because it was astrologically auspicious. At the appointed hour, Amy sat at the computer and played Winston Churchill's funeral on YouTube so she could weep along to the hymn "I Vow to Thee, My Country."

The shallow had become profound.

I have a game I occasionally play with my daughters. Beginning when they were adolescents, when they would occasionally show me a piece of writing, I would ask, "Would you like me to tell you how great it is, or how you might make it better?" They went through every possible response before finally settling on what would be their pet answer: "Both!"

Praise is great, but praise with a gentle nudge can sometimes be even better. Nudging has become a popular idea in recent years, as behavioral scientists have repeatedly found that our ability to make smart choices is not as good as we'd like. As two masters of this field, the Nobel laureate Richard Thaler and Cass Sunstein, write in their book, *Nudge*, "Human decision making is not so great." It's even harder, they add, in situations that are rare, fraught, and filled with emotion—in other words, exactly the kinds of situations we face in moments of life transition. Some of the reasons they cite: We prefer the status quo, we tend to play it safe, we follow the herd.

Often a slight push, a delicate prod, or a loving poke is all we need. A quarter of people in my conversations preferred these kinds of reactions from their loved ones. As Amy Cunningham said, they want someone to sharpen their thinking, remind them of their dreams, and encourage them to strive for their best possible selves.

People like Eric Westover, who sank into self-pity after losing his legs in that motorcycle accident near Lake Michigan. He was comforted when his boss at Costco assured him that his job was safe, but what he really needed was a push to reengage with the world. "My sister kind of forced me on Facebook. First, she put up a GoFundMe page, and that was huge for me. It was emotional because there were all these people that would donate that I hadn't heard from in years. I knew they had families and hard times of their own, but they wanted to help. Then we started getting all these followers on Facebook. It just touched my heart."

People like Janay Brower, whose husband had listened for so long to her frustration with her job running the homeless coalition of Grand Rapids that he finally said, "Janay, it's time. You gotta go." "Even the morning I was going to resign, I was like, 'I can't do it! I can't do it!'" Janay said. "And he's like, 'You can't do it? It's making you sick. You have to do it.' He even took a new job, so he was able to take care of us financially, which was a huge burden off me."

People like Chris Cassirer, the son of high school sweethearts whose mom, a nightclub singer, came out as lesbian when Chris was eight years old. Raised by two moms in blue-collar New Jersey, Chris was bullied and knifed in high school, called a "faggot," and his hair was burned. He fell into drugs, dropped out of college, learned from a transsexual aunt that he was the product of his mother's affair, and then lost his dad to a massive heart attack. Just when his life was most chaotic, a therapist gave him a copy of Viktor Frankl's *Man's Search for Meaning*. "It changed my life," Chris said. "The point at which he was in the concentration camp and everyone was dying around him, and he realized no one can take away your choice to have hope. It made me think back on what my dad told me the day he died. 'You're going to be great someday.' I realized I had to choose to make that true."

Chris eventually became the president of a university in Minnesota.

All he needed was a well-timed nudge.

Slappers: "You Don't Know What the Fuck Is Going on in Your Life"

Helen Churko grew up in a sickly family in the Washington Heights neighborhood of New York City. "My mother was in an oxygen tent because of extreme asthma and couldn't walk more than a block. My father had a series of nervous breakdowns beginning when I was sixteen. I always thought my birth had caused my mother's illness. I didn't learn until I was thirty-five that it actually started six months after I was born. My father told me one day by accident. We sat at the kitchen table and wept."

So Helen became a caretaker—for family, for friends, for clients. For four decades she was a successful lecture agent and late in her career became a certified life coach, too. But all the while she was worried about herself. Having had her heart broken in her teens, Helen struggled with her weight and self-confidence. "Somewhere along the way, it became clear to me that I needed to get in touch with my own self and that this was the most important work for me to do."

She did est training, Landmark Forum, *The Artist's Way*; she joined a book group and a writing group; she spent five days at the world headquarters of Brahma Kumaris atop Mount Abu in Rajasthan, India, working with two hundred other people on how to improve the world. But when she lost three close friends and both parents in six years, and then her company was sold, dashing her dreams of taking it over, Helen lost her way. "It was like not knowing who I was anymore."

One day she was sitting with friends, complaining. "I was sort of yammering on about some fantasy idea I had about my life, when my friend Wendy did that Cher thing where she slaps Nicolas Cage across his face—twice—in *Moonstruck* and says, 'Snap out of it!' It was exactly what I needed to hear to get past whatever crap concept I was putting out there."

A slapper. A lot of us need one. A few of us prefer one.

In 44 BCE, the Roman orator Cicero wrote a treatise called *How to Be a Friend*. In it, he makes the point that good friends tell you what you need to hear, not what you want to hear. "Nothing is worse or more destructive among friends than constant flattery, fawning, and affirmation. Call it what you will, it is the mark of a weak and false-hearted man to tell you anything to please you except the truth." Modern social science backs this up. Children raised with tough love are more likely to have well-developed character; adults confronted with painful truths at work are three times more engaged and view their bosses as five times more effective.

Yet we consistently sidestep telling the truth to those around us. We choose harmony over bluntness. Two researchers studied whether this kind of conflict avoidance is a good idea. They found that kind communication promotes happiness, in that it increases short-term pleasure, while honest communication promotes greater meaning, in that it prioritizes long-term fulfillment. Their conclusion: "Individuals find honest communication to be more enjoyable, meaningful and socially connecting than they expect."

My conversations reflect this bias. Slapping was not the most popular behavior people craved from their mentors, but the people who embraced this kind of blunt talk felt they could not live without it.

People like Amber Hansen, a painter and printmaker from South

Dakota who was on the brink of earning her master's degree in art from the University of Kanas when she flunked the review of her work. "It was this huge failure, because this was everything I had worked towards my entire life. Suddenly I wasn't an artist; I didn't belong. And if this wasn't working, what else was there? I cried and cried." Then a friend told her to stop crying and take a trip. "I went to Berlin for ten days, traveled all through Germany, then went to Amsterdam, and when I got back I switched to film and made a body of work about my childhood dreams." This work earned her the MFA.

People like Janelle Hanchett, the California native who struggled for years to get sober until she met her sponsor, Dave. "The first time I met him he looked at me and said, 'You're a bad woman. I'm not here to love you, you've got plenty of people loving you, but did that ever help you to recover from alcoholism? I don't care about your bullshit lies. In your case, if it looks like a duck, and it quacks like a duck, it's probably a fire hydrant. You're so full of shit, you don't know what the fuck is going on in your life.' And he was right. I had to have someone like Dave to slap me around and make me question my perception."

People like Lisa Porter, the theater professor from San Diego, who sat for a tarot card reading on a yoga retreat and mentioned that her daughter, Daisy, who has special needs, was suffering. "This woman looks at me and says, 'How do you know she's suffering? I think you're suffering.' That was the turnaround in my thinking. I said, 'Oh, wow, you're right. I'm projecting all this suffering onto her. She seems perfectly happy. She's not walking around saying, 'Gosh, I wish I could engage with all the bullshit a typical thirteen-year-old does.' It took a stranger to make me realize that."

Modelers: "Madonna Is the Only One Who's Been There All Along"

Michael Angelo didn't have any role models growing up in Plainfield, New Jersey. "My parents were bat-shit crazy. They were good people, but they were raised by crazy people and knew nothing better." Steeped in fairy tales and all things Disney, and attracted to boys from a very young age, Michael did what many people in marginal groups do: He turned to outsiders for guidance. In his case, celebrities.

"In high school I started experimenting with my style, and Cyndi Lauper was where my eye went. My bangs were orange and hanging over one eye, I had this vintage jacket covered with rock-and-roll pins, and a giant pink triangle. I basically got my ass kicked."

Michael started playing hooky and fleeing to Manhattan on school days; he barely graduated; he enrolled in beauty school and started working in salons. And along the way he adopted a lifelong, long-distance fairy godmother. "Madonna is the only one who's been there all along, right? She was like a big sister, a Tinker Bell on my shoulder. There were all these things she was experimenting with as a human—kabbalah, yoga, BDSM—that kind of lit the way for me. When she got into introspection, that's when I finally moved out of this unhealthy relationship I was in for many years. I was like, 'Enough of this nonsense. Time to get grounded.' I sincerely mean it when I say that she sang every song on *Ray of Light* to me personally."

Not all role models are people we know. I was originally suspicious of this notion, but it came up repeatedly, especially among people whose life stories diverged in some ways from those around them. And maybe I could relate. As a teenager in Savannah, Georgia, in the 1970s with some unusual hobbies—juggling and mime, to name two—I didn't know anyone within five hundred miles who shared these interests. I had to scrape together tips from old paperbacks or counselors at sleepaway camp. Magazines became my mentors. Later, when I dreamed of being a writer, I learned more from Pat Conroy, who wrote about the off-the-beaten-path part of the world I was from, than anybody I knew.

Today, anyone who has a nontraditional interest or is somehow outside the mainstream has a much wider array of options. The internet brings role models right to our noses. My wife, who started an organization that supports entrepreneurs around the world, has identified what she calls the *multiplier effect*: even a single role model can inspire an entire country or an entire continent. Researchers at Johns Hopkins found a similar effect in elementary schools: Students of color who have teachers of color are less likely to drop out. The same applies to aging: Middle-age people with role models for successful aging handle the transition more successfully.

Perhaps most surprising: You don't need to know these people well. A Stanford sociologist has identified what he calls the *strength of weak ties* under which a casual acquaintance often has more impact on your life than people you know. The reason: Your friends are usually too similar to you. The people I spoke with went even further. Sometimes the person who most changed their life was a neighbor, sometimes a stranger, sometimes a person they had never even met.

People like Elisa Korentayer, who, while living in a tiny apartment in New York and feeling frustrated by her fizzled romantic life and stalled tech career, had a neighbor move in upstairs. "She disappeared for a few weeks and came back looking absolutely blissed out. One day I stopped her. 'Where were you and why do you look so happy?' She said, 'Oh, I was at an artist residency!' I said, 'What's that?' She said, 'I go for six weeks, I write poetry, they feed me, they house me, and it's great.' I said, 'That sounds like heaven.'" That weekend Elisa applied to twenty such programs and was accepted at the one in Minnesota that eventually led to her meeting her husband and moving to the Midwest.

People like Kirsty Spraggon, who, when she relocated from Australia to Los Angeles in part to move beyond the shame she felt from herpes, found guidance in books, audiotapes, and YouTube videos. "My mentors have all been motivational speakers," she said. "Oprah. M. Scott Peck; I love *The Road Less Traveled*. At the moment I'm listening to Deepak Chopra. I'm constantly evolving, and I consider them my teachers. They meet me exactly where I need at that moment."

People like Sal Giambanco, who, after leaving the Jesuits following nine years in the brotherhood, had no assets, no income, no home, and no prospects. "In the Jesuits you take a vow of poverty, so when I went to get an apartment, I flunked the credit test. The only place that would have me was Section 8, subsidized housing." Sal sent out four hundred résumés and got two callbacks. "One was from a woman who said, 'I don't have a job for you, but you look interesting. I just wanted to wish you good luck.' The second was from a man who was looking for someone to do personnel work. 'I'm not sure you're the right fit for this,' he said, 'but everyone else who applied for this job is a used car salesman, and I'm pretty sure you're not a used car salesman. I'm going to take a chance on you.'" Sal went on to head personnel for PayPal and to pursue a distinguished career as an executive coach in Silicon Valley.

"I always remember that theme," he said, "and to this day I continue to take chances on people who are outside the bell curve of what's normal. A complete stranger changed my life; I want to be that person for someone else."

Naysayers: "My Parents Compared Me to Willy Loman"

The question I asked in my interviews that produced these answers was "Was there a mentor, friend, loved one, or wise outsider who offered advice during your transition?" The conversations that followed were almost always about what types of advice the person found most helpful. But they weren't always about that. Every now and then, another kind of figure came up. This figure gave a different kind of feedback that proved surprisingly crucial in helping the person soldier through a challenging time.

That figure was a critic, a killjoy, a doubter, a detractor.

A naysayer.

We know this figure from popular culture. Oprah Winfrey never forgot the local news director in Baltimore who fired her after seven months and told her she was "unfit for television and too emotionally invested." Tom Brady, who was already reverse-motivated for most of his career because he was drafted in only the sixth round of the NFL draft, became even more indignant the year he was suspended for four games for "Deflate-gate." He even preserved the NFL's suspension letter among his keepsakes for additional incentive. "Just a nice way to remember," he said. Brady appeared in the Super Bowl that year and won it the next.

Madonna, in accepting a woman of the year award from *Billboard*, noted that when she first moved to New York as a teenager, she was bullied, held up at gunpoint, and raped at knifepoint; in the middle of her career, she was called a whore, a witch, and Satan; late in her career, she was treated worse—she was ignored. "To the doubters, the naysayers, to everyone who gave me hell and said I could not, that I would not, that I must not—your resistance made me stronger, made me push harder, made me the fighter that I am today. Made me the woman that I am today. So thank you."

The naysayers people told me about were not this violent, but they were just as scarring. Many were parents. Brin Enterkin was a B student in high school when she had the idea to build a school for girls in Cambodia. "My parents said, 'It's probably not a good idea.' And I thought, *They don't believe I can do this. I'm going to show them.*" And she did. When Christy Moore dropped out of high school after getting pregnant, her father told her she'd never amount to anything. "He said I wouldn't even earn my GED." She went on to earn her PhD. Shannon Watts was a freshman in high school when she came home with an assignment asking parents to compare their children to a character in history. "Because it was a Catholic school, most parents came back with Joan of Arc or the Virgin Mary. My parents compared me to Willy Loman from *Death of a Salesman*. I think there was a reason I was an only child." Shannon went on to found the leading gun control advocacy group in the country.

Other naysayers came from work. Tyler Dennis, the son of two social scientists at the University of Wisconsin, was a nineteen-year-old undergraduate when a diagnosis of testicular cancer prompted him to abandon his interest in the arts and return to the land. He was working in the organic gardens at the prestigious Stone Barns Center outside of New York City when he floated the idea of opening his own vegetable farm. "My boss was really adamant that I couldn't do it. 'Small-scale farmers barely eke out a living; it's a very small pie that we're competing for.' I'm sympathetic, but I also can't stand being told what to do, and it was extremely encouraging to just go do it." Today he owns Alewife Farm and is featured on the Stone Barns website.

When five-foot-one Ann Marie DeAngelo first tried out for the Joffrey Ballet, the director told her, "We can't use you right now because you're too short." Ann Marie was incensed. She went back to work, made the troupe, became its leading ballerina, and was later named associate director. "There was a quote from Calvin Coolidge that my mother used to say: 'Nothing in this world can take the place of persistence. Talent will not—nothing is more common than unsuccessful men with talent. Genius will not—unrewarded genius is almost a proverb. Education will not—the world is full of educated derelicts. Persistence and determination alone are omnipotent.'"

From naysayers to nudgers, comforters to slappers, outside voices play a pivotal role in our life transitions. They are Sancho Panza to our Don Quixote, Huck to our Tom, Laverne to our Shirley. They are co-narrators as we reframe and rewrite our life stories. They are buoys in our loneliest tides. They are the confidants, the companions, and sometimes even the critics who inch us one step closer to finally achieving our new selves.

CHAPTER 12

Launch It

Unveil Your New Self

One day it just happens. A tinge of normalcy appears, a glimmer of light, an inhale that need not pass a clenched jaw, an exhale that doesn't end in a sigh. The past no longer casts such a long shadow; the future begins to come into view. Even when this moment comes early in the transition, before a person says their full goodbyes or fully weathers the mess, the symbolic importance is still the same.

It's time to launch fresh projects, share your work, celebrate your progress.

Unveil your new self.

"I Used the New Me to Free Lots of People Who Were Just Like the Old Me"

Steven Hassan was the third child of middle-class parents in Flushing, Queens. His mother taught eighth grade; his father ran a hardware store. "When I turned seventeen, both my older sisters got married and left the house," Steven said. "My father asked me if I wanted the hardware store. I was writing poetry and short stories, I imagined myself becoming writer. I said, 'Absolutely not,' and enrolled in Queens College."

Steven studied creative writing. "I was an introvert, terribly shy, and I was really interested in sex," he said. In his junior year, he was sitting in the cafeteria one day when three smiling Japanese girls started flirting with him. "They asked if they could sit at my table, engaged me in conversation, and invited me to come over to their house to meet some friends from all over the world."

The evening was innocuous enough; the students talked about uniting people of different backgrounds; Steven thanked them and headed outside. They followed and asked if he'd return the next day. He politely declined. "I remember they came all the way out to the car, it was snowing, a bunch of people, not even wearing shoes. They surrounded my car and more or less said they wouldn't let me leave unless I promised to come back. I remember thinking, *These are crazy people*, but I've always been a very principled person and I felt guilty."

Steven went back, then agreed to attend a weekend getaway. A van drove them forty-five minutes outside of the city. When they passed through the gates, his hosts announced they were having a joint workshop with the Unification Church. "I went, 'Whoa! I'm Jewish. Nobody said anything about a church.' And they said, 'What's wrong, Steve, are you biased? Do you have something against Christians?'"

They also said the van wasn't going back until the next morning. That night they sang songs, ate, socialized. "It reminded me of summer camp," Steven said. The two-day workshop became three, then seven; Steven missed classes, he quit his part-time job, he turned on his family. "And I came to believe we were at a pivotal time in history. I had the question answered in my mind of who's the messiah on Earth. Who was going to save the planet, end all wars and starvation, create a world where everyone would live together in harmony like the Garden of Eden."

That someone was the Reverend Sun Myung Moon. Steven had become a Moonie.

And not just any Moonie. Steven rose to become a personal favorite of Reverend Moon. He cut his hair, donned a suit, gave over his bank account, and was told to pick a country he would rule when Moon controlled the world. He achieved this status because he proved to be exceptional at recruiting members, at persuading them that Satan had taken over their families, at helping them believe he knew their one true purpose.

He also slept only three to four hours a night, gave up masturbation and sex, and went on regular hunger strikes. "I drove myself to the brink," he said. Then, at 5:30 a.m. one Friday, two years after he joined, Steven was driving a van to pick up members outside Baltimore. He had not slept for two days. "And I drove into the back of a tractor trailer at eighty miles an hour," he said. "The van was crushed, and I was pinned. The door had to be sawn off."

Steven broke his leg badly that day. He was hospitalized for weeks. But that meant he got sleep and food. He asked permission from his "divine family" to call his actual family, specifically his immediate older sister. "We were very close growing up," he said. "She told me she loved me and that I had a nephew I hadn't met. 'I want him to know his uncle Stevie.'"

Steven told her he would come, as long as she didn't tell their parents. She broke the agreement. "My parents hired a team of ex-members who began deprogramming me," he said. "On the one hand I was a relatively easy case. They took my crutches so I couldn't run away." But he was also hard, because of how indoctrinated he had become. One morning his father took him for a drive, and Steven came close to snapping his father's neck. "I would have died, too, but I actually believed it was better to do that than betray the messiah."

But then his father turned to him and started to cry. "If I were your son, your only son, what would you do?" he asked. "I had seen my father cry only once before," Steven said. "And this was the first time I allowed myself to think—even for a moment—from his perspective." Steven agreed to talk to the deprogrammers for five days. If that didn't work, his father agreed to drive him back to the group.

They never made the trip. Steven learned about brainwashing; he heard comparisons between the Moonies and the Nazis; he read psychiatrist Robert Jay Lifton's book on mind control under Chairman Mao. He then went through what amounts to a classic life transition. He felt ashamed and guilty. He was sad to give up the friends and sense of purpose he felt inside the group. He returned robustly to an earlier passion, reading.

And then, after taking time to decompress, he faced a choice: Who did he want to be now? He could paper over his time in the Moonies, resume his life, no one would ever know. Or he could channel what he learned into something positive, answer the calls he was already receiving from other desperate families.

His father took the first position: "You've paid your dues, move on with your life." But Steven wasn't so sure. He tracked down Robert Jay Lifton at his apartment on Central Park West. "Here I am this depressed, college dropout, ex-Moonie, trying to figure out what to do with my life, and he had white hair and was the world's leading authority on mind control. I told him his book had saved my life. He said, 'Which book?' When I explained, he said, 'I only studied these matters secondhand. You lived them. You should explain what it was like to people like me.'"

Lifton helped Steven enroll at Yale; he later earned a master's in counseling. Along the way he developed his own theory of how groups manipulate the behavior, thoughts, and emotions of members.

Finally, Steven was ready to go public with his new identity. He started giving speeches, went on television, spoke to Congress. He filed Freedom of Information Act requests about Moon; he headed up a group of ex–cult members; he founded an organization to help family members free their children from cults, sex-trafficking rings, and terrorist cells. He also got married and later remarried after his first wife drowned; he and his second wife adopted a son.

Steven credits his new self not to Lifton, his father, or even his sister, but to Moon himself. "Being in the Moon cult gave me the grandiose expectations of having a much bigger impact on the world. Prior to that I was going to write poetry and maybe teach at community college. I would have been nervous to get up in front of a class of twelve. But in the cult, I was expected to go onstage and speak extemporaneously in front of a thousand people.

"The ironical, weird story of my narrative," he continued, "is that being in the cult gave me the confidence to help get people out of cults. By going public, I used the new me to free lots of people who were just like the old me."

The shape of his life reflects this growth: It was a cone, opening outward.

The First Normal Moment

When I started this project, I was focused on big themes—the large-scale trends and social shifts that have left people feeling anxious, unsettled, off-kilter, off-schedule. But time and again in my conversations, I was caught off guard by small themes—the microsteps and minipatterns that seem to hint at larger truths. One of those was what I call *the first normal moment.*

Seth Mnookin is the obsessive-compulsive teen from Brookline, Massachusetts, turned Harvard grad who descended into drug addiction in his twenties. The low point in his life occurred in New York City when he was just starting to use heroin. "One thing heroin does is make you incredibly constipated," Seth said. "There was a time when I had lost my job, my roommates were trying to quarantine me, and I hadn't taken a shit in days. I knew that just to be able to function and get outside and score again, I had to somehow go to the bathroom. So I put my hand up my ass and was chipping away at this rock of feces for like an hour. It was degrading, it was demeaning, it was depressing; but it was clearly what needed to be done in the situation."

Four years later, when he finally got sober and secured his first job in journalism, Seth found that one of the most challenging aspects of returning to normalcy was, well, doing normal things. "The hardest part was trying to figure out how to pay a bill. It was physically unlike anything I had ever been through. One of the weird things that still brings me joy—now that I'm married with kids and have a tenured job at MIT—is writing checks. I get really excited to pay my bills on time because it means I have money in a bank account."

Not long after, I was speaking with Michael Angelo, the former bullied teen who became an elite hairstylist in Manhattan. After getting divorced, Michael was adrift. "I've been surprised how fragile I've been," he said. "I used to be able to do anything. I opened a salon in the Meatpacking District, I kept it open through two major disasters, when the economy fell apart and my team fell apart. I've stayed at that ship through massive storms. But now I don't know where to get an egg sandwich.

"There are so many epic tales written about big transitions," he continued. "The hero's journey, Stella gets her groove back. But they don't write fucking movies about somebody who's trying to pay the cable bill. In my case, when I called my accountant and had him take over the bills my husband used to pay, that's when I knew I would make it. That was my normal."

A month later, a close friend who lost his seven-year-old daughter and his wife to cancer within eighteen months of each other told me that he, too, found the most empowering thing he did was pay his cable bill.

As happened earlier with multiple people having boots as mementos, here again were three people, three different circumstances, the same observation.

What is it about paying the cable bill—or mowing the lawn, or unclogging the sink—that is so profound?

Over the years, psychologists have observed that to live a meaningful life is to construct a sweeping metanarrative about what matters most to us—work, family, service, worship, beauty, etc. The advantage of articulating our overarching sources of identity is that it allows us to contextualize and persevere through the day-to-day unpleasantries that afflict everyone. As Roy Baumeister, a leading researcher in this space, put it, meaning "flows downward more easily than upward."

My conversations were a reminder that the reverse can also be true: If we lose touch with our larger sources of meaning, we can focus on the tiniest, flukiest things that get us through the day, and build upward from there. In times of trouble, we latch on to small things. We focus on seemingly minor or random acts that become irrationally important symbols of our ability to persevere. One of these is the first normal act. The first time we laugh after a devastating loss, the first time we sit on the toilet after a long convalescence in bed, the first time we go to the supermarket after a public humiliation.

Over time, these small wins aggregate into larger victories and fuller narratives. And while those aggregations are critical, that first win is often the one that takes on mythic weight. It's the first mile marker on the marathon to recovery, the first stitch on a broken heart. Samuel Johnson once observed that he could be sunk in a stage of lethargy so "languid and inefficient that he could not distinguish the hour upon the town clock," but the mere act of standing up out of his chair would often be enough to spark a better mood. Johnson didn't have cable bills to pay, of course, but he did understand that sometimes it's necessary to act first, let the emotions follow, and allow the simplest of gestures to kickstart our rebirth.

Here are some other examples of the first normal moment:

- Weeks after Kacie Case's one-year-old son was diagnosed with type 1 diabetes, she was scheduled to take him from Texas to Washington, DC. "I'm sitting in the hospital thinking, *We should cancel this trip. I have to travel with all this medication, all these syringes, all these emergency things.* And one of the nurses said, 'We can help you.' They prepped me to get through security, I set up a station in my friend's house, and we were fine. Looking back, that trip gave me so much confidence. I don't think we would have moved into an Airstream and lived on the road, if it hadn't been for that experience."
- After Chris Waddell broke his back on the ski slope, his initial months back at Middlebury were "just rainy and muddy and nasty and depressed." His coach took him to New Zealand that summer to join the US Paralympic team. "I was just awful that first day. The head coach was looking at me like, *The guy can't even make it a hundred yards.* But early that week, when I made my first real curve turn on the monoski, that was the breakthrough I needed." He went on to win thirteen Paralympic medals and become the most decorated male monoskier in history.
- Janelle Hanchett had not been sober long when she and her husband drove their children to Half Moon Bay in California. "It was one of the first trips we took as a family after I was reunited with them. I was driving, and I couldn't see clearly through the window with all the dead bugs and stuff. My husband said, 'Turn on the wipers.' Now I had been drunk and drug-addicted for years, I didn't have any wiper fluid in my car. And I laughed. *Oh, come on, like I have wiper fluid.* And he said, 'I put some in when we stopped for gas.' So I turned them on, and the kids in the back seat just started laughing, and as ridiculous as that moment was, it was one of the most joyful moments in my life,

because I realized, first of all, that this was an incredible signal that I had a life that was working."

The Best-Laid Plans

While the first normal moment may be the first step toward normalcy, it's hardly the last. Over time, people begin a host of new initiatives. They grow tomatoes, join Toastmasters, tackle Proust, clean out their closets, walk the Camino, volunteer at the homeless shelter. They start *personal projects.*

The idea that personal growth involves setting goals has a long history. In the 1840s, Kierkegaard said that when one personal dream gets crushed, we must turn to another, a process he likened to crop rotation. In the 1960s, psychologists identified *the plan* as a central feature of human behavior. Individuals who overcome obstacles have been shown to be self-determined, intentional, and future-oriented. They make plans.

In the 1980s, Cambridge psychologist Brian Little began using the idea of personal projects to develop a more robust understanding of how people navigate difficult times. Little was part of a daring movement that pushed back against the prevailing wisdom that all people have fixed personality traits—extraversion, introversion, and so on—an idea that had reigned for fifty years. Little showed that while some of our traits are stable, others are shaped by our surroundings or circumstances. In response to life events, we develop new ways of living, new habits, and new projects.

The hundreds of studies on personal projects have shown how central they are to our identity. On average, we pursue up to fifteen projects at a time, everything from *get a pilot's license* to *hike the Grand Canyon* to *repair the hole in the wall before Fred gets home.* Women tend to want support for their projects; men want independence to finish theirs. We're more likely to complete these projects if we state them as determinations—*clean out the garage*—as opposed to aspirations—*find time to clean out the garage.*

Inspired by this research, I included a question on this topic: "Please tell me three personal projects that are on your plate right now." When our team analyzed the answers, an interesting pattern emerged. People's projects tended to correspond to the ABCs of meaning. Some were agentic (*write a memoir, get my yoga certification*). Others were belonging-oriented (*help my mom move into assisted living, be a better dad*). Others involved a cause (*rewrite the Thirteenth Amendment, quell gang violence*).

Of the more than five hundred personal projects we analyzed, 56 percent were As in my model; 27 percent were Bs; 17 percent were Cs. People clearly seek out projects that focus on themselves, then others, and finally the larger world. A trumps B trumps C.

Looking deeper, we found that a quarter of our subjects had all three projects in one category. (The bulk of these were agency.) Four in ten had two projects in one category and one in another. (Again, agency doubled up most, followed by belonging, then cause.) But I was most fascinated that around one in three people had one project in each category, suggesting their three sources of meaning were most balanced.

Here are some examples of people who had one project in each category:

- Beverley Bass, the first female pilot in American Airlines history, was flying a 777 from Paris to Dallas on 9/11 that was one of 225 planes forced to land in Gander, Newfoundland, and Labrador, a story that later inspired the Tony Award–winning musical *Come From Away*. She mentioned hiring a personal assistant (A), helping her daughter get hired by American (B), and growing an organization she founded for female airline pilots (C).
- Brittany Wilund, the daughter of evangelicals in South Carolina who fled to Hawaii to pursue a career in pottery, said conducting interviews with interesting people for inspiration (A), building a new bus for her

and her boyfriend to live in (B), and converting an old sugar mill into an artists' cooperative (C).

- Brad Corrodi, the former Booz Allen consultant who struggled to find fulfilling work, listed fixing the lights in his shed (A), carpooling his children (B), and bringing more tech jobs to his community in Princeton, New Jersey (C).
- J. R. McLain, the trucker turned nurse, named collecting rocks near Portland (A), mentoring disadvantaged children by taking them mountain climbing (B), and promoting single-payer health care (C).
- Khaliya, who was born Kristin White in New York, married the son of Prince Aga Khan, the spiritual leader of fifteen million Ismaili Shia Muslims, then got robbed, divorced, and became an expert in global health, said writing a memoir (A), trying to have a baby with her new husband (B), and working to change how we view mental illness (C).

Keep It Moving

One day, late in my interviews, I had a thought: A lot of people, in the course of their transitions, seem to move. I hadn't been seeking out such stories, but a pattern seemed to be presenting itself. I went digging through the transcripts to see if any evidence emerged.

Boy did it.

Sixty-one percent of people mentioned that their transitions included some kind of movement. They sold a house, changed their workspace, emigrated, entered a nursing facility. The messy middle was the least popular time for these moves, with 26 percent of people mentioning this phase; the long goodbye and the new beginning both tied at 37 percent. What explains these high numbers?

On one level, moving is the oldest story of all. From Moses to Confucius to the Dalai Lama, our greatest religious stories have been journeys of discovery. Van Gennep, in his original research into rites of passage, saw transitions as fundamentally an act of movement, a passing from one place to the next. The hero's journey is full of similar tropes.

More recently, psychologists have begun to observe that in times of trauma, people get stuck, both physically and emotionally. Movement gets us unstuck. It restores agency by giving us the feeling we're acting on our situation; it nurtures belonging by bringing us into contact with new people; it gives us a cause by giving us something to focus on. A trio of researchers in New Hampshire asked people about memorable experiences in their lives. Moves generated twice as many memories as comparable experiences. Their explanation: Each time we move, we go through our possessions, engage and reengage old memories, reconnect with milestones of meaning we may have forgotten.

To be sure, some of the moves we make, especially ones at the beginning of a transition, tend to be isolating: Michael Hebb taking only his golf clubs and moving into an Airstream outside Portland after his humiliating fall from grace as a restaurateur; Amichai Lau-Lavie moving to a hippie compound in Israel's Negev desert after coming out as gay to his ultra-religious family. But more tend to symbolize healing. They are signs—dramatic, visible public signs—that we're turning a corner, literally and figuratively, and taking up residence in a new mental space.

Some we make for personal reasons. Carolyn Graham, after going through therapy following the breakup of her second marriage, built a treehouse in her backyard in central Florida. "It was in an old oak tree, no glass windows, all screens. I rented out my house and moved into the treehouse. I had lights, beautiful running water, I used the bathroom outside."

Some we undertake for medical reasons. Eric Westover, after enduring a downturn in his marriage following the biking accident that took his legs, moved into a ranch-style home in Grand Rapids that was easier for him to navigate. "After everything that happened, my wife really wanted to do the move ourselves. We had some guys help us with the furniture, but we did everything else. It took us six weeks. At the end, we said, *Finally, we can live.*"

Some we make for work reasons. Jenny Wynn, after being promoted to senior pastor of her Oklahoma City church following the death of her predecessor, took a sabbatical and asked the board to redecorate and repaint her new office in her absence so that when she started as the first female spiritual leader, the community would find it easier to accept her in her new role.

Others we tackle for family reasons. Jan Egberts, after becoming a single dad following the suicide of his wife, quit his job as CEO of a public company in New Jersey and moved his three sons to his native Amsterdam. "I said, 'Why don't we make a fresh start in Holland?' They liked the idea, they had a very close relationship with my mother, so we rented out our house, stayed in a boardinghouse for a while, then finally built a house of our own."

But everyone, in a sense, moves for the same reason—they need a change in scenery, a new setting for their life story. Khaliqa Baqi, who left her husband and the spiritual retreat they were building in rural Oregon, went on a vision quest and then settled in Portland, where she became a medical chaplain. "I think of transition itself as movement," she said. "Sometimes that movement is manifested by physically moving from one place to the other. But it's also an internal transition that involves moving from what you might call one native land to another. You leave an identity, a knowingness, something you've probably called home. And you do that because the soul has a certain trajectory. That trajectory is not linear. It's possible that something that once brought you joy all of a sudden is empty to you. But the soul moves on, and your ego has to learn to follow. You have to let go of that old identity, go into the emptiness, and find your new life's dream."

Open the Second Eye

Small steps and big moves are important milestones toward recovery, but sometimes you need a gesture with more transcendent resonance. You need a ritual. As popular as rituals are in marking the beginning of a transition, they're equally popular in marking the end. Meaningful acts that proclaim the unveiling of the new you were a powerful theme in my conversations. They hark back to an old Japanese tradition: *opening the second eye.*

Robert Yang was born in Southern California to parents who fled China to escape Mao. "I was that friendly, non-sexually-threatening, sociable-nerd type in high school, which means I didn't get picked for anything. Also, I'm gay, but I wasn't out the entire time I was in school."

Robert attended the University of California, Berkeley, but still felt socially awkward. "One of my roommates was a very straight, small-time drug dealer, and I kept asking for love advice because I had no idea how to ask a guy out or anything." Robert eventually started dating, moved to New York for graduate school, and later married a New Zealander. Along the way, he started mixing his love life with his nerd life and designed cutting-edge gay video games. The first one was a simulation of gay divorce; later ones became more graphic and sexual. Far from fringe, his work earned him a professorship at NYU. The first line of his bio reads: "Robert Yang makes surprisingly popular games about gay culture and intimacy—he is most known for his historical bathroom sex simulator The Tearoom and his male shower simulator Rinse and Repeat, and his gay sex triptych Radiator 2 has over 150,000 users on Steam."

Robert was describing how stressed he was after graduate school, when he was trying to design games that were both fulfilling and successful, but he felt enormous pressure from his parents to achieve traditional milestones of success. He used a ritual from Japan to help. "I had one of those daruma dolls," he said, referring to the red papier-mâché dolls that are modeled after the founder of Zen Buddhism and sold with the eyes blank. "You're supposed to paint one pupil black at the outset of a project, to symbolize your aspiration, then paint the other one when you finish. When I got the job at NYU, I opened the second eye."

In Japanese, *opening the second eye* means you realized a personal goal. It's a technique that helps you both visualize your dream and memorialize its achievement. I have a daruma doll in my home from finishing my first book, which describes the year I spent teaching junior high school in rural Japan.

You might think triumphant rituals like this are superfluous. After all, reaching a personal milestone would hardly seem to be a scary thing you need to tame or normalize in some way. But as anyone who's been through a long medical treatment, served in combat, or dropped out of the world for a while to complete a daunting project knows, fear of reentry is a real and terrifying thing. I remember thinking at the end of my year of chemo, *Now what?* I've done all I can do; I've been in this oddly sheltered place, a place where I didn't have to make many decisions or follow social norms, a place the poet Hakim Bey called a *temporary autonomous zone*. But now that I'm forced to leave, the prospects of being ordinary again seemed intimidating. I couldn't go back to who I was, yet I wasn't yet sure who I wanted to become.

What I needed, I now realize, was some way of marking the milestone. Some meaningful act, gesture, or ceremony to crystallize to myself and signify to those around me that a changed-and-still-changing me was emerging from that unordinary realm and returning to this ordinary one.

Some people mark the occasion by giving themselves a reward:

- Brett Parker, the New York City lawyer and Parkinson's patient who ran seven marathons on seven continents in seven days, got a tattoo of the number seven on his leg. "It's my way of saying, 'Fuck you,' to the disease."

- Jamie Levine, the Goldman Sachs dad who moved his family from London to Boston because of the Hail Mary cure that might save his daughter's liver, had T-shirts and a bib made with a graph showing Scarlett's spiking-then-plunging bilirubin number. "It was like, 'This number is her death, this is her life.'"
- Leigh Wintz, after finalizing her divorce and reaching her weight loss goal, bought a horse. "I was never going to do something so extravagant. I know what a commitment it is, blah blah blah blah. But I had enough money, I was looking for a way to reward myself other than food, so I did!"

Others mark the occasion by designing a personalized ceremony:

- Kate Hogue, the Missouri preacher and tornado survivor, designed a special service involving a blessing, a shawl, a loaf of bread, and a candle that she performed at the housewarming of any family who'd lost their previous home in the disaster. "It was a way of saying, *That was the old time, this is the new time, we bless the time to come.*"
- Leo Eaton, after the long walkabout across Europe he took with his wife Jeri's ashes, finally ended on Crete, where he and Jeri had lived for years. "I went to this little garden right outside our village. We grew our vegetables there, we grew our grapes, we made our wine. I went with some friends to the spot we used to call *the libation of the gods.* We scattered some of her ashes and placed others under her favorite olive tree, and as we were walking away my friends said, 'Jeri's home now, don't worry, we'll look after her.'"
- Michael Angelo, the hair salon owner, and his husband, Scott, tried for years to save their marriage, but when nonmonogamy made things worse and a cross-country trip ended in tears, they stayed up all night in a hotel room in Utah. "I slept for maybe an hour," Michael said, "and when I rolled over and looked at him, I knew it was time to go. For the

first time, we started talking instead of fighting; we started listening instead of defending. And I thought, *There's so much I want him to know if this is the last time I'm going to see his face.* And I don't know what came over me, but I kept looking at his ring, and I thought of him taking it off himself, and that was so unbearable to me. So I took his hands in mine, took his ring off his finger, and said, 'I love you. You are free to go. Be as great as you know how to be. I wish you happiness, success, and fulfillment.' And he took my ring off, placed it in my palm, and reminded me that I was the love of his life and that he didn't hold any of what had gone so awfully wrong against me. He said, 'Michael, really, truly, from my heart, I forgive you.' We showered and got dressed. We had a beautiful lunch and ordered a piece of strawberry cheesecake, it was the perfect miniature of our wedding cake, then he drove me to the airport, and I flew home to start my life over. Sometimes the happiest ending isn't the ending you expected."

Show Your Work

A final step in the long arc of unveiling a new self is not intimate, unspoken, symbolic, or unsaid. It's public; it's social; it's scary; it's necessary.

It's sharing your transformation with others.

People haven't always disclosed their private milestones in public, especially ones involving intimate details. In the ancient world, confession was not commonplace. Sophocles was not talking about his stint in rehab; Jeremiah was not revealing that he and his wife had trouble getting pregnant but were *finally having a baby*!

It wasn't until the modern era that this type of personal revelation became widespread. The cultural historian Paul John Eakin observes that the modern autobiography seems to have emerged concurrently with the appearance of personal spaces. It took the rise of privacy for us to eliminate privacy in our public personas. The spread of online culture has meant we increasingly spill our most personal details in front of everyone we know—and many that we don't.

Whatever the origins, among the people I spoke with, sharing that they'd reached the end of their transitions was a meaningful part of the process. They celebrate their cancerversaries or soberversaries, they hashtag #MeToo or #ItGetsBetter, they announce their divorces or downsizings on social media. I once gave a speech at a hospital in New Jersey in honor of National Cancer Survivors Day, which is the first Sunday in June. The director explained that one reason patients like to come is to show off to their nurses and their doctors that their hair has grown back, that they can get dressed up, that they have an identity beyond hospital gowns and fearful expressions. AA members have a similar bonding tradition of sidling up to fellow former drunks and saying, "I'm a friend of Bill W.," a badge of honor that says, *I, too, went through Bill Wilson's twelve-step program.* (AA members worried about falling off the wagon in an airport are encouraged to page, *Friends of Bill W., please come to gate . . .*, and a fellow traveler will appear.)

And why shouldn't we celebrate these moments? It's worth being proud of these accomplishments because they are, indeed, accomplishments. We've endured yet another life transition and picked up a few skills along the way. In narrative terms, we've reached the point where our story starts to cohere, and we're ready to start sharing it with others.

Here are some examples of how people unveiled their new selves:

- Lisa Ludovici was two years into her life as a medical hypnotist before she got the courage to update her LinkedIn profile. "I would sit there in my apartment all day, typing and retyping my profile, and I just couldn't do it. I was afraid of what people might think of me. *Whack job. Are you kidding? That's weird!* Finally, when I hit publish and declared, *I'm a medical hypnotist*, all the fear went away."
- Christian Picciolini had been out of the neo-Nazi movement for a decade when he wrote an article for a magazine in which he denounced

his years of hate. "The publication of that article was pivotal for me, as it was the first time I'd openly spoken about my past in a large public forum." The following year he cofounded Life After Hate.

- Carl Bass was some years into his reluctant tenure as CEO of Autodesk when he took the stage at his company's annual customer event in Las Vegas. "Having started out as someone who was afraid to talk to fifteen people, to now standing on stage in front of fifteen thousand, and feeling for the first time *I deserve to be here*, it felt huge."
- Tiffany Grimes, having opted to stay with Dade as he transitioned, further decided with him to start a YouTube channel. "There were not a lot of people doing that at the time. We had been watching a lot of videos, and they were so helpful to us, but no one had done that as a couple. So we decided to document our transition together, including my process of understanding and accepting as he went through the physical changes."
- David Figura, having aborted his extramarital affair en route to the motel, interviewed men about their anxieties and wrote a book called *So What Are the Guys Doing?* On the eve of publication, he shared the book with his son. Alex got about three chapters in and threw it across the room. "You're just pissing me off," he said. "You were going to cheat on Mom and leave us." "I got really mad," David said. "I told him, 'For God's sake, read the friggin' book.' About a month later he calls me at work and says, 'I finished the book. Thank you, Dad.' And I was in tears. All I could say was, 'It's partly because of you, Alex—but also because I love your mother—that I didn't take that step that night.' And I gotta tell you, that sort of openness has made us stronger in our love and appreciation for each other."

Small wins, big changes, private rituals, public declarations are all part of the process of embracing the new beginning. They are incremental steps toward the largest task of all: revamping your story of yourself.

CHAPTER 13

Tell It

Compose a Fresh Story

The last of the tools is the first one that drew me in—and the one that undergirds all of the others. It's the one essential act of surviving a major life change, yet it's the one we spend the least amount of time talking about. It's updating your personal story.

"We Have to Try to Have Another Baby. Now."

Aaron Koffman was the only child of incompatible parents in Los Angeles. "My mom wanted four kids; unfortunately, my parents' marriage didn't survive six months of my life." Aaron had what he called a ping-pong childhood. He spent every other weekend with his father until he was ten, then moved in with his father and spent every other weekend with his mom, until his father got remarried, and, well, everything got worse.

"I basically had to parent myself," he said. "I had to find ways to entertain myself, I had to find ways to educate myself. At my bar mitzvah, we ended up having two parties because there was no universe under which my parents were going to be in the same room together. All that led me to want to get as far away as possible, so I enrolled at Syracuse University at sixteen."

It was a horrible mistake.

"I was too young," Aaron said. "Two weeks in, I was like, *What the hell was I thinking? This is a different country where I speak the same language.*" Aaron returned to California, got a job, volunteered for Habitat for Humanity, and fell in love with urban planning. The boy who came from a broken home would devote his life to building homes. He went to Berkeley for college, then MIT for graduate school, and then, stirred by 9/11, moved to New York to help rebuild the city.

But what he really wanted to be was a dad. "I wanted to correct all this instability with stability," he said. After a few serious relationships, he met his wife, Heather, a community lender, at thirty-three. Four years later they were married; she got pregnant on their honeymoon. Their son, Bodie, was born the last week of August. Aaron called it the high point of his life.

The low point occurred nine months later.

"The story strangely starts in the morning," he said. "It was raining. A friend of mine was in from LA. Our nanny, who we shared with another family upstairs in a situation I didn't really love, was late. She was pregnant, she was a model, she was a bit of a diva, she came in and said her husband told her she should quit. I looked at her and thought, *I should just fucking say I'm done with your shit.* But I was late to meet my friend; I knew I couldn't do it without talking with Heather; so I hopped in an Uber."

His day never improved. The rain continued. His wife was working late. The real estate company where Aaron was a partner was closing a big deal. At five thirty he texted the nanny that he'd be running a little late and ducked into the subway. As soon as he stepped aboveground, the nanny called.

"She never calls," he said. "And she was screaming that Bodie was not waking up from a nap. It's that thing you fear as a parent. I started running like I haven't run in twenty years."

By the time he arrived on his block, his heart was pounding so hard he feared he was having a heart attack. He turned the corner and saw the EMT truck, then the fireman working on his nine-month-old son. "And I screamed, '*WHAT IS HAPPENING!*' The fireman says, 'We got him down. We're giving him air. We're going to Brooklyn Hospital.' And I'm, like 'Why the fuck are you going to Brooklyn Hospital when there's an emergency room two blocks from here?' 'That ER can't handle it,' the fireman said."

Bodie's ambulance left. Aaron got in a second ambulance and followed. "It's hitting me now that this may be the worst possible nightmare. I'm trying to tell myself that he got the care he needed. Maybe he choked on something. But he's going to be okay. Then all of a sudden, when his ambulance passed the Brooklyn Bridge, I realized that it didn't have its light on. That's when I knew."

Bodie Fairfax Koffman was declared dead at 7:00 p.m. on the last Thursday in May, his nine-month birthday. "My legs just came out from under me," Aaron said. "I fell to the floor and screamed—screamed—'*NOOOOOO!*' We used to celebrate his milestones. My wife is a great baker. Today was going to be three-quarters of a cake."

The story swept the New York City tabloids. The case was the subject of multiple police investigations; no charges were ever brought. The death was deemed an accident. Aaron was furious at the nanny ("I wanted to kill her"), but Heather convinced him to dampen his hostility. Mostly, he was just devastated.

"I thought, you have to be kidding me. I know my struggles are nothing compared with many children, but I had a hard childhood. I have had a hard adulthood. Heather lost her father to a stroke when she was twenty-five. And I really thought the universe was just going to take care of us now. I couldn't believe this was happening."

What followed, for Aaron, was the most painful of his many painful life transitions.

The biggest emotion he struggled with: sadness.

Rituals he used to mark the event? He didn't shave for a year; he wore Bodie's favorite color, blue, every day for that year; he got a tattoo on his forearm of a capital *B*. "I needed my memory of him to be physical," Aaron said. "I roll up my sleeves a lot, I wanted to be reminded of him every day. The tattoo is blue, like Bodie's eyes."

His memento: "I kept some dirty clothes at the instruction of another parent who lost their child. I didn't want to lose his scent."

What did he shed? The joy of pushing his stroller every day; taking pictures.

How did he structure his time? Sandbox. "Both our jobs told us to take as much time as we needed. In the early days we didn't want to leave the apartment. I would sometimes go into his nursery and just lie down on the rug. But basically we had nothing to do. One day we had an appointment at eleven thirty for the detective to come over, and he canceled at ten. Heather just started bawling, like, *What are we doing today? How are we going to fill this time?*"

Creative habits he started? "A friend of mine gave me a beautiful glass jar and a deck of flashcards and said, 'Anytime you think about him, just write down a thought or a memory, fold it up, and put it in the jar.' For a second I would be surrounded by happiness, and it was wonderful."

Did his transition involve a move? "We canceled a move. We were three weeks away from moving into a new apartment; we were finally going to get some space. But we canceled everything because we had to be here. I had to lay on the rug every day; I slept on the rug. It was a real source of comfort just to be in his room."

Finally, how did he write a new story?

"We started right away," Aaron said. "Bodie died on a Thursday. Heather had her period the next morning. The funeral wasn't until Tuesday. And in that window of time we went through a lot. I had no interest in killing myself, but I felt like death was the only way I could get through this because it would mean not feeling the pain anymore. But we realized that dying would just kill off Bodie's legacy. Also, we needed to be here for each other.

"That Monday night we stayed up late to write our eulogies," Aaron continued. "And something about the act of writing down our thoughts, of talking about it together, of thinking about how we could keep our story alive, we both decided, in that moment, *We have to try to have another baby. Now.*"

Heather got pregnant on the first try. Nine months after their nine-month-old son died, Heather gave birth to a baby boy. Bodie's story wasn't over—memorials were planned, money was raised, parks were renovated in his honor—but Aaron's story had a new beginning. The light refracted, the beam splintered, the whole he had been trying to hold together his entire life had fractured, then adhered again. His story prevailed. And in one sense, he wasn't surprised. The experience somehow fit the fractal nature of his story. The shape of his life, Aaron said, was a prism.

Write the Next Chapter

If a transition is the process of making ourselves whole again after a shattering life event, repairing our life story is the crown jewel of that process. It renders complete the art of completing your new self. The story is the one part of a transition that ties together all the other parts. *I used to be that. Then I went through a life change. Now I am this.*

Stories, we've been reminded in recent years, are the primary psychic unit of being alive. One of the distinguishing features of human beings is our ability to take seemingly unrelated events and convert them into coherent narratives that we package for private and public consumption. And this ability is built into us. Half our brains are involved in imaginative work, including converting our lives into ongoing chronicles, then making meaning from those accounts. "We dream in narrative," the literary scholar and poet Barbara Hardy remarked, "daydream in narrative, remember, anticipate, hope, despair, believe, doubt, plan, revise, criticize, construct, gossip, learn, hate, and love by narrative."

There are downsides of narrative, of course. Our minds are so desperate to find patterns in the world that we often simply make them up. Shown a series of random blinking lights, we invent persuasive explanations of their messages, even when there are none. Observing sports teams and financial markets, we create compelling narratives from artificial concepts like *momentum* or *hot streaks*, then lose our shirts betting on these fictions.

I heard sobering examples of how people are tempted by dangerous narratives. After doctors told Peggy Fletcher Stack, the religion writer from Salt Lake City, that one of her twin daughters would not live past two, Peggy tried to convince herself the child never existed. "I just lay in my bed and thought, *Well, I really only wanted one child, so I'll just pretend I had one child.* When I told Mike my idea, he said, 'Absolutely not! Camille will always be part of our family. We'll recognize her in heaven.' He was so right."

Michelle Swaim, the anorexic, obsessive jogger who slipped on the ice, quit jogging, and went on to adopt eleven children, persuaded herself for years that she was wronged by her husband because it was his job to make her happy. "Once I realized, *Oh, that's not his job. That's my job*, I started growing up and making decisions to finally make myself happy."

But the upsides of personal storytelling far outweigh the traps. Storytelling allows us to take life events that are exceptional, unforeseen, or otherwise out of the ordinary and domesticate them into meaningful, manageable chapters in the ongoing arc of our lives. This act of integration is storytelling's greatest gift. It conventionalizes the unconventional. It transforms the untellable into a tale. It allows us, in the evocative words of novelist Hilary Mantel, to seize the copyright on ourselves.

I heard some stirring examples of how people use personal narratives to heal themselves.

For years, Rockie Lynne Rash had been reluctant to tell the story of his abandonment and difficult childhood until his record label introduced him to a songwriter who had a similar upbringing. "Abandoned, not a great family, the whole thing," Rockie said. "He and I wrote this song called 'That's Where Songs Come From.' It says I don't want to be pitied, I'm the lucky one, 'Oh, can't you see, that's where songs come from.' The whole experience was a huge, cathartic moment for me."

Mary-Denise Roberts was serially sexually abused as a girl. "There were at least three different adult men, in three different locations, who always had their hands on me," she said. Mary-Denise fled her troubled past for various trouble spots around the world as a professional peacemaker and aid worker. But she completely repressed her childhood terrors until, divorced and remarried, she joined a writer's group in Atlanta. "I was telling a very sanitized version of my life story, using lots of lingo and jargon," she said. "And my teacher stalked me. 'You need to write about the thing you don't ever want to write about, the most horrible thing ever.' I finally sat down and wrote out the whole story, and I couldn't stop. That was the moment—it was pretty messy; it wasn't without tears—that I realized I could tell it. That I should tell it."

Davon Goodwin, the Pittsburgh-born botany lover who was injured by an IED in Afghanistan, was also reluctant to tell his story until that day his mother forced him to share it out loud in church. "I think the key to recovery is you gotta get your story out," he said. "Otherwise, it will control you. I'm not saying I don't have bad days, but that was the day I started to control it, instead of it controlling me."

Keep Your Distance

Telling a successful personal story is central to finalizing a life transition, but how exactly do people do this? Are there shared qualities that transformational stories have? One thing I listened closely for in my interviews—and we later coded for—is whether there are particular signposts people employ to say to themselves and to those around them, *I've absorbed the jolt, I've endured the exile, I'm back in the game.* Are there specific ways, when telling their story, people convert their meaning vacuums into meaning moments?

We identified three.

The first is they put some distance between the present and the past. They create a time gap between the story they told when their life first ventured off course and the story they tell today. They shift from *this is happening to me now* to *that happened to me then.*

One barometer of this change is verb tense. The more we describe our disruptive events in the present tense—*I open the door and see the body on the ground*—the more visceral they seem, but the less meaning we're able to draw from them. The more we use past tense—*I opened the door, saw the body, and began to realize my life was about to change*—the more removed the events become and the easier it is to integrate the events into the larger flow of our narratives. As my friend Catherine Burns, the artistic director of the Moth, puts it, "The best stories are vulnerable but not raw; they come from scars not wounds."

I encountered this issue in two ways. First I spoke with a number of people—the book editor whose wife left him and whose boss fired him within months of each other; the single mom who was just released from federal prison for a crime she said she didn't commit; the dad whose daughter was in her third stint in rehab—who were still reeling from the unexpected explosion in their lives. These conversations were among the most wrenching I had, yet because the events were so recent, the person was still processing their feelings.

On the flip side, some of the more poignant stories I heard took years before the person could get the proper distance to find meaning in them.

I'm thinking of Chris Shannon, the air force technician who had a near-death experience after losing his leg in a motorcycle accident (he's the one whose femur got lodged in the radiator). Today he alternates between mentoring young people in Oregon and traveling the country in a camper. "Losing my leg really did change my life," he said. "I have some anxieties about things, but I really have no fear. I'm much more appreciative. Hell, I even appreciate being run over."

I'm thinking of Kate Milliken, the New York television producer whose broken engagement led to a health crisis that left her unable to walk. In the cab on the way to her doctor, she almost turned on her video camera. Then she caught herself. "It's too early to tell this story," she said. After receiving a diagnosis of MS and sinking into depression, Kate turned to alternative treatments, fell in love, married, and had children. She also made thirty-two mini-films about her journey. "It took me a while, but I was eventually able to see what happened as transcendent. Instead of seeing the wall, now I see a sea of possibility."

I'm thinking of Kate Hogue, the young preacher who almost died in the tornado in Joplin, Missouri. In the immediate aftermath, Kate did a lot of preaching, mostly to comfort her neighbors. "I spoke about how grateful I was for all that we have." But the experience felt hollow, she said, because inside she was questioning her faith. "I thought, *What does it mean that God was watching over me, but not my friend Tripp, who died?*"

It took Kate five years, including enrolling in a PhD program, entering counseling, and using a form of therapy called eye movement desensitization and reprocessing, to finally put the event behind her. "I think anytime you experience trauma, you realize how little control you have over those kinds of things. But the control you do have is to decide how to make meaning once it has happened. To me, the good stories are the ones where something terrible happened and you did something about it that is positive and life affirming. Now I'm one of those stories."

Make Pigs Fly

The second technique that transformative personal stories display is they use positive language.

The novelist John Steinbeck had a quirky logo he drew after signing his name. It was a pig with wings. He called it Pigasus, which he wrote out in Greek letters. Late in his life, he accompanied the illustration with the Latin words *Ad Astra Per Alia Porci*, which he translated (incorrectly, it turns out) as "to the stars on the wings of a pig." His explanation: We must all try to attain the heavens, even though we are bound to the earth.

For half a millennium, the expression *when pigs fly* has been used in multiple languages to mean a circumstance so improbable that its completion is nearly impossible. It's a figure of speech known as an adynaton, a way of saying something that will never happen. Steinbeck adopted this phrase because he had been told by a naysayer professor that he would be an author "when pigs fly."

More recently, neuroscientists have discovered that imagining this kind of unimaginable outcome is vital to recovering from a life interrupted. The more we are able to conjure up a future that seems out of reach—*I will find another job, I will laugh once more, I will love again*—the more we're able to advance toward it. A big reason is mirror neurons, the part of our brains that mimic the actions we observe. When we see someone jump, laugh, or cry, our brains imitate the same activity.

A similar response occurs with stories. If we read about someone jumping, laughing, or crying, our minds perform the same actions. And it doesn't stop there. The same mirroring happens with stories we *tell*. If we tell ourselves we will get better, or calmer, or happier, our minds will begin to simulate that outcome. This response doesn't mean we'll achieve these results right away, but it does mean we set in motion that possibility.

Steinbeck was right: We can make pigs fly.

All this neuroscience helped me figure out something I kept hearing in my conversations that at first I couldn't understand. People described being in uncomfortable situations in which they began telling themselves stories they didn't yet believe. *Fake it till you make it* was the most common explanation. That expression is often linked to William James's observation that if we first act a certain way, our feelings will follow. But I was hearing something different. People were saying that if we tell ourselves a certain story first, our feelings will follow.

In Steinbeck's terms: First we have to persuade ourselves we can make pigs fly; only then do we have a chance of helping them fly.

Here are some examples of how people told themselves upbeat stories as a stepping-stone to renewal:

- When Ellen Shafer moved back home to North Dakota from Minneapolis after her husband lost his job, she found it degrading to go from running big-city ad campaigns to working at a small agency. Moving in with her parents for a time didn't help. "My husband was thrilled, because my mom made great midwestern food every night and did our laundry. But I don't care how old I was, I was suddenly back in sixth grade." So she made up a story about why they had come home. "I told everyone I was doing all these exciting projects for Target, but in the end I was just trying to persuade people to buy more stuff they didn't need. So I came back to Fargo to help smaller business make an impact in a smaller community. It was a rationalization, but the more I told it, the more I came to believe it. Now I love it here."
- Brenda Stockdale, who tamed her lupus with mind-body therapy and now runs a practice to help others use biobehavioral self-care, said even small acts of affirmation can rewire your mind. "In moments of great horror there's a loss of identity," she said. "All it takes are tiny moments of immediacy: a bite of food, an aroma, a hummingbird on the feeder, the smell of fresh cut grass. These micromoments are around us all the time, but we usually ignore them. Once we notice them, our

biology follows, and suddenly that hummingbird, or that grass, leads us to a fancy vacation; we're in a hammock in Tahiti. I found that if we take advantage of these moments, if we give ourselves permission to follow where they lead, our minds will take us to our healing place."

- Sasha Cohen, after back-to-back disappointments in ladies' figure skating at the Winter Olympics, was haunted by failure. "For a long time I couldn't shake the question, *Why wasn't I good enough?* People would come up to me and say, 'Why did you fall?' But now, when I look back, I've reframed the question. I know that I didn't have such quick reflexes; that there were things I couldn't do easily that other people could do in their sleep; that I always did every jump a little different each time. Now I think, *Maybe I got as far as I did because of how much I pushed myself mentally with the body I had. Maybe I should give myself credit that I hung in there and overcame a lot of obstacles. Maybe I should see it as a story of grace instead of a story of disappointment.*"

Nail the Ending

The third way we can tell our personal stories in a way that maximizes their benefit is to nail the ending.

Dan McAdams, the scholar who did more than any other to promote the significance of life stories, has been thinking about narrative identity for more than thirty years. His signature insight is that the way we shape those stories affects the meaning we take from them. The two most common examples are *contamination narratives* and *redemption narratives.* In contamination narratives, we describe major events as making our lives worse. The event may be positive or negative, but the story we tell about it ends on a downbeat. *I loved becoming a mom, but then my husband cheated on me. I recovered from my stroke, but I can't ride my bike again.*

In redemption narratives, we describe major events as making our lives better. The event may be positive or negative, but the story ends on an upbeat. *Winning that award was great, but I was especially touched I could share the recognition with my colleagues. My father's death was long and painful, but it really brought our family closer.*

The important thing about scripting a happy ending is that it need not happen quickly. Ruminating on a disruptive life event, thinking about it from multiple angles, even obsessing over the details is not only healthy, it's necessary, McAdams says. But equally necessary—and even healthier—is finding a way to articulate something constructive that came out of the experience and committing to make it happen.

The larger point here is worth emphasizing: We have a choice in how we tell our life story. We do not write it in permanent ink. There are no points for consistency, or even accuracy. We can change it at any time, for any reason, including one as simple as making ourselves feel better. After all, a primary function of our life story is to allow us to place experiences firmly in the past and take from them something beneficial that will allow us to thrive in the future. Only when that happens will we know our transition is complete.

Only then will we have nailed the ending.

In my conversations, I encountered many people who transformed their lifequakes into life stories with upbeat endings. Christy Moore said of getting pregnant at seventeen and dropping out of school that it saved her from a life of doing drugs or flipping burgers. "I can't imagine not having my daughter, who was literally the perfect baby and child. I can't imagine not being a doctor. I attribute it to God. It was all a divine plan that I had no idea was coming."

Davon Goodwin called the IED that nearly ended his life in Afghanistan a blessing. "Without it I wouldn't have graduated college in three years," he said. "Without it I wouldn't have found my way back to botany. I'm not going to accept the things that are wrong with me. I acknowledge them, but I'm not going to accept them as limitations."

Sean Collins, the onetime Benedictine monk who left the monastery because he was gay, told me that one of the worst things that ever happened to him occurred when he was seven and a boy at school called him a "faggot." "Of course what I heard is that he'd figured out my secret," Sean said. "When my mom picked me up from school, I was crying. I told her why, and she immediately headed toward the boy's house. I begged her, 'Please don't do this. *Please!*" The kid's mother answered the door, and Sean's mom lit into her. The boy appeared and started laughing. Sean sobbed again on the way home and was still sobbing when his mom called him for dinner. "She looked at me with such disgust and said, 'You know, maybe he was right.'

"And it was at that moment I thought, *You cannot trust anyone with this information, because eventually they will turn on you. I am never going to tell my parents anything that's personal.*"

And for the longest time, he didn't. This event was the defining moment in his longtime, rocky relationship with his mom.

"Years and years passed," Sean said. "I was thirty-two before I brought up that story again to my mother. She apologized, then she said, 'You know, during the war, if I hadn't met your father, there was this woman I was very fond of.' And she admits that she had a relationship with this woman before World War II. She comes out to me, twenty-five years after that incident. My being honest with her allowed her to be honest with me, and it made me realize how similar we were, after all."

Chris Waddell knows as well as anyone the challenge of nailing the ending. When he first became a paraplegic at twenty, he thought his life was over. Then he went on to a glorious career as a Paralympian. When that ended at thirty-four, he again thought his life was over. Retiring from competitive skiing was "far more difficult" than breaking his back, he told me. "I had no idea who I was, and I felt betrayed by my passion. It just dropped me off a cliff."

So he decided to climb another cliff. Specifically, he hatched a dream to become the first disabled person to summit Tanzania's Mount Kilimanjaro, the tallest mountain in Africa. Since he couldn't use his legs, though,

Chris would need to scale all 19,341 feet by pedaling a four-wheel mountain bicycle using only his arms. He raised money, trained for the altitude, built a special vehicle, and recruited an international team to assist him by securing him to a winch, laying down boards on the mountain, and helping him navigate the boulders, altitude, bodily demands, and stress. At forty-one years old, he set off.

The seven-day climb was brutal. At times he moved only a foot a minute. International media were rapt by his heroism.

But then, a mere hundred feet from the summit, the boulders became too large, the wheels of his vehicle too meager, the path unpassable. He had to abandon his dream.

"I was crushed," he said. "I could see the top. My sole job was to get there. It was not about *one man gets broken and overcomes anything*. To me, that's a ridiculous cliché. It was about promising that I would do this. It was about so many people having sacrificed to give me that opportunity, and now I've just failed everybody." His partners persuaded Chris to let them carry him the final inches to the summit, where he posed for pictures and listened to the local guides sing celebratory songs in Swahili, all while he felt fraudulent and guilty.

"And it wasn't until much later, when I started telling the story to schoolkids, that I realized the lesson was there all along. *Nobody climbs a mountain alone.* That was the thing I had to discover: the value of the team. Because for me to say I climbed it myself was complete fantasy. There were so many people who worked so hard. Making it to the top on my own would have perpetuated a lot of what I was trying to eliminate: the sense of separation. That people with disabilities need to be apart. We don't. We need other people. That's why I talk about that day as a gift. It taught me what I most needed to learn: that I'm just like everybody else."

It taught him the value of rewriting his life story to give it a heroic ending.

CONCLUSION

In Between Dreams

The Secrets of Successful Transitions

Edwin Jacob Feiler Jr., was born on Wednesday, January 23, 1935. His mother was a math teacher, his father a jack-of-all-trades lawyer.

"On 1/23/45 I was ten years old," he said. "I was proud of that fact and loved to share it. I was born in Savannah, Georgia, and my life, in one way or another, has revolved around this city, which I love, and which my family has been a part of for more than 150 years. My children once joked that I have been a *professional Savannahian*. The nickname stuck. It's an honor I am proud to carry."

Two significant world events shaped my father's childhood. The first was the Great Depression. "My family lived modestly in a snug, six-room house that had two bedrooms and one bath. Heat came from a small, coal-fired furnace."

The second was World War II. "Everything was devoted to the war effort. There was gas rationing, so we couldn't just drive around." Also, there were few toys. "My main hobby during those years was building model airplanes. The models came in cardboard boxes that I would purchase from Getchell's Variety Store. Authenticity was very important to me. Kits contained plans, balsa wood strips, templates for wings and body parts, decals, and tissue paper.

"It was painstaking work," he continued. "The glue had to dry before the next connection could be completed. I had a series of strings across the ceiling of the bedroom I shared with my brother, Stanley, to display the finished models. I still have a scar on my left wrist where I cut it when an X-Acto knife slipped."

Being Jewish in the segregated South of the 1940s came with complications. "When I was in junior high school, I wrote a book report about a biography of Babe Ruth," he said. "At the same time there was a movie out called *The Babe Ruth Story.* The teacher insisted I had only seen the movie. I did not back down, because I had read the book. 'You Jew boys always do that,' she said. After school, I went home and told my mother, who immediately walked the two blocks to Washington Avenue Junior High School. She spoke to the principal, and the next day I was in a different class."

"How did you feel about that?"

"I was sort of embarrassed, but I felt I had done the right thing. I hadn't seen the movie, which I later heard was the worst movie ever made."

My father's love of military-style precision carried forward. He became an Eagle Scout, earned a Navy ROTC scholarship to the University of Pennsylvania, and served as a lieutenant junior grade on the battleship USS *Wisconsin.* "The junior officers sat on a different side of the wardroom, where the nightly movies were projected onto a cheesecloth screen," he said. "Thus, our view of the movies was backwards—in baseball movies, the runner appeared to be going to third base."

But the defining event of his life, he said, occurred in Baltimore in 1957.

"Matchmaking was very much at the heart of the college experience in those days," he said. "I had pretty much decided that I did not want to stay in the New York–New Jersey corridor after school. The folks were too pushy and acquisitive for me. My desire was to be back home in Savannah, because it was 'a good place to raise kids.' Most of the girls I dated were midwesterners who met this criteria, but my aunt Gladys, who was living in Baltimore, suggested I call up this girl, Jane, whom I had met a few years earlier.

"We went out twice and found immediate compatibility," he continued. "She was smart, attractive, and would graduate from Michigan the following year. I especially adored her obvious artistic talents and excellent taste. Thus began an intense period of quick visits and frequent correspondence."

In June 1957, warships from all over the world gathered in Annapolis for the International Naval Review. My father's parents came up from Georgia; Jane came from Baltimore. Despite the obvious culture clash—she was the youngest child of a bookish, Yale-educated urologist; his father hunted squirrels and asked her to call him by the Southern honorific *colonel*—they got along.

But my father was on sea duty that summer, and Jane insisted on dating other men. They met again that August. "That night, before I said anything, she blurted out, 'I love you.' My first response was, 'That means you will have to live in Savannah, Georgia.' We came to immediate agreement after I actually proposed, though she said I had to get her father's consent. He gave it, along with permission to take gasoline for my car from the tank they had in the backyard because he was a doctor."

Edwin Feiler and Jane Abeshouse were married in June 1958. They lived in Annapolis until my dad was discharged, then moved to Savannah, where my father worked alongside his father building low-income housing and my mother taught junior high school art. They had three children, whom they named like hurricanes, with first names starting with A, B, C.

The great tragedy of my father's life, he said, was that his younger brother, Stanley, was diagnosed with MS in 1970. "Stanley had everything," my father said. "He was attractive, smart, popular, had a great education and a prestigious legal practice. I don't think Mother really ever recovered from this." Stanley spent the last years of his shortened life living in my parents' home after his wife pushed his wheelchair to my parents' driveway and left him.

The great pride of my father's life was founding a civic organization called Leadership Savannah in 1975. "The theory was to identify emerging leaders, introduce them to one another, and discuss community issues." His father strongly objected, but he insisted. "If people like me don't do it," he said, "it's not going to get done." The one condition my father made to civic leaders was that the program must have balance. "That meant participation by men *and* women, blacks *and* whites, people who could afford it *and* people who couldn't." That concept wasn't exactly routine in South Georgia at the time; the organization continues to this day.

The great sadness of my father's life was his own diagnosis with Parkinson's disease in his midsixties. For nearly a decade, he was able to conceal his illness from the outside world. He continued to work, serve on boards, be himself. But over time, he could no longer hide his deterioration. The disease slowly undermined his business life, his family time, his community service—the three pillars of meaning that were as balanced in him as anyone I've ever met. As my father neared eighty, the emotional toll nearly overwhelmed him, and he began planning to end his life.

The plan failed. I once asked him how he felt about what he'd done. "Ashamed," he said. The months that followed were among the worst I can remember. The conversations our family was forced to have were aching, unbearable. My mother gave up much of her life to care for her husband of nearly sixty years.

The sheer weight of confusion, emotion, and pressure we were all under is one reason the storytelling project I began with my dad—emailing him a question every Monday morning—was so profound. At the simplest level, it gave him something to do; it gave my mother a break; it gave us all something to talk about. But in reality it gave us so much more.

My father spent his final years, often slumped in a wheelchair at home, painstakingly turning the 150-plus stories he wrote into a sixty-thousand-word autobiography, demonstrating the same care and precision, insistence on accuracy and detail, he used with those model airplanes he strung on his ceiling as a boy. Every story had to be accompanied by a photograph, a news clipping, a love letter; every fact had to be double- and triple-checked, preferably by a grandchild; every list had to include a Harvard comma. For me, reading those stories, draft after draft, was like a journey into the origins of my own mind.

And when I sat with my dad on one of his final days—his body weakened from the disease that had slowly decimated his legs, his fingers, his bowels, and his bladder, but his mind still as sharp as ever—and asked what he had learned from becoming a writer in his eighties, he said, "It certainly stimulated my thoughts. I was forced by your questions to relive some of the past. I had been an avid photographer, so I had lots of pictures, but I didn't have the stories."

"And what did it force you to do?"

"Think about my past—who I'd met, what I'd done, how I'd done it, what I thought about along the way, whose lives I influenced."

I asked what the most valuable part of the process was.

"I felt extraordinary about the fact that this publication will outlast all of us."

"If you could give one message to your grandchildren from this experience, what would it be?"

He thought for a second and made the rarest of things for a Parkinson's patient: a smile. "Write the stories."

The Meaning of Your Life

After a century of study, scholars still can't agree on an answer to the simplest of questions: What is a story? If there's any consensus, it's that a story contains at least two objects, acts, or events, connected over time. A snowball is not a story; a bloody nose is not a story; the connection between a snowball and a bloody nose is a story. Also, stories contain problems that protagonists attempt to resolve. A mother comes upon a child with a bloody nose and a snowball. Now that's the beginning of a story. That leads to the final necessary ingredient for a story: Something interesting has to happen. Otherwise, why tell it?

But there is one thing about stories that most everyone agrees on: A story has no inherent meaning. Somebody has to give it meaning—the teller, the hearer, or some combination.

The same applies to our lives.

The first big lesson of the Life Story Project is that our life is a story. It has multiple events, connected over time. It has problems that protagonists attempt to resolve. It has interesting happenings. But on a fundamental level, our life story has no inherent meaning. We must give it meaning. Just as we must give our lives meaning and our stories meaning, we must give our life stories meaning.

Each of our lives is a life story project of its own.

Learning to make meaning from our life stories may be the most indispensable but least understood skill of our time. Paul Wong, a meaning researcher in Toronto, calls meaning-making "the best kept secret to the greatest human adventure." In our culture these days, happiness gets all the attention, but meaning is arguably more important. In a landmark study published in 2013, Roy Baumeister and three colleagues found that happiness is fleeting while meaning is enduring; happiness concentrates on the self while meaning concentrates on things larger than the self; happiness focuses on the present while meaning focuses on stitching together the past, present, and future.

In a pointed conclusion, Baumeister and his colleagues write that animals can be happy—after all, it's just a passing feeling—but only humans can find meaning, because only humans have the ability to take events that are fundamentally unhappy and turn them into empathy, compassion, and well-being. "Indeed the meaningful but unhappy life is in some ways more admirable than the happy but meaningless one," they write. "Put another way, humans may resemble many other creatures in their striving for happiness, but the quest for meaning is a key part of what makes us human, and uniquely so."

The fundamental goal of tending our life stories is to do so in a manner that maximizes the meaning we take from them. Fortunately, we're good at doing that. If anything, the pursuit of meaning may very well be easier than the pursuit of happiness. It begins with telling a personal story—taking two events, making a connection between them—then drawing a meaningful conclusion from the result. *When I was nine, I saw a bully give a kid a bloody nose, so I made a snowball and said, "If you do that again, you'll regret it." That's why I went into law enforcement. My whole life has been about standing up for the underdog.*

Though I didn't know it when I began, storytelling projects like the one I did with my dad have been shown to give greater meaning to life. James Birren, the founder of gerontology, calls them *guided autobiography.* Lives are made up of memories, but when those memories remain episodic and disconnected, their impact dissipates. Countless studies have found that carefully cultivating our memories improves quality of life, increases self-esteem, heightens well-being, elevates our sense of serenity, even reduces clinical depression. Had I known that last fact earlier, I might have started asking my dad questions long before I did.

I went to see James Birren in his book-lined home north of Los Angeles not long after I started sending questions to my dad. Professor Birren, who was ninety-six, brightened at the opportunity to talk about his work. The thing he was most proud of, he said, was recognizing the healing power of stories for older people. As we age, we feel a greater sense of alienation, loneliness, and loss of purpose; we also feel bored. Storytelling ameliorates those feelings. By climbing to a summit and peering out on our lives, we feel closer to events that might seem far away and to people who might seem long forgotten.

Professor Birren also told me something else. The same process of reviewing your life that he originally envisioned for older people also works for people of all ages. But it performs different functions. Older people use life review to make sense of their past and construct a narrative of a life well lived; younger people use life review to gain insight into the present and help them make a pressing life decision. Later in our lives, we use stories to better learn who we were; earlier in our lives, we use stories to better learn who we are. In both cases, storytelling helps prepare us for the future.

As I departed, Professor Birren directed me to a bookshelf and asked me to retrieve a black volume. Nothing appeared on the spine. On the cover was cursive white text that said, *James Emmett Birren: A Memoir.* He took out a pen and signed the title page with the same gentle script.

> *To Bruce: With best wishes for fuller life stories.*

The Theme of Your Life

What is the primary meaning most people distill from their lives? The last question I asked in every interview addressed this question. "Looking back over your entire life story with all its chapters, scenes, and challenges, do you discern a central theme?" I was moved by how many people immediately answered, "Yes!"

Five categories emerged. *Struggle,* which was the choice of 31 percent of our respondents; *self-actualization,* which was the selection of 28 percent; followed by *service* with 18 percent, *gratitude* with 13 percent, and *love* with 10 percent. Because these answers are a proxy for the meaning we take from our life stories, it's worth taking a closer look.

Struggle

The largest category was people who said life was full of ups and downs, and their lives were about learning to adapt to these changes. The popularity of struggle is yet more reinforcement for the idea that people view life as irregular and nonlinear, not predictable and expected. This notion calls to mind Viktor Frankl's observation that our need for meaning is greatest when life is harshest. "If there is meaning in life at all, then there must be meaning in suffering."

The people in this category used expressions like life is *a difficult climb, a long journey, a rollercoaster, a cycle of starts and stops.* They are people like Amy Murphy, who said her life was about chaos, "Chaos I create and chaos that is thrown at me"; Darrel Ross, who said his life was about adversity, "Tough things and tough times are going to happen, but most actually build and prepare you, not destroy you"; and Wendi Aarons, who said her life was about agility, "You have to figure out how to deal with life, and be adaptable."

Theme of Life: Struggle

The prodigal son
In order to win, you have to take risks
Life is long Leap of faith
A cycle of start and stop
Chaos I create, and chaos that is thrown at me
Hope and perseverance
Death and resurrection
Connecting the dots, and seeing where that gets you
Change is life
Take what's come and work with it
Getting hit with curveballs
Embracing uncertainty

Self-actualization

The second biggest category included people who said their lives were about being true to themselves, accepting themselves, or improving themselves. People in this category used phrases like *put myself first, get out from under the spell of my parents, be genuine and authentic.* They are people like Joe Dempsy, who said the theme of his life was self-respect, "You are who you are and don't apologize for it"; Antonio Grana, who said the theme of his life was independence, "I had to learn how to individuate from others, take back my identity for myself"; and Karen Peterson-Matchinga, who said the theme of her life was self-respect, "When I am true to myself, it is always the right answer."

Theme of Life: Self-actualization

My insecurities drive my life, they're the reason I do everything
Figuring out who I am and where I fit in
A desire to be genuine
Maslow's Hierarchy of Needs is true
Losing myself in the midst of adventure and exploration
Evolution and the process of discovery
You are who you are and don't apologize for it
Who am I and where do I belong?
Growth Quest for meaning
When I am true to myself, it is always the right answer
Keep getting bigger
Trying to be a better person and husband
My work is who I am

Service

The third most popular category was people who said their lives were devoted to making the world a better place. They are people like Nancy

Davis Kho, who said her life was about "taking the good I've been given and trying to magnify it"; Leo Eaton, who said his life was about "trying to let my work make a difference;" or Matt Weyandt, who said his life was about "trying to make the world better, even if it's just in a small way."

Theme of Life: Service

Connection to the natural world
Trying to let my work make a difference
God must become more and I must become less
Do good, avoid evil, speak up
Mission: creating opportunities for people
A journey to enlightenment and helping others
Pushing boundaries
Embody the all-beautiful love of God
Do the right thing
Doing something to make the world better even just by a tiny bit
Fulfillment of our potential as human beings
Social justice
Desire to make a difference
Leading by example

Gratitude

The next category was people whose lives were defined by feeling appreciative, lucky, or joyful. These people used phrases like *be happy where you are, everything is possible, earning the gift of life*. They are people like Nisha Zenoff, who said, "Life is a love fest. I am blessed and have this amazing life"; David Parsons, who said his life has been characterized by "God's grace, God protecting me, and God caring for me"; and seventy-eight-year-old Mary Ann Putzier, a former nun turned artist who did her interview soon after burying her husband and while undergoing chemotherapy, and who summed up her life by saying, "I've just been very lucky." Six months later she died.

Theme of Life: Gratitude

Everything's possible with God
Enjoying the struggle
Earning the gift of life
I am blessed and have this amazing life–it's a gift
Optimism
God's been with me so nobody can be against me
Playfulness
I'm lucky
Existence is extraordinary
I had a dream and pursued my dream and loved it
We get it all from the Good Lord
Embracing opportunities
Be happy with where you are
God's grace, God protecting me, God caring for me

Love

The final category comprised people who said their lives were built around relationships. These people used phrases like *dedication to wife and kids, had my mom there to comfort me through everything, err on the side of love.* They are people like Moselyn Bowers, who said, "Success without someone to share it with is nothing," and Lisa Heffernan, who said, "Learning to build relationships rather than destroy them." And, to my surprise, my dad, who first mentioned his sixty-one-year marriage to my mom, then told a story. "A few years ago, I was having lunch at the Commerce Club in Atlanta with a United States senator's chief of staff. 'How are you?' he asked. My answer was, "We have three children who get along well with one another, understand the value of money, and have a work ethic. Everything else is in second place.' My lunch mate said, 'I know everybody in this room, and no one else can make that statement.'"

Theme of Life: Love

Err on the side of love
Dedication to life and kids
Had my mom there to comfort me through everything
Family and music
Fear of not being loved and letting go
Success without someone to share it with is nothing
Let love lead
Connection Love
I love to talk and I love to listen
Redeeming a childhood
Learning to build relationships rather than destroy them
To be loved and trying to get up
Having loving relationships

Five Truths of Transitions

My father elected not to organize the stories in his autobiography chronologically. Instead he divided them into sections—family, school, business, travel, politics, photography, and so on. At the end of the book is a section entitled "Legacy." It contains a story called "Solving a Big Problem," a letter called "Advice from Your Grandfather," and a list called "What I Learned in 1975."

The 1975, in this case, refers to the recession that peaked that year. For my father it was the defining nonlinear event in his life, because it upended the stable-but-staid professional life he had enjoyed since returning to Savannah and opened the door to the more-risky-but-at-times-more-lucrative professional life he would pursue for the rest of his career.

"What I Learned in 1975" was his ode to a transition well handled.

I kept a similar list as I was working on the Life Story Project. It might have been called "What I Learned from Talking to 225 People About Their

Lives." Since the theme of these conversations was that the linear life is dead, the nonlinear life involves more life transitions, and life transitions are a skill we can, and must, master, I actually named the list "Five Truths of Transitions."

1. Transitions Are Becoming More Plentiful

If I didn't find the idea of the linear life so misleading, I would find it almost quaint that for generations, people embraced the idea that our lives follow three, five, seven, or eight predictable stages. Insofar as that road map brought people comfort in the past, it can bring us comfort no more. We need different maps for different times. Crises aren't just for midlife anymore; turning points don't care how old we are; urges to overturn our routines don't follow handy charts printed in undergraduate textbooks. Life changes happen when they happen, often when we least expect them to happen, and at a pace that would have seemed unthinkable even a few years ago.

The average adult will experience one life disruptor every one to two years—that's more frequently than many people see a dentist. One in ten of those—around three to five in an adult life—will be so big that the person will undergo a major life change. Considering that nine out of ten of us live with other people, that means virtually every household in the United States has at least one person in it who's undergoing a significant reorientation of their lives, sometimes more than one person, sometimes multiple people undergoing the same transition. It's time we see ourselves as what we are: a people in perpetual flux.

2. Transitions Are Nonlinear

Life is not the only thing that's nonlinear; the transitions that fill our lives are nonlinear, too. The first century of thinking about transitions—that they involve three precise stages we pass through at three precise times—has become grossly outdated. Transitions are not hopscotch, they're pinball; they're not connect-the-dots, they're freestyle drawing. People gravitate to the stage they're best at—the long goodbye, the messy middle, or the new beginning—and bog down in the one they're worst at. Even the most adept of us at managing life transitions have parts of the process we don't handle well.

The same goes for the microsteps we use to manage these times. Transitions involve tools that everyone can master and that everyone deploys in their own idiosyncratic way. The full tool kit involves accepting the situation, marking the change, shedding old ways, creating new outlets, sharing your transformation, unveiling your new self, telling your story. While not always easy to execute, these tools can prove remarkably restorative and reliably reinvigorating. Transitions have endured as a coping mechanism because transitions work.

3. Transitions Take Longer Than You Think (but No Longer Than You Need)

The moment in my conversations that was universally the most awkward was when I asked people how long their major life transition took. Even the most well-spoken individuals stammered and stumbled and seemed reluctant to admit what turned out to be my most consistent finding: longer than they wanted.

The average length of a life transition is around five years. Fewer than one in four said it took under three years; more than half said it took between four and ten years; one in seven said it took longer. Again, multiply these figures by the number of transitions we're likely to face—three, four, five, or more—and it's clear that transitions are a lifetime sport that no one is teaching us how to play.

There is an upside to our ineptitude. With a little work, we can get better at transitions. There are skills we can learn and mistakes we can avoid.

Also, these times of being betwixt and between do end. Sure, some emotions might linger and some scars might endure, but more than 90 percent of people said their transitions ultimately did come to a conclusion. Transitions take longer than we think, but not longer than we need—and not forever, either.

4. Transitions Are Autobiographical Occasions

The legendary neurologist Oliver Sacks once wrote, "It might be said that each of us constructs and lives, 'a narrative,' and that this narrative *is* us." If he's correct—and I believe that he is—that means a breach in that narrative is an existential event. The disruptors, pivots, junctures, deadlocks, lurches, and lifequakes that dot our lives are narrative breaches that must be tended, in part, with narrative repairs. We must fix the plot holes in our life stories.

A life transition is both the setting and the mechanism to do just that. It is an autobiographical occasion, when we simply must take the opportunity to revisit, revise, and ultimately restart our internal autobiographies, making some tweaks, adding a new chapter or two, elevating or devaluing certain themes. And ultimately making sure that we maintain the balance among the three primary strands of our autobiographical selves: our me story, our we story, and our thee story.

5. Transitions Are Essential to Life

The last item on my list is the one that had been my moon shot motivation all along: We need to rebrand life transitions. Instead of dismissing them as hostile terrain we have to soldier through, we should see them as fertile terrain we can gain sustenance from. "We regard discomfort in any form as bad news," writes the Buddhist nun Pema Chödrön. But feelings like disappointment, embarrassment, irritation, resentment, anger, and despair, instead of being bad news, she writes, "show us, with terrifying clarity, exactly where we're stuck."

And therein lies their power. Transitions are filled with tumult and unrest, but they're also filled with helpful purging and dazzling creativity. In other words, they're chaos. And as a new generation of scientists has taught us: Chaos is not noise, it's signal; disorder is not a mistake, it's a design element. If we view these periods as aberrations, we risk their becoming missed opportunities. If we view them as openings, we just might open up to them.

Transitions are not going away; the key to benefiting from them is to not turn away. Don't shield your eyes when the scary parts start; that's when the heroes are made.

Now I Know My ABCs

Not long after my interviews concluded, I was telling a friend how moving the experience had been. I've been fortunate to have many rewarding professional experiences, I said; this was the most profound.

"Why?" she asked.

Her question caught me off guard. I thought for a full minute, then told this story. About a third of the way through my conversations, I was in Boston doing interviews. Late one Friday afternoon, a man I had never met, John Mury, drove to my in-laws' home. I first encountered John when he wrote me an email about a failed link on my website and thanked me for the "self-disclosure" in my work. The phrase jumped out at me, and I invited him to share his story.

John, whom we've encountered briefly in this book, was the son of an Irish Catholic US serviceman and a North Korean woman he met while serving in South Korea. When John's mother moved to the US, she was crushed to find the streets were not paved with gold. She cut her wrists and tried to drown herself in a bathtub while pregnant with John, then felt him kicking and changed her mind. "She decided to live for me," John said.

"Actually, I think she decided to live through me." His parents separated a few years later.

John grew up angry and violent, caught between two cultures and two warring parents. At eighteen, two weeks into his freshman year at Carnegie Mellon, he was walking along a street in Pittsburgh and heard the voice of God. He became a believer, transferred to a Bible college, and then moved to Massachusetts to open a church. He also married and had three children. "Cleverness and hard work were my idols," he said.

He then experienced a horrific epidemic of disruptions, a ten-car pileup virtually unrivaled in the otherwise boisterous collection of life stories I heard. First, his wife came down with a form of gastric cancer so rare that only seventy families in the world experience it, most of them from the Maori tribe in New Zealand, and had to have her stomach removed, then much of her intestine; not long after, she had a double mastectomy. Next, their youngest child was diagnosed with autism, their oldest child became hyperactive, and their middle child was overwhelmed by all the chaos. On top of that, John's brother, who moved nearby to help, died unexpectedly. And John's church failed. In the midst of all this, his wife was treated for stress, John was medicated for mood disorders, and their marriage buckled.

"My cleverness and hard work were not going to work anymore," he said. "I needed help."

Hearing this story was almost as cathartic as telling it, and by the end we both were in tears. As I ushered him to the front door, we gave each other a big hug.

Just then, my mother-in-law, Debbie, appeared. John is quite handsome, and Debbie had a bit of a schoolgirl crush on him. "Who's *that*?" she said after he'd gone. When I told her what John had just shared, she slumped against the wall. "Why would this man drive an hour on a Friday afternoon, share that unbelievable story, then give you a hug at the end?"

My answer to her helps explain why this experience was so rewarding. Sharing stories enriches all three of the ABCs of meaning.

A) Stories empower us. They give us a sense of agency. Like nearly everyone else, John ended our conversations by expressing how appreciative he was for what was essentially his gift to me—his time, his honesty, his self-disclosure. For a long time I wondered why. Part of the reason, I came to believe, touches on something scientists have discovered about memory. Memories, unlike what I learned about them as a child, are not stable—neat little packages stored away in our brains like keepsakes we pull out of the closet when we need them and stuff back when we don't. Memories are living, breathing entities that change with each summoning. Every time we recall a memory, we recall it in a slightly different way.

The same applies to stories. Every time we tell our life story, we tell it in a slightly different way. It could be the audience we're telling the story to or the circumstance we're telling it in. Whatever the reason, we generate the meaning we need in the moment. That act of reinterpretation is fundamentally an act of agency; it gives us a sense of control and confidence at exactly the moment we feel out of control and lacking confidence. Retelling our story accelerates our recovery.

B) Stories connect us. They give us a sense of belonging. They can take two people with no previous relation and give them a relationship for life. There is power in telling stories, of course. There is power in hearing them. But there is greater power in the interaction between the two. Just as nearly everyone said they learned something valuable from our conversation, I felt the same way. We created something together that neither one of us could have created on our own. And when it was over, both of us wanted the same thing: To do it again. To hear another story. To share the process with almost anyone we knew.

And I do mean anyone. When I started this project, I was very intentional about seeking out people of a certain age or a certain life experience. My wife was the first to tell me I was wrong. She was right. Twenty-five-year-olds turn out to have high points, low points, and turning points, themes, patterns, and shapes just as much as seventy-five-year-olds do. Life stories that appeared to be about one thing often turned out to be about another. I would go into an interview expecting to hear a story about illness or job loss only to discover one about domestic violence or near death. Everybody has a story, and not always the story the listener or teller expects to hear. The sharing is what brings out the surprise.

C) Which leads to the final takeaway: Stories inspire us. They give us purpose, focus, and cause. They make us more human, and more humane. And yet, for whatever reason, we've pulled back from this oldest of pastimes. It's easy to think we live in a moment when *TELL YOUR STORY* is flashing in bright-colored lights all around us. Yet other than carefully curated snippets—the passing social media post, the fleeting holiday card—we actually don't do it very often. Certainly not in a way that's comprehensive, reflective, vulnerable, and meaning-making. We have become a generation of unstorytellers, which is one reason we're a generation of malcontents.

We need to return to the campfire.

And we can. It's as simple as saying to someone, *Tell me the story of your life.* And when they're finished, say, *I'd like to tell you mine.*

Whatever happens next, both of you will emerge with a story to tell of your encounter—and a new, meaningful experience you share.

Out of the Woods

At the end of my conversation with John Mury, I asked him the shape of his life. His answer: a winding river. "This may sound corny, but there's a Garth Brooks song that really made an impact on me," he said. "It's called 'The River.' A dream is like a river, he says, always changing as it flows; we are merely vessels, who must change as we go. That's what I feel like today. A huge part of my narrative coming out of this darkness is that my responsibility is not to change the world, but to be the right kind of person in the world."

Unbeknownst to John, I spent a year traveling with Garth decades earlier for a book I was writing about country music. I heard him perform

"The River" countless times. There's a line near the end of the song that captures perhaps the greatest insight I took away from listening to more than a thousand hours of life stories. It's exactly the lesson I most needed to hear years earlier when my own life veered off course, hurtling me into a bog of anxiety, frustration, and fear.

Even though we can't control the river—even though life is ever flowing, ever changing, ever threatening, ever maddening—we must "choose to chance the rapids / and dare to dance the tide."

We must never give up on the happy ending.

We must insist that our oscillating narratives can turn upward as well as down.

We must write the legends of the nonlinear age. And sing them as loud as we can.

And they should tell us that the best way to respond to a period of personal upheaval—the close of one story, the end of one dream—is to push through the darkness, paddle through the torrents, persevere through the woods. And to know: We're not alone. The woods are full of people just like us. All those disturbances we run into along the way—the bend in the river, the howl in the night, the wolf in the path—are what everyone encounters in between dreams.

And they're what allow us to dream again. Because once we're out of the woods, we're into the light, we're on dry ground, we're beyond the wolf; once we've exhausted all the arrows in our quiver and fear we'll never have the courage to fight again, it's time to do the most frightening and necessary thing we can do.

Plunge back into the woods, dive back into the waters, face down another wolf.

Dream another dream.

It's time once more to utter the most spellbinding, life-affirming words we can utter. The words that suggest a story is coming. Maybe even a fairy tale.

Once upon a time.

i am
tired of
your shit.

ACKNOWLEDGMENTS

The idea seemed so simple: Ask people to share their life stories. And yet, everything depended on how those people reacted. I'd like to extend my profound gratitude to the 225 people who agreed to participate in the Life Story Project. These extraordinary individuals, all but a handful of whom were complete strangers to me at the outset, answered my probing questions, shared their heartfelt stories, examined their most intimate moments, and offered up a tearful stream of insights with humor, passion, and emotion. I am eternally thankful for their honesty and transparency, and will always marvel at how their lives aligned so magically with one another. I hope in a small way the ideas in this book honor your remarkable lives.

I did not find these people by myself. I would like to thank the many people I encountered along the way, including those on social media, who recommended a person or two, and to each person I interviewed who passed the baton to others. Deep bows to Laura Adams, Sunny Bates, Subodh Chandra, Anna Marie Clifton, Christina Cohen, Carol Danhof, Gail Davis, KJ Dell'Antonia, Leo Eaton, John T. Edge, Laurie Hill, Jodi Kantor, Tom Kohler, David Kramer, Cindi Leive, Connie Mitchell, Betsy

Musolf, Esther Perel, Brian Pike, Courtney Richards, Lani Santo, Lauren Class Schneider, Pattie Sellers, and Lindsey Lusher Shute.

I was extremely fortunate to have a wonderful team of young minds to help me code, analyze, and compile a robust data set from these stories, then bring that data to life visually. I called this group *The Meaning Lab*, and they came from a wide variety of backgrounds and worked with impressive rigor and camaraderie. I am pleased to honor the contributions of Jerimee Bloemeke, Kannan Mahadevan, Spencer Feinstein, Robin Xiao, Nina Premutico, Brad Davis, George Tolkachev, Lucy Ackman, and Claire Walker-Wells. A particular salute to the wonderful Elda Monterroso, who escorted the work from beginning to end, and to Kirk Benson.

In the many years I worked on this book, I interviewed scores of scholars across an array of disciplines about the many themes and topics this project touched on. I am especially grateful to those I consulted regularly: Marshall Duke, Robyn Fivush, Dan McAdams, Jennifer Aaker, Kathleen Vohs, and Cheryl Svenson.

David Black patiently endured years of rethinking and reimagining as this book slowly found its shape. Scott Moyers offered his masterly mix of support, confidence, and probing, all of which made his ultimate enthusiasm all the more meaningful. Thank you. I am in awe of the acumen and skills of the unrivaled team at Penguin Press: Ann Godoff, Matt Boyd, Sarah Hutson, Danielle Plafsky, Gail Brussel, and Mia Council.

I am blessed to be surrounded by an extraordinary assembly of people who are always looking out for the greater possibilities in my work. Thank you to the incomparable Craig Jacobson, as well as to Alan Berger, Elizabeth Newman, and Eric Wattenberg. A special shout-out to Laura Walker for your friendship and generosity, and to Nick Baum for your inspiration. And forever admiration to those allies who point me in the right direction: Greg Clayman, Beth Comstock, David Kidder, Charlie Melcher, Andrew McLaughlin, and Kaja Perina.

To my council: Josh Ramo, Ben Sherwood, Max Stier, and Jeff Shumlin.

To my Rottenberg family: Dan and Elissa, Rebecca and Mattis, and especially Debbie Alan, who sprung open many doors around Boston. To my siblings: Cari and Rodd introduced me to some remarkable people and housed me along the way; Andrew once again read every draft of this book, providing remarkable clarity and insight. To my parents: In the thirty years I've been writing books, my mother, Jane Feiler, rarely showed more enthusiasm than she did for this project. That encouragement helped sustain me immensely. Dad, this project began with you and never would have happened if you didn't answer that first question about your childhood toys. Thank you for your love of storytelling and for allowing me to hear and share your life story. That you got to see this book in its entirety is yet another of your many gifts to me.

I am singularly fortunate in getting to share my life with the storied Linda Rottenberg. Well known around the world for her legendary energy, passion, and vision, Linda is less well known for what may be her greater skill: living with a professional creative person, with all the emotional volatility, late-night wonderings, and never-ending demands that requires. That Linda excels in all these is the one linear thing in my otherwise nonlinear life.

Eden and Tybee: During the many years I've been working on the Life Story Project you have become storytellers of your own. Your love of theater, books, dance, and song makes you both a rarity in this digital age and heirs to the oldest of traditions. My greatest joy in life is watching you seize authorship of your own life stories and waiting with breathless anticipation for where you will take those stories next.

One thing I know for sure is that your family will always be a part of that narrative, especially your beloved cousins: Max, Hallie, Nate, Maya, Judah, and Isaac. At this ending moment of the Life Story Project I can do no better than what my father said at the end of his Life Story Interview. My wish for all of you is that you fulfill the dedication of this book:

Tell the stories.

THE LIFE STORY INTERVIEW

This is an interview about the story of your life. I'm interested in learning how you think about your life and how you turn the ups and downs of your life into a coherent narrative. Our conversation is not meant to be exhaustive. The way it will work is: I'll ask you to focus on the overarching story, then a few select events, and especially the larger themes of your life—what we might call the overall shape of your life. Obviously I'm not trying to judge you. My goal is to understand how we all live now—how we navigate the transitions, disruptions, and reinventions in our lives in a way that allows us to live with meaning, balance, and joy. I think you'll enjoy the conversation.

The Story of Your Life

Please tell me the story of your life in fifteen minutes. (Most people take longer.) Please do so as if you were talking to someone you just met over coffee, and you want to tell them about who you are as a person—what's important to you, how you got that way, who you are now. I'm especially interested in how the different chapters of your life are connected and might have influenced each other.

The Key Scenes in Your Life

Now that you've described the overall arc of your life, I'd like you to focus in on a few key scenes. A key scene is a moment or period that's particularly good, bad, vivid, or memorable. For each scene, I'd like you to describe in detail what happened—what led to it, what you were thinking and feeling during it. Then I'll ask you how this scene fits into your overall life story.

1. High Point

Please describe a scene, episode, or moment in time that stands out as especially positive. This might be *the* high point of your entire life, or just a particularly happy or wonderful moment.

2. Turning Point

Again, looking back over your life, can you identify a key turning point that marked an important change in your life story?

3. Meaningful Experience

Many people report having an experience in their lives that was deeply profound, that provided a sense of transcendence, a feeling of oneness with the world. For some this experience is spiritual, for others natural, for others artistic. Can you identify one such moment?

4. Low Point

The next scene is the opposite of the first one. Thinking back over your life, can you identify a scene that stands out as a low point, maybe even *the* low point in your life story? Even though it's unpleasant, please tell me what happened: who was involved, what were you thinking and feeling?

5. Easy Transition

Reflecting back on your life, think of key transitions—these could involve home, work, family, health, or religion. Please identify one such transition that others might have found difficult that you got through, relatively speaking, without too much difficulty.

6. Tough Transition

The next question is the opposite. Of the key transitions in your life, can you identify one that others might have found easy to navigate that really threw you for a loop?

Secrets of Successful Transitions

I'd like to focus on the biggest transition in your life that we've talked about so far. I have a series of questions about that time.

1. Was this a voluntary or involuntary transition? Was it easier or harder because of this?
2. Did you give this period a name?
3. What was the greatest emotion you struggled with during this period?
4. Did you initiate, create, or have any rituals, celebrations, or formal markers?
5. Did you keep any mementos from the past?
6. Did you mourn the past?
7. Can you tell me about a habit from the past you had to give up?
8. How did you structure your time during this period?
9. Can you tell me three creative activities you did to help rebuild the new you?
10. Was there a mentor, friend, loved one, or wise outsider who offered advice?
11. Did you experience this time as an autobiographical occasion?
12. Transitions are divided into three stages—the long goodbye, the messy middle, the new beginning. Which stage was the hardest for you?
13. How long did this entire transition take?
14. Did you have an expression of freedom, joy, or new beginning at the end?

The 5 Story Lines of Your Life

The next section is about the prominent story lines of your life. A story line is an ongoing source of conflict, struggle, or challenge—or just an area that you've given a lot of focus to. I'm going to mention five large arenas of life. Please tell me what's been the dominant story line in your life, then the second and third. The five story lines are: IDENTITY, LOVE, WORK, BODY, BELIEFS.

The Future

Next, I'd like to turn to the future for a few questions.

Please tell me three personal projects that are on your plate right now. A personal project could be as small as emptying out the cat litter or as big as ending world hunger.

Your life story includes key chapters from your past along with how you see or imagine the future. What's the next chapter in your life story?

Please describe a dream you have for the future of your life story.

The Shape of Your Life

Now, two questions to end.

Looking back over your entire life story with all its chapters, scenes, and challenges, do you discern a central theme?

Looking back over your life story in a slightly different way, what shape embodies your life? Please explain why you chose this.

FURTHER READING

In the many years I worked on this project, I read more than three hundred books and upward of seven hundred academic studies. Any source I relied on heavily is mentioned in Sources. Instead of listing everything I consulted, I've opted to highlight selected recommended books for those interested in particular themes explored here.

Storytelling. For the scientific roots of storytelling: *On the Origin of Stories*, Brian Boyd, Belknap Press of Harvard University Press; *The Storytelling Animal*, Jonathan Gottschall, Houghton Mifflin Harcourt; *Louder Than Words*, Benjamin Bergen, Basic Books.

In the field of narrative psychology: *The Stories We Live By*, Dan P. McAdams, Guilford Press; *How Our Lives Become Stories*, Paul Eakin, Cornell University Press; *Making Stories*, Jerome Bruner, Harvard University Press; *Memories That Matter*, Jefferson Singer, New Harbinger Publications.

A warm place in my heart for the grumpy anti-storytelling manifesto *Keeping It Fake*, Eric Wilson, Sarah Crichton Books.

Shape of Life. The idea of shape of life has been explored in a number of thoughtful academic books, among them: *Aging by the Book*, Kay Heath, SUNY Press; *The Oxford Book of Aging*, Thomas Cole, Oxford University Press; and *Time Maps*, Eviatar Zerubavel, University of Chicago Press.

I also enjoyed these explorations of the idea of adulthood: *The Prime of Life*, Steven Mintz, Harvard University Press; and *Midlife*, Kieran Setiya, Princeton University Press.

Meaning. The best overviews of meaning research I know are *The Human Quest for Meaning*, Paul T. Wong, Routledge; *The Power of Meaning*, Emily Esfahani Smith, Broadway Books; and *Meanings of Life*, Roy Baumeister, Guilford Press. I can also recommend the following: *The Happiness Hypothesis*, Jonathan Haidt, Basic Books; *On Purpose*, Paul Froese, Oxford University Press; and the wonderful *Shop Class as Soulcraft*, Matthew B. Crawford, Penguin Press.

Transitions. A number of diverse books explore this underdiscussed topic: *The*

Rites of Passage, Arnold van Gennep, Routledge; *Remembered Lives*, Barbara Myerhoff, University of Michigan Press; *Adapt*, Tim Harford, Farrar, Straus and Giroux; *Rising Strong*, Brené Brown, Random House; *Option B*, Sheryl Sandberg and Adam Grant, Alfred A. Knopf.

Psychology. Some excellent new books have creative explorations of the psychology of change, recovery, and renewal: *The Brain's Way of Healing*, Norman Doidge, Penguin Books; *In the Realm of Hungry Ghosts*, Gabor Maté, North Atlantic Books; and *Supernormal*, Meg Jay, Hachette Book Group.

Chaos Theory. For readable approaches to the science of complexity: *Chaos,* James Gleick, Penguin Books; *The Drunkard's Walk*, Leonard Mlodinow, Vintage Books; *Messy*, Tim Harford, Riverhead Books; and *Sync*, Steven Strogatz, Hachette Books.

Memoir. Among the scores of books about how to tell your personal story, I'm pleased to recommend these choices: *The Art of Memoir*, Mary Karr, HarperCollins; *When Memory Speaks*, Jill Ker Conway, Vintage Books; *Writing About Your Life*, William Zinsser, Hachette Books; and the absolutely delightful *I Is An Other* by James Geary, Harper Perennial.

Finally, this list would not be complete without the essential book that expertly mixes personal stories and careful analysis, *Far from the Tree*, Andrew Solomon, Simon & Schuster.

SOURCES

All interviews quoted in this book were recorded and transcribed. In keeping with long-standing custom in academic writing on life story interviews, I allow people to tell their own stories in their own words. I contacted no individuals referred to in these stories for alternative viewpoints. My general philosophy was to respect, consider, and analyze people's life stories, accepting that they contain certain events that others might interpret in a different way.

In addition to quoting from the large trough of stories I collected, I drew on the wide literature of narrative psychology, positive psychology, applied neuroscience, sociology, anthropology, economics, and chaos theory, along with history, philosophy, literature, and art history. In this chapter-by-chapter accounting, I offer sources for all the quotations and academic references included in the book.

Introduction. The Life Story Project

For a full listing of my previous work, see the front matter to this book. My experience in Japan is detailed in *Learning to Bow*; in the circus in *Under the Big Top*; and in the Middle East in *Walking the Bible*, *Abraham*, and other books. My cancer journey is detailed in *The Council of Dads*. All the books mentioned here are published by William Morrow.

The research on family history from Marshall Duke and Robyn Fivush is discussed at length in my book *The Secrets of Happy Families*, also published by Morrow. "The Stories That Bind Us" appeared in *The New York Times* on March 17, 2013. For more information on how to read the book we self-published of my father's stories, please visit www.brucefeiler.com.

Kierkegaard's *people baths* are described in Sarah Bakewell's *At the Existentialist Café* (Other Press), p. 17–18. Dan McAdams describes the history of narrative psychology in "The Psychology of Life Stories" (*Review of General Psychology*, 2001, vol. 5, no. 2), and "Personal Narrative and the Life Story" (*The Handbook of Personality*, 2008); as well as two important books, *The Stories We Live By* (Guilford Press) and *Power, Intimacy, and the*

Life Story (Guilford Press). For the full text of my Life Story Interview, please see the back matter of this book. Jim Collins describes his collaborative coding techniques in *Good to Great* (HarperCollins).

Aristotle describes *peripeteia* in *Poetics*, Section VI, 350 BCE. The Bruner quote, "A story begins with some breach..." comes from *Making Stories* (Harvard University Press, 2003, p. 17). The James quote "Life is in the transitions..." comes from his 1904 essay "A World of Pure Experience" (*The Journal of Philosophy, Psychology and Scientific Methods* vol. 1, no, 21). *Lupus in fabula* is discussed in Umberto Eco, *Six Walks in the Fictional Woods* (Harvard University Press, p. 1).

1. Farewell to the Linear Life

Karen Armstrong describes rewriting our cultural stories in *A Short History of Myth* (Canongate). For the history of life shape, I drew on Thomas Cole, *The Oxford Book of Aging* (Oxford University Press) and *The Journey of Life* (Cambridge University Press); Kay Heath, *Aging by the Book* (State University of New York Press); Anthony Aveni, *Empires of Time* (University Press of Colorado); James Gleick, *The Information* (Vintage). "All the world's a stage" is delivered by Jacques in *As You Like It*, Act II, Scene VII, written in 1599. The sources for the staircase images appear in the front matter.

My discussion of the origins of mechanical time is informed by Leonard Mlodinow, *The Drunkard's Walk* (Vintage); Paul Davies, *About Time* (Simon & Schuster); Eviatar Zerubavel, *Time Maps* (University of Chicago Press); and Roy Baumeister, *Identity* (Oxford University Press). The grandfather clock story comes from Cole, *Journey*. The popularity of midlife, adolescence, et cetera are discussed in Heath, *Aging*, p. 1ff. Morton Hunt has written a wonderful one-volume *The Story of Psychology* (Anchor Books), which includes biographies of Freud, Piaget, and Bowlby. Elisabeth Kübler-Ross outlined the stages of grief in *On Death and Dying* (Routledge); Joseph Campbell introduced the hero's journey in *The Hero with a Thousand Faces* (New World Library).

My history of Erik Erikson relies on Hunt; Erikson discusses his ideas in detail in his books *Identity and the Life Cycle* (Norton); *Gandhi's Truth* (Norton); and *The Life Cycle Completed*, with Joan Erikson (Norton). "As our world-image..." comes from *Insights and Responsibility* (Norton). George Bonanno's critique is found in *The Other Side of Sadness* (Basic Books), p. 22.

Elliott Jaques published "Death and the Mid-Life Crisis" (*International Journal of Psychoanalysis*, XLVI, 1965, p. 502–14). The history of the midlife crisis is told in Dan McAdams, *The Stories We Live By* (Guilford Press); Daniel Levinson, *The Seasons of a Man's Life* (Ballantine); Steven Mintz, *The Prime of Life* (Belknap); Barbara Bradley Haggerty, *Life Reimagined* (Riverhead Books); Kieran Setiya, *Midlife* (Princeton University Press); James Hollis, *Finding Meaning in the Second Half of Life* (Gotham Books). The Levinson quote "Single, most frequent age..." is in Levinson, *Seasons*, p. 53.

Gail Sheehy published *Passages: Predictable Crises of Adult Life*, with E. P. Dutton (Bantam), along with multiple revisions over the years. She details the history behind the book, including Roger Gould's lawsuit, in her 2014 memoir, *Daring* (HarperCollins), p. 210–34.

2. Embracing the Nonlinear Life

The literature on chaos theory and complex physics is robust. I was helped enormously by James Gleick's *Chaos* (Penguin Books); John Briggs and F. David Peat, *Seven Lessons of Chaos* (HarperCollins); John Gribbin, *Deep Simplicity*, (Random House); Steven Strogatz,

Sync (Hyperion Theia). Lorentz's original essay "Deterministic Nonperiodic Flow" appeared in *Journal of the Atmospheric Sciences*, 20 (2). The quote "We begin to envision . . ." comes from Briggs, *Seven Lessons*, p. 5, and the Gleick quote from p. 24.

T. H. Holmes and R. H. Rahe published "The Social Readjustment Rating Scale," in *Journal of Psychosomatic Research*, vol. 11, issue 2, 1967. The statistics on the deck of disruptors come from the following:

Love. On the marriage rate, Mintz, *Prime*, p. 169; on households headed by married couples, Mintz, *Prime*, p. 98. On children raised by single parents, divorced parents, https://census.gov/topics/families.html; on adult children living at home, Pew Research Center, 2016.

Identity. On moves, "Reason for Moving: 2012 to 2013," United States Census Bureau; "Who Moves? Who Stays Put? Where's Home?" Pew Research Center, 2008. On gender, "Facebook's 71 Gender Options Comes to UK Users," *The Telegraph*, June 27, 2014. On mobility, "Harder for Americans to Rise from Lower Rungs," *New York Times*, January 4, 2012.

Beliefs. On changing religions, "U.S. Religious Landscape Survey," Pew Research Center, 2008; on interfaith marriage and no religious affiliation, "America's Changing Religious Landscape," Pew Research Center, 2015. On political beliefs, "Americans Continue to Embrace Political Independence," Gallup, 2019; on millennials, "Half of Millennials Independent," *Politico*, 2014. On travel, Monthly Tourism Statistics, travel.trade.gov.

Work. On the number of jobs, Bureau of Labor Statistics, August 22, 2019; on changing jobs and skill sets, Mintz, *Prime*, p. xii; on duration, Jenny Blake, *Pivot* (Portfolio), p. 4; on automation, Carl Bededikt Frey, Michael Osborne, "The Future of Employment," Oxford Martin Programme of Technology and Employment, 2013; on disengagement, Blake, *Pivot*, p. 4; on a different career, Roman Krznaric, *How to Find Fulfilling Work* (Picador), p. 11; on the side hustle, "How Many Americans Have a Side Hustle," *The Motley Fool*, June 25, 2018; on a portfolio, Krznaric, *Fulfilling Work*, p. 85.

Body. On puberty, "Early Puberty," *Scientific American*, May 1, 2015; on late menopause, Heath, *Aging*, p. 74; on epidemics, "Depression, Anxiety, Suicide Increase in Teens and Young Adults," CBS News, March 14, 2019; on longevity, "U.S. Life Expectancy Declines Again, a Dismal Trend Not Seen Since World War I," *Washington Post*, November 29, 2018. On chronic conditions, Mintz, *Prime*, p. 312; on cancer and other conditions, Mintz, *Prime*, p. 314. On Americans over 65 in 1920, "65+ in the United States," Hobbs and Damon, United States Census Bureau, 1996. On future number of Americans over 65, "An Aging Nation," Ortman et al., United States Census Bureau, 2014.

The results of the midlife study were published in *How Healthy Are We?*, edited by Orville Brim, Carol Ryff, and Ronald Kessler (University of Chicago Press). The quote "little evidence" appears on p. 586. "Quarter of participants" appears on p. 30. The *New York Times* headline is from February 15, 1999. On views of middle age, Heath, *Aging*, p. 5. The research into pliability and change across the life span is discussed in Gabor Maté, *In the Realm of Hungry Ghosts* (North Atlantic Books), p. 363; Briggs, *Seven Lessons*, p. 96; Brian Grierson, *U-Turn* (Bloomsbury, 100ff). "Brain remodels itself . . ." comes from Jeffrey Schwartz, quoted in Maté, *Ghosts*, p. 363.

Data for jobs and moves op cit; accidents, "How Many Times Will You Crash Your Car?" *Forbes*, July 27, 2011; for marriage and divorce, "The Marrying—And Divorcing—Kind," Pew Research Center, January 14, 2011; for cheating, "Sorting Through the Numbers on Infidelity," NPR, July 26, 2015. On heart disease, "Nearly Half of Americans

Have Heart Disease," *USA Today*, January 31, 2019; on addicts, "Alcohol and Drug Abuse Statistics," American Addiction Centers, July 29, 2019. On diets, "Weight Loss," *Express*, February 8, 2018; on financial struggles, "76 Million Americans Are Struggling Financially," CNN, June 10, 2016.

3. Lifequakes

Maynard Solomon has written a wonderful biography, *Beethoven* (Omnibus Press); Fitzgerald chronicled his emotional breakdown in a series of essays that were later gathered in a book, *The Crack-Up* (reprinted by New Directions).

Weber's *metanoia* is described in Grierson, *U-Turn*, p. 7; James's *mental rearrangements* is in his *The Varieties of Religious Experience*, Lecture IX.

4. The ABCs of Meaning

Viktor Frankl wrote extensively about his life in his autobiography *Reflections*, translated by Joseph and Judith Fabry (Basic Books). I've also drawn on William Blair Gould's biography *Frankl* (Brooks/Cole Publishing) and Alex Pattakos, *Prisoners of our Thoughts* (Berrett-Kohler Publishers). "What troubled me . . ." comes from *Reflections*, p. 29; "honor thy father and mother . . ." from *Reflections*, p. 83. "Dream" comes from Victor Frankl, *Man's Search for Meaning*, translated by Ilse Lasch (Beacon Press), p. 29; "suffering" from p. 117, and Frederich Nietzsche from p. 104.

"Sickness of the century" comes from *Reflections*, p. 66; "fullness" from Hollis, *Finding Meaning*, p. 8; "central concept," from Jerome Bruner, *Acts of Meaning*, p. 33.

Agency. "Heart" from Mintz, *Prime*, p. 292; "in charge" from Bessel van der Kolk, *The Body Keeps the Score* (Penguin Books), p. 97. Happier, healthier from Roy Baumeister, *Meanings of Life* (Guilford Press), p. 215, 227; on deluding yourself, Baumeister, *Meanings*, p. 42. "Action" is from Aristotle, *Nicomachean Ethics*, Book II.

Workers. Mintz, *Prime*, p. 49; workspace is from Tim Hartford, *Messy* (Riverhead Books), p. 58; on schedules, Krznaric, *Fulfilling Work*, p. 133–34. On General Mills, Matthew Crawford, *Shop Class as Soulcraft* (Penguin Books), p. 67; On Ikea, Michael Norton, Daniel Mochon, Dan Ariely, "The 'IKEA Effect,'" (Harvard Business School, 2011); on the nursing home, Brian Little, *Me, Myself, and Us* (Public Affairs), p. 102.

Belonging. For "Most reinforced," see Brim, *Healthy*, p. 336; "89 percent" from Eric Klinger, *Meaning and Void*, cited in Baumeister, *Meanings*, p. 147; "Stanford study" from Howard Friedman, Leslie Martin, *The Longevity Project* (Plume), p. 182. "Only thing" from Joshua Wolf Shenk, "What Makes Us Happy," *The Atlantic*, June 2009.

"Cultural organ" appears in van der Kolk, *Body*, p. 86. "Cancer patients" from Baumeister, *Meanings*, p. 259; Alzheimer's is in *The Human Quest for Meaning*, edited by Paul Wong, p. 92; on alcoholics, Maté, *Hungry Ghosts*, p. 33; on trauma victims and PTSD, William Bridges, *Transitions* (DaCapo), p. 53, 96; "blitz" from van der Kolk, *Body*, p. 212.

"Workplace" from *How to Be a Positive Leader*, edited by Jane Dutton and Gretchen Spreitzer, (Berrett-Koehler Publishers), p. 12. "New hires" from "Inside Google Workplaces," CBS News, January 22, 2013. "Feedback" from Dutton, *Positive Leader*, p. 25–27; on emails, "Alignment at Work," Gabriel Doyle and others (*Proceedings of 55th Annual Meeting of the Association for Computational Linguistics*, 2017), p. 603–12.

Cause. "Volunteer" from "Volunteering Makes You Happier," *Fast Company*, September 3, 2013. "No cause" from Paul Froese, *On Purpose* (Oxford University Press, p. 4);

"third of us" and "perform work" from Emily Esfahani Smith, *The Power of Meaning* (Broadway, p. 93). "Hospital study" from Dutton, *Positive Leader*, p. 57. "Caregivers" from Strogatz, *Sync*, p. 263–64.

5. Shape-Shifting

I drew on R.W.B. Lewis, *Dante* (Penguin Lives) and Marco Santagata, *Dante* (Belknap). "Mortality" from Frankl, *Recollections*, p. 29. "Escape," see Ernest Becker, *The Denial of Death* (Free Press), p. 25ff.

Peter Brown has written the seminal biography, *Augustine of Hippo* (University of California Press). "Inward healer" from *The Confessions*, translated by Maria Boulding, p. 198. Robert Zussman's "Autobiographical Occasions" appeared in *Qualitative Sociology*, vol. 23, no. 1, 2000 and "Stories about lives" from p. 5.

I am indebted to David Reynolds, *Walt Whitman's America*. "Contradict myself" from *Leaves of Grass*, Section 51. For more on self-organizing, see Briggs, *Seven Lessons*, p. 16. "Psychic adaptation" and "counterbalancing" come from Grierson, *U-Turn*, p. 73. "Core constructs" and "goggles" from Brian Little, *Who Are You, Really* (Simon & Schuster), p. 26.

6. Learning to Dance in the Rain

Van Gennep's biography is covered in "Arnold Van Gennep," *American Anthropologist*, vol. 84, no. 2, 1982. "Translators" appears in Arnold van Gennep, *The Rites of Passage*, translated by Monika Vizedeom and Gabrielle Caffee (Chicago), p. vii. "Bridges" is from *Rites*, p. 48. "reorientations" is from Bridges, *Transitions*, p. xii.

"Place" from *Rites*, p. 17. "Phases" from *Rites*, p. 21. "Betwixt" from Victor Turner, *The Ritual Process* (Aldine), p. 95. "Endings" from *Transitions*, p. vii. "In that order" from *Transitions*, p. 10.

7. Accept It

I often rely on *The Torah*, translated by W. Gunther Plaut (Union for Reform Judaism) for quotations from Genesis. "Other religions," Briggs, *Seven Lessons*, p. 9. "Return" from Mircea Eliade, *Myths, Dreams, and Mysteries*, translated by Philip Mairet (Harper & Row), p. 80.

Moses. "Who me?" from Exodus 3:11. "Facticity" from Bakewell, *Existentialist*, p. 157. "Fate" from Solomon, *Beethoven*, p. 149, and "resignation," p. 61. "Strange" from *Oxford Book of Aging*, p. 328. On 12-step programs, I am indebted to Ernest Kurtz and Katherine Ketcham, *The Spirituality of Imperfection* (Bantam) and Nan Robertson, *Getting Better* (Authors Guild). "Acceptance" is in Pearl Buck, *A Bridge for Passing* (Open Road), p. 46. "James-Lange" is in Grierson, *U-Turn*, p. 143.

For the "body-first" view of trauma, I have drawn on van der Kolk's *The Body Keeps the Score*. "Begun to solve" is from *U-Turn*, p. 153. For an overview of "negative visualization," see "How to Harness the Power of Negative Thinking," *Greater Good Magazine*, October 31, 2012. "Worse" is from Sheryl Sandberg and Adam Grant, *Option B* (Knopf), p. 25.

Fear. "Triggers" comes from Brian Boyd, *On the Origins of Stories* (Belknap), p. 55; "indicator" from Steven Pressfield, *The War of Art* (Black Irish), p. 40; "selves" from Hazel Markus and Paula Nurius, "Possible Selves," *American Psychologist*, vol. 41, no. 9, 1986. "Brave" from Pema Chödrön, *When Things Fall Apart* (Shambhala), p. 5.

Sadness. "Quickly" comes from Buck, *Bridge*, p. 37. "Pleasure" from John Green, *The Fault in Our Stars* (Dutton), p. 262. "Slow motion" from Bonanno, *Sadness*, p. 32.

Shame. "Guilt" comes from Brené Brown, *Daring Greatly* (Avery), p. 71.

8. Mark It

Ritual. "Alone" comes from Christine Downing, *A Journey Through Menopause*, Spring Journal, p. 5. "Punctuation marks" from Jeltje Gordon-Lennox, *Crafting Secular Ritual* (Jessica Kingsley Publishers), p. 30. "Integrate" from Downing, p. 7.

Mourning. "Sweet" is in Elizabeth Gilbert, *Eat, Pray, Love* (Riverhead Books), p. 164. "Sad words" is from John Greenleaf Whittier's poem "Maud Muller." "Mourning" is in Amy Greenberg, *Lady First* (Knopf), p. 203ff. "60 percent" from Bonanno, *Sadness*, p. 60ff, and "Consistent" from p. 6.

Mementos. "Things" from Mihaly Csikszentmihalyi and Eugene Rochberg-Halton, *The Meaning of Things* (Cambridge), p. 91.

9. Shed It

Lost. "Forest dwelling" comes from Bridges, *Transitions*, p. 43. "Crossing the threshold" from Campbell, *Hero*, p. 64. "Middle" is in Margaret Atwood, *Alias Grace* (Anchor), p. 298. "Discover" is in André Gide, *The Counterfeiters* (Vintage), p. 353. "Rock bottom" is in J. K. Rowling, *Very Good Lives* (Little, Brown), p. 33. "Decades" is in Erikson, *Identity*, p. 228.

Shedding. "Habits" is taken from Charles Duhigg, *The Power of Habit*, Random House, 2012, p. xvi. "Flung" from Mark Twain, *Pudd'nhead Wilson's Calendar* (Dover), p. 26.

10. Create It

Matisse. I relied on Alastair Sooke's *Henri Matisse* (Penguin Books) and *Henri Matisse: The Cut-Outs*, edited by Karl Buchberg, Nicholas Cullinan, Jodi Hauptman, and Nicholas Serota (Tate Publishing). "Calm" is in Sooke, p. 3, and "Resigned," p. 5. The Beethoven quote is in Solomon's *Beethoven*, p. 149.

"Social exclusion" comes from Marie Forgeard, "Perceiving Benefits After Adversity," *Psychology of Aesthetics, Creativity, and the Arts*, vol. 7, no. 3. Poincaré is in Nancy Andreasen, *The Creative Brain* (Plume), p. 43.

Baldwin. Quotes come from *The Writer's Chapbook*, edited by George Plimpton (Public Library). Baldwin's appearance at Yale was featured on page 1 of the *Yale Daily News*, November 3, 1983, though the quote I remembered does not appear. The story of expressive writing is told in James Pennebaker, *Opening Up by Writing Down* (Guilford Press). "Decrease" is from Pennebaker, p. 18, "immune system" from p. 21, "jobs" from p. 23, and "why" from p. 72.

Tharp. Twyla Tharp has written the indispensable guide *The Creative Habit* (Simon & Schuster), and "Truly original" is from p. 67ff.

Feldenkrais. My account draws on Norman Doidge, *The Brain's Way of Healing* (Penguin Books), especially chapter 5, p. 160ff. "Knife" is found on p. 164.

11. Share It

"Subjective experiences," Diana Tamir and Jason Mitchell, "Disclosing information," *Proceedings of the National Academy of Sciences of the United States*, vol. 109, no. 21. "Money" is from Tamir and Mitchell. "Group therapy" is from Pennebaker, *Opening*,

p. 3. "Adolescence" is in Robyn Fivush, *Family Narratives and the Development of an Autobiographical Self* (Routledge). Also, McAdams, *Stories*, p. 79. For more on "significant others," see Kurtz, *Spirituality*, p. 87.

Comforters. For "Mammals," see Bridges, *Transitions*, p. 95. "Adoptability" is from Meg Jay, *Supernormal* (Twelve), p. 139. For the founding of AA, I have relied on Kurtz's *Imperfection*, including "another alcoholic" and "mutual give-and-take," p. 84.

Nudgers. "Decision making" is in Richard Thaler and Cass Sunstein's *Nudge* (Penguin Books), p. 7.

Slappers. For "Nothing," see Marcus Tullius Cicero, *How to Be a Friend* (Princeton), p. 155. "Tough Love" is in Jen Lexmond and Richard Reeves, *Building Character* (Demos), p. 13; "Painful truths" and "Individuals" are from Emma Levine and Taya Cohen, "You Can Handle the Truth," *Journal of Experimental Psychology*, vol. 147, p. 9.

Modelers. Endeavor, the organization cofounded and run by my wife, Linda Rottenberg, has done extensive research on the multiplier effect. See, "The 'multiplier effect' in Argentina," Endeavor, February 13, 2012, endeavor.org/blog. "Hopkins" is in Seth Gershenson, Cassandra Hart, Constance Lindsay, and Nicholas Papageorge, "The Long-Run Impacts of Same-Race Teachers," IZA Institute of Labor Economics, 2017. "Aging" is from D. S. Jopp, S. Jung, A. K. Damarin, S. Mirpuri, and D. Spini, "Who Is Your Successful Aging Role Model?" *The Journal of Gerontology*, vol. 72, no. 2. "Stanford" is in Mark Granovetter, "The Strength of Weak Ties," *American Journal of Sociology*, vol. 78, no. 6.

Naysayers. For "Unfit," see "5 Things You Didn't Know About Oprah Winfrey," *Vogue*, January 29, 2017. "Remember" is taken from "Tom vs. Time," Tom Brady's Facebook show, episode 1. "Doubters" is from "Madonna Delivers Her Blunt Truth During Fiery, Teary Billboard Women in Music Speech," billboard.com, December 9, 2016.

12. Launch It

Jerome Bruner's books, *Making Stories* and *Acts of Meaning*, helped introduce the idea of life as a metanarrative. "Downward" is in Baumeister, *Meanings of Life*, p. 21. "Languid" is in Robert Richardson, *William James* (Mariner Books), p. 244.

"Crop rotation," is in Tim Harford, *Messy*, Riverhead Books, 2016, p. 28; "plan" is in Bruner, *Making Stories*, p. 28. Little outlines the history of "personal projects" in *Me, Myself, and Us*, "Identity" is on p. 187, "fifteen" on p. 183; "women" and "men" on p. 196, and "state" on p. 208.

For "Discovery," see Ronald Grimes, *Deeply Into the Bone* (University of California), p. 103. For "Movement," see Van Gennep, *Rites*, p. 181. "Unstuck" is in van der Kolk, *Body*, p. 53. "Trio" is in Kenneth Enz, Karalyn Pillemer, David Johnson, "The Relocation Bump," *Journal of Experimental Psychology*, vol. 145, no. 8.

For "Temporary," see Hakim Bey, *TAZ* (Autonomedia).

"Autobiography" is from Paul John Eakin, *Living Autobiographically* (Cornell), p. 91–92.

13. Tell It

See "Psychic unit" in McAdams, *Stories*, p. 23. "Half" in Scott Barry Kauffman, *Wired to Create*, (TarcherPerigee), p. xxviii. "Dream" in Barbara Hardy, "Towards a Poetics of Fiction," in *Novel* (Duke University Press). "Blinking" in Boyd, *Origins*, p. 137. "Hot streaks" in James Geary's *I Is an Other* (Harper Perennial), p. 39. "Copyright" in Hilary Mantel, *Giving Up the Ghost* (Picador), p. 66.

"Tense" is from Denise Beike and Travis Crone, "Autobiographical Memory and Personal Meaning," in *Quest*, p. 320–23. "Scars" is from Nancy Groves, "The Moth in Australia," *The Guardian*, September 4, 2015. Burns credits poet Nadia Bolz-Weber with introducing her to the phrase.

For the history of "Make Pigs Fly" I have relied on The Martha Heasley Cox Center for Steinbeck Studies; their website sjsu.edu contains a letter from Elaine Steinbeck. For the neuroscience of active verbs, I have drawn on Antonia Damasio, *Looking for Spinoza* (Harvest); Benjamin Berge, *Louder Than Words* (Basic), p. 235; Benedict Carey, "This Is Your Life (and How You Tell It)," *New York Times*, May 22, 2007; Geary, *Other*, p. 89; Pennebaker, *Opening*, p. 151; János László, *The Science of Stories*, Routledge, 2008, p. 141; Wong, *Meaning*, p. 318.

The best summation of McAdams's research into narrative structure can be found in his "Personal Narrative and the Life Story," in *Handbook of Personality* (Guilford Press). Pennebaker builds on this in *Opening Up*, p. 143–52.

Conclusion. In Between Dreams

The best overview of recent writing about narratology I know is Anthony Sanford and Catherine Emmott, *Mind, Brain and Narrative* (Cambridge). "What is a story?" draws especially on p. 1–8. "Best kept secret" is from Wong, *Meaning*, p. xliii. "Landmark study" is in Roy Baumeister, Kathleen Vohs, Jennifer Aaker, and Emily Garbinsky, "Some Key Differences between a Happy Life and a Meaningful Life," *The Journal of Positive Psychology*, vol. 8, no. 6, p.505–16.

My conversation of guided autobiography draws on James Birren and Kathryn Cochran, *Telling the Stories of Life through Guided Autobiography Groups* (Johns Hopkins), as well as my personal interview with Birren. For "Countless studies" see Ursula Staudinger, "Life Reflection," *Review of General Psychology*, vol. 5, no. 2.

"Suffering" in Frankl, *Search for Meaning*, p. 67. "Constructs" from Oliver Sacks, *The Man Who Mistook His Wife for a Hat* (Touchstone), p. 110. "Bad news," Chödrön, *Fall Apart*, p. 12.

For information about doing a Life Story Project with a loved one similar to the one I did with my dad—where I send a handpicked question every week, they reply with a story, then their stories are bound together at year's end in a beautiful, keepsake book—please visit brucefeiler.com and click on the above icon.

To contact me directly; to learn more about speaking, events, or my other work; or to sign up for my newsletter, please visit brucefeiler.com.

INDEX

A PENGUIN READERS GUIDE TO

LIFE IS IN THE TRANSITIONS

Bruce Feiler

About This Guide

The questions, discussion topics, and other material that follow are intended to enhance your group's conversation of Bruce Feiler's *Life Is in the Transitions*, a groundbreaking and deeply human investigation into the ways society has shaped our life narratives over the generations, and how individuals can reclaim a sense of agency, resilience, and healing during life's inevitable and unexpected transitions.

Questions and Topics for Discussion

Introduction

1. Bruce opens the book with the emotional story of his father and how the storytelling project he did with his dad inspired his quest to collect life stories across the country. How did Bruce's personal struggles—from his cancer to his family—help shape his experience working on the book and your experience reading it?

2. Bruce's Life Story Project combines the old-fashioned technique of collecting stories with the more modern approach of analyzing those stories for data, themes, and takeaways that can help anyone going through challenging times. The same applies to how he put together the book. How do you think the mix of stories, data, and analysis affected you while reading *Life Is in the Transitions?*

3. Bruce worked on this book for many years and completed it before the pandemic. Yet it was published in the middle of the pandemic. How did the timing influence how you read the book?

Lifequakes

1. Bruce draws a distinction between *disruptors*, which are more everyday breaks in the normal, and *lifequakes*, which are larger on the Richter scale of consequences and have aftershocks that last for years. How do these terms resonate in your life? Do you think the

number of disruptors and lifequakes in contemporary life is growing or shrinking? Why?

2. Bruce's research shows that we go through three to five lifequakes in the course of our lives and they last an average of four to five years. That means you or someone you know is in one now. Is that true for you? Are you, or is someone in your family, in a lifequake today?

3. Bruce divides lifequakes into voluntary and involuntary, personal and collective. The pandemic is the first collective-involuntary lifequake most of us have lived through. How does going through a lifequake with others affect the experience? What are the positives and negatives?

Transitions

1. Bruce talks about the three stages of transitions—*the long goodbye, the messy middle*, and *the new beginning*—and says that each of us has a *transition superpower* and a *transition kryptonite*. Thinking of your own transitions, which of the three phases are you good at and which are you weakest at? Why do you think that is?

2. Using Bruce's model, if you're in a life transition now, which phase are you in? Did you pick up any techniques or strategies to make this part of your journey go better?

3. In chapter 9, Bruce writes about getting lost as part of the messy middle of transitions. Reflect on a time when you or someone you know got lost, what they discovered in that period, and how they returned.

4. While not all transitions or lifequakes have to do with death explicitly, there is a commonality between Bruce's discussion of transition and the grieving process, as discussed in chapter 8. How does his nonlinear model of transitions compare with the popular idea of the "five stages of grief" and other clichés about grief and mourning?

The Transition Tool Kit

1. Bruce identifies seven tools for navigating life transitions—Accept It, Mark It, Shed It, Create It, Share It, Launch It, Tell It. Which

one most surprised you? Which one are you good at, which one do you need to work on, and which one did you get motivated to go out and try?

2. One of Bruce's findings is that the top three emotions people struggle with in their transitions are fear, sadness, and shame. Guilt, anger, and loneliness also came up. What about you? What is the hardest feeling you grapple with in times of change?

3. Have you ever performed a ritual in service of working through a transition, whether or not you knew it at the time? What kind was it—personal, collective, name change, or cleansing—and how did it make you feel?

4. If you could pick one habit from your life to shed, what would it be?

5. Bruce also talks about astonishing acts of creativity that people turn to: singing, dancing, cooking, painting, writing. What new skill or talent have you embraced during a difficult time?

6. The importance of sharing your transition with others is one of Bruce's tools and a larger theme of *Life Is in the Transitions.* In the conclusion, he tells the story of bonding with John Mury who had a ten-car pileup, and the moving story of his own father, who found hope and purpose in revisiting his own life story. What insight did you gain in how to get through your own lifequakes?

The Life Story Project

1. Bruce shares many of his interviewees' stories throughout the book—Loretta Parham, whose daughter died in a car accident leaving her to raise her two granddaughters; Chris Waddell, who turned his life-altering injury into Paralympic success and also climbed Mount Kilimanjaro; Fraidy Reiss, who left her religious community to protect herself from her husband; Ann Ramer, who had two children with multiple cancers; Tiffany Grimes, who worked to accept her partner's transition to a new gender; and Zach Herrick, who lost his face in the Afghanistan war. Did any story or stories resonate with you in particular? Whose transition did you most cheer? Whom would you most like to meet?

2. Have you experienced an "autobiographical occasion"? If so, was it on a private or public scale?

3. If you could do a Life Story Project based on Bruce's questions with anyone in your life, whom would you choose? (PS: If you'd like to have Bruce email your loved one a question every week, please visit brucefeiler.com.)

The Shape of Your Life

1. Bruce spends a lot of time debunking the idea of the linear life and exploring how our lives take all different shapes. He also discusses how many people grew up with the idea of linearity and are still haunted by that idea. Are you one of those people? Have you struggled to accept that life is nonlinear or did an event earlier in your life teach you about life's ups and downs?

2. One of Bruce's questions is, "Looking back on your life story, do you detect a central theme?" Having read the book, what answer would you give?

3. Consider Bruce's provocative and creative question, "What shape is your life?" What shape comes to mind for you? And which of the ABCs of meaning does it fit into—line (agency), circle (belonging), or star (cause)? What does this reflect about your general tendencies toward prioritizing your *me story*, your *we story*, or your *thee story*?

Beyond the Covers

1. One theme of *Life Is in the Transitions* is that younger generations are more open to the nonlinear life and more accepting of the quickening pace of personal change. If you can, find someone of an older or younger generation whose upbringing was different than yours and discuss how your experiences with linearity and nonlinearity, stability and change are both similar and different.

2. Bruce replicates his Life Story Interview at the end of the book. You might enjoy using these questions to write or talk about your own life or that of someone you love.